BRIAN MOORE
THE FINAL SCORE
An Autobiography

BRIAN MOORE
THE FINAL SCORE

An Autobiography

Brian Moore
with Norman Giller

CORONET BOOKS
Hodder & Stoughton

First published in Great Britain in 1999
by Hodder and Stoughton
First published in paperback in 2000
by Hodder and Stoughton
A division of Hodder Headline

A Coronet Paperback

10 9 8 7 6 5 4 3 2 1

A CIP catalogue record for this title is available from
the British Library.

ISBN 0 340 74831 1

Printed and bound in Great Britain by
Mackays of Chatham plc, Chatham, Kent

Hodder and Stoughton
A division of Hodder Headline
338 Euston Road
London NW1 3BH

For Betty,
who waited so patiently

Photographic acknowledgements

The author and the publisher would like to thank the following for permission to reproduce photographs:

AllSport, Barry Connor, *Evening Standard*, London Weekend Television Ltd, Susan Marden-Cook, E. J. Shakespeare, Bob Thomas, *TV Times*.

All other photographs are from private collections.

Author's acknowledgements

I would like to thank my good friend Norman Giller for his invaluable guidance in helping me to gather up the threads of my thoughts and memories. My thanks also to publisher Roddy Bloomfield for his encouragement, and to Marion Paull for her copy editing skills. My acknowledgements, too, to David Wills for all the sound advice over many years and many projects. Most of all I thank my sons, Chris and Simon, for their love and support, and, of course, Betty for always being there. I hope that one day my grandson Calum will read this so that he knows that his Grandad did more than just sit and *watch* the television!

CONTENTS

AT THE TOP OF THE MOUNTAIN

IT is just over a year since I lay down the commentary microphone for the last time. I have vivid memories still of that
roaring, delirious French crowd in Paris on the night of the World
Cup final as I said, 'And the final score is France 3, Brazil 0.'

This was the final score of my final match, and the end of a
career that had taken me from a Kent country boy's life to the
twin worlds of football and broadcasting. The question that has
been put to me hundreds of times since I decided to give up one
of the greatest jobs on earth is: why have you retired?

It was Don Revie who first planted thoughts of retirement in
my mind. I had gone to visit him in Scotland, where he had set
up home, during the spring of 1988. This once great bear of a man
was reduced by motor neurone disease to a dwindling, but still
spirited, figure in a wheelchair. Those glorious but controversial
days as manager of Leeds United and England were well behind
him.

'When are you going to retire, then?' he suddenly asked.
Frankly, the question shook me.

'Good heavens, Don, I'm still in my mid-fifties,' I replied. 'I
love my work and I haven't given it a moment's thought.'

'Well, take a tip – don't leave it too long. I did, and look what's
happened to me.'

Don, despite his somewhat flawed public image, was a
man of great warmth. I often found him filled with what seemed

to be private misgivings; he was sometimes cruelly misunderstood. He died less than a year later aged just sixty-one. The date was 26 May 1989, the very day that I was commentating on the match in which Arsenal dramatically won the League Championship with virtually the last kick of the season at Anfield. Who can forget it?

The timing of Don's death somehow doubled the impact of what he had said to me. I remembered those words: don't leave it too long.

It took ten years for me to put his advice into practice. So it was in the Stade de France on Sunday, 12 July 1998, that I commentated for the last time. France triumphed in the World Cup final, the mystery of Ronaldo had still to be solved and, like Brazil, my time was up.

I told the viewers that I hoped football fans everywhere had shared, in some small part, the enjoyment and excitement I'd experienced in the previous thirty years or more...because I was putting the finishing touches to a working life that, quite simply, could not have been bettered.

So back to that often-asked question. There is nothing slick or clever about the answer. I love football as much as ever I did. Nothing in my working life can ever replace the rush of adrenalin I felt when leaving the commentary box – a privileged messenger – on those occasions when the words had come out in more or less the right order and the game had been stunning.

As I bowed out, my old bosses at ITV had, without argument, gathered the strongest portfolio of high-profile games in all my thirty years with them. I could still have played a major part in all of that. But I had made a conscious decision to go while still successful. To finish with an FA Cup final followed by a World Cup final was to go out at the peak of my profession. It's worth recalling that during France '98 we reached an ITV all-time record audience of 27 million viewers: England v Argentina at St Etienne on 30 June.

By the time the next World Cup is here I shall be seventy, and by then the words may be less willing to come out in the right order. There also comes a time when you've had your fill of frozen outposts of Europe on bitter winter nights.

More important still, I wanted extra time with my wife, Betty, who, for more than thirty years, like the wives of most broadcasters, has too often taken a back seat to a television assignment. It was pay-back time.

For me, now, it is also play-back time. One of my first radio commentaries in the early 1960s was alongside the legendary Raymond Glendenning. I grew up with him on our Bakelite wireless. He was the man I always wanted to be. There he was sitting next to me at a game at Portsmouth, overcoat fashionably long, those little wire-rimmed spectacles, famous handlebar moustache, hair slicked back, and that wonderfully rich, evocative voice that has not been bettered in sports broadcasting before or since.

I mention it because my old friend Harry Carpenter tells a story of his boxing days with Raymond that will ring a bell with all commentators. Harry often found himself at a fight trying to sum up a round that had been pretty uneventful but which Raymond, with the throttle full out, had made sound like a spectacular three minutes of devastating punching from first to last. Harry felt he had to have it out with the great man. Raymond listened politely.

'Take your point, old boy,' he said, 'but, you see, my job is to stop people reaching for that little switch marked "off".'

That's commentating in a nutshell. On television, however, you have to find the balance between what the viewer can see and how you interpret it; and if the action is good, milk it for all you are worth.

Peter Black, distinguished former television critic of the *Daily Mail*, once wrote that every commentator had to have a bit of the ham actor in him. He was right, and for a little over thirty years I tried to heed that advice and keep people on the edge of their favourite armchair.

I had the opportunity to thrust a microphone in front of such sporting legends as Jesse Owens, Stanley Matthews and Bobby

Moore, Sir Neville Cardus and Sir Gordon Richards, Bjorn Borg and Niki Lauda; I've shared a mike with Eamonn Andrews, the greatest pro of them all, Sir Alf Ramsey, Kevin Keegan, Ron Atkinson, Brian Clough and the matchless George Best.

I watched Jimmy Greaves play as a youth international and I have seen, at close range, Michael Owen at the dawn of what should be a glorious career; I accepted the holiday of a lifetime from Elton John and I have sat in the studios of Lord Snowdon and David Bailey – not bad for someone once described by a television critic, himself no oil-painting, as having a face like an old football. 'Correction,' he wrote, 'I mean a *tired* old football.'

I've worked on nine World Cups and two Olympic Games, and I have climbed into commentary boxes in just about all the great sports arenas in the world, from the Maracana in Brazil to the Lenin Stadium in Moscow, from Wembley Stadium to the Azteca in Mexico, and from the Nou Camp in Barcelona to the Yankee Stadium in New York. Could a country boy like me ever have dreamed such a dream?

Getting my story down on paper has been a new experience. All my working life I either got it right or got it wrong. There were no grey areas and all the verdicts were shaped by split-second judgements. Now, as I dredge my memory and set it all down, my guiding light has been a piece of advice I once received from the late Lord Ted Willis, prolific writer, creator of 'Dixon of Dock Green' and a wonderful friend. 'Never use a one pound word when a sixpenny one will do,' he said.

For a football commentator like me, that was never a problem. I've made a good living with sixpenny words.

1

THE LAST COMMENTARY

WHERE better to start than at the finish! I still can't believe how relaxed and comfortable I felt as I prepared for my last commentary after more than thirty years at the microphone. The stage could not have been bigger – the World Cup final between France and Brazil. Neither could the setting have been more spectacular – that gloriously futuristic flying saucer of an arena, the Stade de France in Paris.

Usually in the days before a game of this magnitude, I would have lived a clenched-fist kind of life, uptight, impatient and not very easy to live with, but now I was so uncharacteristically laid-back that I even managed an afternoon nap before going to work. For someone who has always slept badly – I've tried hypnotherapy, relaxation tapes and pills with little success – that truly was something.

It could only be that I was at ease with my decision to end thirty years at the sharp end of television for something quieter and free from stress. I had that comforting deep-down feeling that I had chosen the right time to get out. The old comedians say you should always leave them laughing. Well, I was leaving the stage with the crowd roaring.

As usual I was at the stadium early. A family joke is that I get them to airports in time to wheel out the aircraft and at football matches to help mark out the pitch, but that is my way.

Early-bird Moore. The kick-off was at nine o'clock Paris time; I arrived at four forty-five!

I had prepared well the previous day – any commentator will tell you that homework, and plenty of it, is our lifeline. You want to know something about every player? I'll tell you. About the Cup itself? I even know the Italian who designed it. How about the history of the tournament? Weren't we in the very city where Jules Rimet dreamed up the whole beautiful idea? And so on and so on. You show me the commentator who does not do his homework, and I will show you a man on a tightrope without a safety-net. The more facts you have at your fingertips, the better you are prepared for any emergency. But as I settled alongside my co-commentator, Kevin Keegan, for my final assignment, I was unaware of the huge emergency developing just a hundred metres or so away in the Brazilian dressing-room.

As the match atmosphere started to build, I took a panoramic look at my commentating colleagues ranged row upon row alongside me, below me and above me. Just about every football nation in the world had their Moores and Keegans adjusting their headsets, shuffling their papers, casting anxious eyes at their monitors and waiting for the kick-off of what we antici-pated being one of the biggest games of our lives.

At times like this, commentators are just as nervous as the players. They cannot wait for their first pass, first shot, tackle or save; we cannot wait to get our first words in, to pick up the rhythm of the match and, hopefully, make the right identifica-tions and interpretations.

Quite a few of my commentating friends spared the time to come to my commentary position and, with a handshake, wish me well in my retirement. John Motson was among them. He'd soon be rattling away for the BBC but I was touched by his gesture and, I have to say, I might even have glimpsed a small tear of emotion in his eye as he left.

John is a good friend; there's no animosity between the BBC and ITV commentators. In fact, two days earlier I'd enjoyed a private lunch at one of Paris's finest eateries down by the Parc des Princes with Motty's great BBC rival and friend Barry Davies. There's so much tub-thumping and point-scoring in the days before ITV and BBC go head-to-head on a match like this; I'm never sure how much good it does. What I do know is that it doesn't get close to shaking the foundations of our friendships.

All, then, was moving in an orderly way towards the kick-off when the calm was shattered by the news of Ronaldo. A printed team-sheet is handed to us about an hour before all major games and this one contained a bombshell. Brazil's No. 9 was missing. Ronaldo, the world's most famous footballer, was out of the world's most important game. Edmundo, No. 21, was there in his place. I still have my copy of the team-sheet, signed by Brazil's coach, Mario Zagallo.

The buzz among the world's TV men grew to shouts in dozens of tongues. While I gathered up the news and its consequences, Pele, the most famous Brazilian of them all, climbed quickly past me to his TV perch three rows back, pursued, as ever, by a swarm of reporters. I grabbed one.

'Why no Ronaldo?' I asked. He didn't understand. 'Ronaldo blessé?' I shouted. Schoolboy French to a harassed Brazilian, in the cold light of day, may not seem so sensible, but he tapped his ankle and said, 'Training.' So that was it.

I passed this snatched intelligence to our news team and to Bob Wilson, who was, as usual, presenting our show and sharing the bits and pieces of information being fed to him on air with the ITV panellists, Glenn Hoddle, Terry Venables and Ruud Gullit. Then I spotted Andreas Brehme, the German whose penalty won the 1990 World Cup final in Rome. I suggested to Kevin, still fluent in German from his Hamburg days, that he should ask Brehme what he knew about the Ronaldo situation. He had also heard that it was an ankle problem.

Armed with the new information from a Brazilian and a German, I had to work out the change in my opening remarks. 'Will this be the night when the true Ronaldo emerges and carries off the trophy for Brazil? etc., etc.' became, 'Can

Edmundo, for all the twenty-eight caps for his country, turn in a Ronaldo-style performance…?' and so on.

Next, I had to change my own team boards, laid out on A4-size cards. Ronaldo was eliminated by a covering sticky label and Edmundo replaced him. But another twist was just around the corner.

In the meantime, FIFA had also been taken in by the ankle injury story. Within minutes they had released a communiqué:

RONALDO WENT TO THE HOSPITAL BEFORE COMING TO THE STADIUM FOR A TEST ON HIS LEFT ANKLE, AFTER HE HAD NOT TRAINED FULLY FOR TWO DAYS. THE BRAZILIAN TEAM DOCTORS GAVE RONALDO CLEARANCE TO PLAY FORTY-FIVE MINUTES BEFORE KICK-OFF, WHEN HE ARRIVED AT THE STADIUM AFTER THE REST OF THE BRAZILIAN TEAM.

No talk yet of the nightmare fit or the emotional disturbance that were to become the after-match story. Within minutes the confusion was further increased when the whisper went round that Ronaldo might be playing after all. This was confirmed by a second team-sheet that reduced Edmundo to the substitutes' bench (and elimination by another sticky label) and had Ronaldo reinstated. And back, too, came those original opening remarks!

The questions were flying everywhere and nobody had the answers. How fit was Ronaldo? Had his team-mates had a big say in the team selection? And, in any case, why had the Brazilians not come out for a pre-match warm-up? It's at times like this, commentators, despite being so near the action, feel so far from a story. Oh, to have been a fly on that dressing-room wall.

What was clear, though, once the game started, was that all was not well in the Brazilian camp. Ronaldo was a sorry figure, the game passed him by and there was a flabby, disinterested look about the team's whole performance.

Soon, dark rumours of commercial pressures surfaced. Did the boot manufacturers Nike – who have a massive contract with the Brazilian FA – lean heavily on Zagallo and his backroom

4

team to make sure Ronaldo was exposed to the world's TV screens for ninety minutes of priceless advertising time? Nike strongly deny any involvement.

I am not sure we will ever know exactly what went on in what had obviously suddenly become an extremely unhappy and disturbed Brazilian camp. Ronaldo's ankle injury later became embellished as either a tongue-swallowing fit or extreme emotional distress.

I can understand the stress. At twenty-one, the hopes of a football-crazy nation rested on his shoulders and he had not a moment to call his own. He could not move anywhere in France that month without cameras, microphones, questions, demands, autograph books all being thrust in his direction. Thousands turned up for every Brazilian training day. There was just no escape from the clutches and the clamour of a media gone mad.

The lad, for that is what he is, lives in an unreal world. Bobby Robson told me of the day he bought him for Barcelona.

'With some of the money he made that day,' Bobby revealed, 'Ronaldo went out and bought an island off Brazil, complete with helipad and a mooring for his boat.' At the time, he was not even twenty.

Bobby is a man whose opinion I respect, and so I bow to his knowledge when he describes him as the greatest talent he has seen since Pele. But that night in Paris you did not need a coaching certificate to see that Ronaldo was in no fit mental state to play. It was cruelly obvious from almost the first whistle, and as early as twenty minutes into the game most of us were looking for a Brazilian substitute. Just before the interval, both Kevin and I took the view that he would not appear for the second half.

But he did, and that convinces me that it was now not a football decision. There had to be other considerations at work. Zagallo, fired soon after the final, seemed no longer to be calling the shots. If indeed commercial considerations did prevail, from whatever direction, football has taken a huge step down a dark corridor from which there is no return. Incidentally, months later there still seemed no end to Ronaldo's mental turmoil – as his flaccid display against Manchester United in the Champions League confirmed.

So France won and won well. The crowds swarmed down the Champs Elysées and cared little for the plight of Brazil as they toasted the goals of Zidane and Petit. There was a brief moment about ten minutes from the end of the game when the thought flashed past me that I would not be doing this ever again. And then it was gone. At the end, I waited for an emotional backlash. It never came. A lot of kind people came and pumped my hand again. You could hardly hear yourself speak for the joyous celebrations of the French supporters over what was an unexpected but, finally, well-deserved victory. What a pity the Brazilians did not come to the party.

My last commentary had gone off into the ether and, I hope, landed pleasantly in the homes of millions of football followers back home. It was once written that I am to television technology what Einstein was to ladies' hairdressing. I confess that it's true, and right up to my final sentence I never understood how my words managed to get from my mouth to television sets thousands of miles away in living-rooms up and down the land. I had been in the caring hands of all-knowing technicians throughout my commentating career; without them, I would have been speechless.

I went back to the Hotel Sofitel in the Paris suburbs to find, among other things, a message of good wishes from Lawrie McMenemy, a note from Alex Ferguson and a very welcome call from Hugh Johns, for so long my eminent predecessor in the ITV commentary box. Then it was up to the twenty-first floor by express lift for our end-of-tournament party. I was so pleased to see Bob Wilson and Glenn Hoddle there with Terry Venables, Ruud Gullit, Ian St John, Barry Venison and my two long-standing co-commentators and good friends Ron Atkinson and Kevin Keegan.

Ron, I know, was very disappointed to miss out on the final. I understand that it had not been an easy decision for our production chief, Jeff Farmer, to pick Kevin in front of Ron. There is nothing to separate them and they have both mastered the art of saying things succinctly, entertainingly and, most important of all, at the right time.

I had no say in the matter of which of them would work alongside me for the final. I have worked happily with both and enjoy their company. If I had been asked, I would probably have dodged the issue. Thank goodness neither Kevin nor Ron ever sat on the fence when called on for opinions to pepper my commentaries.

Kevin arrived at the party with a case of excellent French wine as a retirement present for me – Pommard Premier Cru 1986 to commemorate our work together during the 1986 Mexico World Cup; 1990 Margaux for our time at Italia '90; and a 1994 Pomerol to celebrate the tournament in the United States.

I cannot tell you about the quality of the vintages, but Kevin can. He has become quite a wine buff. Indeed while we were in Toulouse earlier in the tournament he bought himself a wine cellar. It looks like a large, glass-fronted wardrobe and keeps wine at just the right temperature. Kevin arranged to have it shipped back to his home in Cleveland. I shall drink to his continued good health and to our friendship.

By three-thirty the morning after the World Cup final, it was all over. A long day had started with a morning preview programme televised from a Parisian rooftop and ended among many friends, not least the hidden heroes: the technicians, engineers, editorial boys and girls, the secretaries and the drivers. Our team, like France, were winners. They were a joy to work with and saying goodbye to them was more difficult than bidding farewell to match commentating. You can get by without football, but not without friends such as these, whom I had made over the years.

So, after five weeks, the World Cup was wrapped up and France were the champions. It had been a memorable but, in all honesty, not a classic tournament. It had lasted at least a week too long and should have been made up of twenty-four teams instead of thirty-two. I don't often agree with Sepp Blatter, the

FIFA secretary-general, but I am glad he also feels that future tournaments should not stretch beyond twenty-four days. Equally, you can be sure they will stick with thirty-two teams. Vote-catching politics among football's lesser nations will see to that.

It saddens me deeply to say that the biggest blight on France '98 was the lack of sportsmanship among the players. It became known as the Cheat's Charter as players went diving for penalties, imagined or exaggerated injuries, pulled constantly at each others' shirts and almost begged referees to brandish the yellow and red cards at fellow professionals. Adding to their shameful behaviour was the continual sight of players rolling over and over in what for all of us became a sickening indictment of the modern game.

FIFA tiptoed around the whole mess. They ordered referees to get tougher or take the next plane home – what a charming way to promote natural, relaxed refereeing – and when they did get tougher, they were told to ease back a bit. No wonder they were confused. The best referees came to France and had earned their place in the competition. They should have been allowed to take charge in their own style and be judged on that. Turning referees into robots is not the way to cure the game's ills.

Even so, the hard-pressed referees would still have lost out to the sly professionals who were a part of every team. The friend-ship and fellowship among players that I remember from earlier tournaments are now little more than a sepia image. The sight of Bobby Moore and Pele embracing in Mexico in 1970 at the final whistle after Brazil's single-goal victory and that memorable Gordon Banks save, brothers-in-arms, great professionals with huge respect for each other, was never remotely replayed in France.

The knock-on effects could be devastating. The appalling behaviour of the players in France '98 will be mirrored on school playing fields, in parks, in Sunday morning games, from bottom to top, with an agonised, over-the-top reaction to every chal-lenge. The combination of professional players and television is not always beneficial – the good, the bad and the downright ugly are there for all to see and many to copy. Now that is threatening the very roots of the game.

The last thing I want to do is turn this book into a lecture, but the solution to mushrooming problems is that, for a start, referees must be encouraged to show yellow cards every time they suspect a player is cheating. And referees must be supported to the hilt by the authorities, with no back-sliding and no appeals. It means there will be times when a player is punished when he is genuinely injured, perhaps even lying there with a broken limb, but the punishment must stand. It is rough justice, but the players have brought it on themselves. The future of the once beautiful game deserves nothing less.

I talked with Bobby Charlton – a shining example of how men should behave and the game be played – at the airport the morning after the final. He suggested that for future World Cups, or any high-profile game on television, there should be retrospective punishment. Bobby put forward the positive thought that committees should meet the morning after each game and sift through television evidence. If they find a player has cheated – no matter how – he should get his come-uppance. His action may have influenced the game the night before and nothing can be done about that, but he'll find there is no escape for him. In short, cheats must not be allowed to prosper or the game we know and love will be damaged beyond repair. This policy has already been successfully adopted by rugby union – and how ironic that sitting a few yards from us watching the final was England's rugby coach Clive Woodward, who earlier that year had lost one of his leading players, Martin Johnson, from just such a second look at video evidence. Football should learn from rugby's example.

I cannot leave the 1998 World Cup without reference to the mighty duel between England and Argentina in the steep-sided arena at St Etienne in the second phase of the tournament. It was, without question, the most dramatic night of football in my whole broadcasting career and an experience I was fortunate to share with a record ITV audience of 27 million viewers.

Two disputed penalties, a wonder goal by wonder boy Michael Owen, the sending off of David Beckham, a disallowed goal by Sol Campbell, an heroic fight by Tony Adams and Co. and then that penalty shoot-out – just writing those words stirs the blood and gets the pulse racing! But at the end of that extraordinary match my thoughts were not of the approaching close of my career but of the great hole into which I had managed to drop my co-commentator.

It had been a match and an occasion made for commentators and, thankfully, I got it mostly right, like England, until the final kick. The penalty shoot-out was reaching its chilling climax – I could just imagine all the cushions in front of faces at home – when David Batty made his way to centre stage. He *had* to score to keep the game alive; a miss and England were out.

Sitting next to me was the man who once bought Batty for Newcastle and probably knew more about his qualities than anyone. My intention was to say to Kevin Keegan: 'How will Batty handle this?' That would have been a good question to pitch to your co-commentator.

Unfortunately for me, David put the ball on the spot and shaped up much quicker than I had anticipated. It was as though he wanted to get the whole thing over. So all I had time to say was, 'Kevin, you know him – yes or no, will he score?'

I've asked some daft questions in my time, but that's one that will always haunt me. Whatever Kevin thought privately, what could he possibly tell a hushed nation?

'Yes,' he said and the word was hardly out of his mouth before the world knew that he and Batty had got it wrong.

I was furious with myself – the biggest night of all and a real clanger in the last minute. In a different way, I felt just as bad as David Batty and Paul Ince, the earlier penalty-miss culprit. As we came off the air, I put my arm round Kevin and apologised.

'Don't worry about it Mooro,' he was sporting enough to say. 'I can take it. In any case, they never expect me to get it right.'

That was a glancing reference to our commentary together a

few days earlier when England drew level near the end against Romania in Toulouse. 'There's only one winner now and that's England,' said Kevin – a view shared, incidentally, by just about every pundit in the ground. Dan Petrescu's goal for Romania in the final minute shattered all those predictions. The tabloids had their fun with my co-commentator.

We drove back to our hotel in nearby Lyon, had a nightcap and a natter and went to our beds. We have never spoken again about that stupid 'hospital pass' question of mine but I've thought about it often. It underlines how easy it is to hang yourself at the microphone.

Penalty shoot-outs seemed to become part and parcel of my commentary career in the major tournaments, and each time England finished devastated losers. Before St Etienne, of course, there were the heartbreaking exits from Euro '96 and Italia '90 after penalty-decider defeats by Germany.

I have received hundreds of letters from viewers condemning all penalty shoot-outs. I disagree. Would there have been a debate had England won this one in France, or come out top against Germany at Wembley or in Italy? I doubt it very much. You can be sure the topic doesn't register high on the football agendas in Buenos Aires or Bonn! Sadly, it still overshadows everything else on what should have been also been the most remarkable night of my broadcasting career.

You can talk endlessly about counting the corners, playing on with seven men, playing on without a goalkeeper and so on; and about the cruel pressure it puts on players. But penalties still provide the best and most convenient package to round things off if a match is deadlocked. Television schedulers need to know where they stand and, in any case, shoot-outs remain TV's most heart-in-the-mouth sporting climax. Penalty shoot-outs are here to stay, because, in case you hadn't noticed, what television wants television usually gets!

I have tried to think how Glenn Hoddle must have felt that night in St Etienne when Batty's penalty was saved. He was convinced he had a team that, given the right breaks, was good enough to win the World Cup. It's a view I shared, but the dream died with that missed penalty and I wonder just how deeply the defeat affected the England manager.

This was, in fact, the start of Hoddle's demise, although nobody could have known it at the time. I had long been a Hoddle fan. Indeed how could it be otherwise for anyone who saw him play as a teenager onwards at Tottenham, providing passes and pleasure beyond the range of almost every other player. When he became England manager at first he seemed to be a man at ease with himself. But the honeymoon period in that job is never long. The tabloids in particular were after blood. Perhaps Glenn was sometimes a little aloof; maybe once or twice he trailed red herrings across his press conferences. The grumbling began in the ranks of the press. The writers started to feel uneasy, and before long they turned up the heat on the England manager. It started before his book of revelations from the World Cup dressing-room and training camp was published, and when the book came out it could only be seen as a serious misjudgement. It gave his critics the bullets they needed.

The trust of players is the first and paramount requirement of any manager. Casey Stengel, the legendary American baseball coach, once said that the key to a winning team spirit is for the coach to separate the seven players who hate him from the seven who are undecided. Glenn's men had not crossed the line by that much, but now they would certainly begin to have their doubts about him.

From publication onwards, it was all downhill for Glenn Hoddle. His credibility with the English football public, driven by the headlines, began to falter. When the flames started to die down, all the newspapers had to do was toss another log on the fire – perhaps Eileen Drewery, the faith healer; perhaps those disappointing post-World Cup results against Sweden and Bulgaria; perhaps his religious beliefs; perhaps we had a pretty lousy World Cup after all; and if there was nothing new – let's go back to Eileen Drewery.

My thoughts often fly back to Alf Ramsey's reign, with the

1966 World Cup triumph as its glorious peak moment. He remains the role model for all international managers. Players loved him and would almost die for him on the football field. It was because they trusted him, and he, in return, defended them to the hilt – whatever he might have said privately to them. They were made to feel part of an intensely loyal and very special family, and to hell with what anybody outside said about them.

Alf's players knew that he would not be listening to any mixing from outsiders; and he most certainly wouldn't add to any debate by writing about it himself. Alan Ball summed up how all the players felt about Ramsey when he told me: 'We would walk through a wall of fire for Alf.' You have to be a very special manager to win that sort of loyalty. Most of all, Alf knew that loyalty was a two-way street, and he never ever let his players down.

In my view, all England managers should sign a type of official secrets declaration. Hoddle devalued himself with the book, put the respect and trust of his players in jeopardy and, perhaps most worrying of all, allowed himself to be sucked into the tabloid world with his exclusive flag nailed to one masthead. Suddenly he was no longer able to lift himself above the excesses of some of the fruitier publications and writers. He was in there, right up to his neck, with them.

I have got to know Hoddle well enough to understand that he has deep inner strength. He has a strong sense of discipline that made the England players think twice before taking liberties with him; he has an enlightened tactical brain; he was single-minded enough to pick his team and not the media's, bold enough to grasp the Gascoigne nettle; he has an open mind, hence Eileen Drewery. He has all the necessary qualities. He was a good general. Ah, but was he a lucky one? Now we have the answer.

I've always believed that managers should manage; it's their head on the block. When Hoddle left out Beckham or Owen we all had the right to a view. It's a game we all love to play – power without responsibility. But you have to allow the manager to know best and in this case I believe he did. I had no argument with Hoddle's team selection in the World Cup. When Beckham or Owen came on they freshened the side and it looked better for it. Only the manager sees the whole picture.

Unfortunately, Glenn's World Cup was a disappointment. That great sprawling drama in St Etienne obscured the fact that England under-achieved in France '98. Victory over Tunisia and Colombia; defeat by Romania and Argentina – it wasn't good enough. We had talked endlessly about England getting to the quarter-finals, maybe the semi-finals and, then, well who knows? But the fact remains we could not get beyond the second phase. The promise was there; the results were a let-down.

One thing that my co-commentator Kevin Keegan and I got one hundred per cent right on that emotional night in St Etienne was to label Michael Owen as the biggest threat to Argentina. His pace was devastating and his goal, I think, the best of the World Cup.

I first met the exciting young prodigy at an England get-together at Bisham Abbey a few weeks before the World Cup. He was the most composed and mature eighteen-year-old sportsman you could ever meet, and on that day down by the Thames he was put up for the press conference in front of all the leading football writers and hard-nosed newshounds. He was flanked by Glenn Hoddle and press officers ready to deflect any questions that young Michael might find too hot to handle (if only they had been there some nine months later to do the same protective work for the manager!). But the 'minders' were super-fluous. Owen answered brightly, with intelligence and humour, and was not for a moment overawed – a forty-eight-year-old head on an eighteen-year-old frame.

Give thanks, then, for his solid, loving family life and for the fact that, at Liverpool, his feet will be kept firmly on the ground. In this crazy world of football money, he will break all records. Jimmy Armfield, once a distinguished England full-back and captain, told me that it took him three years to learn how to bridge the gap between club and international football. Michael managed it in three months.

His pace is electric and it frightens the very best defenders. His nerve and courage are not in doubt. He took plenty of punishment from wily old pros during the World Cup as they tried to tame him, and he didn't flinch. His finishing reminds me of Jimmy Greaves. I saw Greaves as a youth international fresh out of school in 1957 and afterwards when he was just sensational for Chelsea. I followed him closely, after his spell in Italy, throughout those glorious years at Tottenham.

Similar build, same icy nerve and nimble brain – I can see Greavsie all over again. But, of course, Jimmy went on to prove so much in the years that followed that early burst – forty-four goals in fifty-seven England internationals, and a record 357 first division goals that will never be beaten. That surely is tomorrow's challenge for Michael Owen, to build on the foundation laid with Glenn Hoddle in France.

For the time being, let's revel in that wondrous goal against Argentina. It was a product of all his qualities – speed, strength and power shooting. Incidentally, I have a permanent reminder of it. A few days after I got back home from France, I was given a T-shirt – on the front of it the plan of how the goal was scored and under it my commentary words: 'Beckham to Owen and here's another Owen run. He's going to worry them again, and he might finish it off… Oh! It's a wonderful goal to make it 2–1 for England.'

I can see it all again – my abiding memory of France '98. For fifteen minutes or so after that Owen goal, Glenn Hoddle's team gave us all a glimpse of the promised land. England's football was skilful, imaginative and as good as anything in the tournament. If Paul Scholes had scored from a glorious chance during this purple patch there would have been but one winner and we would have been spared all the agony that came later.

Who knows, maybe we would have been spared the Beckham sending-off? What a reckless and needless moment that was! And how costly for England and Beckham's later peace of mind.

When I first saw it – and indeed after the first replay – I said that the referee had violently over-reacted, but a more revealing angle showed up Beckham's petulance, I revised my view and confirmed that the referee was totally correct.

Now the bandwagon started to roll. The vilification of a fine young footballer reached ludicrous lengths. Forgotten was the acclaim for a hero after his sublime free-kick goal against Colombia in the previous game; now he had become public enemy number one, ripped apart by sensation-seeking columnists and taunted by tabloid headline writers, all for the impetuous actions of one second.

Being a Manchester United player was bad enough, and to have a high-profile fiancée, but now this. Beckham was wrong. We all know it – more importantly, so does he. But somebody had to pay for the nation's despair that night. David Beckham was the convenient scapegoat. Thankfully, he's got plenty of time and talent to turn things around, and he has already started to do it. There was no better player in the Premiership that following season – and, to cap it all, he was the key figure in United's exhilarating triumph. As Beckham was on the receiving end of that red card, he could never have dreamt that within a year he would be celebrating an historic Treble with his team-mates.

What did not help was that his misdemeanour was seen on ITV by its biggest-ever audience. My bosses were doing cart-wheels when they heard next day that the viewing figures for the game had peaked at 27 million. What an audience and apparently it included the Queen, the Queen Mother and the Prime Minister. Rarely, if ever, has a match so captured the collective imagination. Only two television audiences have bettered it, both for the BBC: a Christmas edition of 'Only Fools and Horses' and, strangely, an episode of 'To the Manor Born', no doubt explained by the fact that ITV were on strike at the time!

It was also the night when ITV produced the best and most authoritative programme of the World Cup. In the Paris studio with Bob Wilson were two former England managers, Bobby

Robson and Terry Venables, both of whom had been on the wrong end of penalty shoot-outs (that should have told us something). In the stadium with Jim Rosenthal were John Barnes, former international of great standing, and Ian Wright who, but for an injury, would have been stripped for action. As already mentioned, former England captain Kevin Keegan was my co-commentator. The ITV team proudly got everything almost right. Only the result was wrong.

I rated Bob Wilson ITV's star of the tournament. Bob agreed with the decision to present all our matches (except the Argentina game) from the stadiums and not from the convenience and comfort of a Paris studio. It meant that ITV were right at the centre of the World Cup and not outside looking in; but this had its downside. Bob had to battle daily against crowd noise, strident loudspeakers, hazardous communications and, on one difficult night in Marseilles, a mistral that threatened to blow him, his notes and Ruud Gullit's dreadlocks into the sea.

Bob was truly in the front line. Anyone who knows anything about television will regard twenty-one games in twenty-three days in a maze of cities in those conditions as a considerable television *tour de force*. He was continually being compared with Des Lynam, but in his own way and with his own style, he even matched the BBC master. Bob came through it all superbly. Most of the television critics haven't quite caught on to his strengths yet – but they will.

As I think back on France '98, I cannot help but wonder at how it has all changed. My first World Cup in 1966 – I was a young radio commentator then – was covered on television using probably no more than three cameras at each ground, and an ambitious six for the final at Wembley; and a good job they made of it, too. In the Stade de France for the 1998 final, the director had his pick of more than twenty cameras. Two months earlier when ITV covered the '98 FA Cup final, the director, John Watts, had no fewer than twenty-nine cameras at his disposal.

The whole World Cup circus will move in 2002 to South Korea and Japan. You can just imagine what a technical and logistical nightmare that is going to be for everyone involved. I shall miss some of it, but not all. As I've said, nothing can replace that high all commentators experience at the end of a great game. I shall miss working with many friends, and also describing the blossoming lives of Michael Owen and David Beckham who, I believe, could establish themselves early in the new millennium as two of the world's greatest players.

As for me, when the ball starts rolling in the Far East in 2002, I shall stretch out in my favourite armchair and love every minute of it. And do you realise that Michael Owen will still be only twenty-two!

2

YOUNG MAN OF KENT

I WAS not born with a silver microphone in my mouth; far from it. On that cold winter's day in February 1932 when I arrived, my mother and father were kept warm by their love. They had very little else. I should tell you about their finances. When they were married at St Luke's Church in Gillingham, Kent, two years earlier, they left their modest wedding breakfast at my grandmother's house with one shilling between them and too proud, bless them, to accept a loan.

My father, a farm worker, was on thirty-two shillings and sixpence a week (£1.62½), and he earned an extra sixpence an hour cutting hedges at the weekend, sometimes by moonlight. He could not afford a newspaper, except for one week when he found a sixpenny piece in the street. When first he played cricket for the village, he took sandwiches to eat alone in the church at the top of the village green because he did not have the tea money.

The dangers of writing about how poor you were when you were young is that you risk being dragged into one of those Monty Pythonesque sketches in which everybody tries to outdo the other. I am laying the facts down here only because it is a true illustration of my background, and an important part of my past. When I appeared on Sybil Ruscoe's afternoon show on BBC Radio 5 Live, she said, 'You are proud of your background.' I said that I was not proud of it, but that I *was* proud of my parents and what they provided and achieved with so little.

They drew our family together with love and an intense loyalty, and to this day my sister Sally, brother Trevor and I set aside one day every month to be with each other. We raise a glass to the memory of our much-mourned parents. If wealth could be measured by happiness, they died millionaires. I can't remember a single serious argument between them in nearly 40 years of marriage. My dad's names were Baden Kimberley, an obvious echo from the Boer War, and I carry Baden – after the war hero and scout movement founder – as a second name.

My early life was spent in the Weald of Kent amid the orchards and hopfields. It really was the Garden of England, and I grew up surrounded by splashes of colour and staggeringly beautiful changes of season. My parents lived in a tied cottage in the village of Benenden. This meant we had a roof over our heads for a modest rent, but the downside was that both my father and mother were at the beck and call of the farmer–landlord. Dad was always on call seven days a week, and Mum worked in the big house in the mornings, and would then pick or pack apples in the afternoon before getting herself back to the kitchen to feed our family of five.

She would be horrified that I'm writing this now, but they were hard but happy days. Even on Christmas Day our family would be split because Mum had to leave our table and an excited young family in the early afternoon to wash up at the big house. All these years later, I still cannot easily forget the lack of thought or compassion of those people in the big house for our family, particularly when there were women-folk there who could for once have got their hands wet. Still in later years I find myself weeping silent tears over the festive plight of my parents.

The last remnants of the feudal system were still in evidence in the Kentish countryside in the 1940s and, for all I know, there are traces of it there now. Workers touched their caps to passing gentry, referred always to young members of the privileged families as Miss Jill or Master John, could be sacked on the spot – as my dad once was – and left homeless, and certainly would always be told how they were expected to vote come a General Election; not that the last demand impressed my dad in the slightest. He was a proud lifelong supporter of the Labour Party, and so am I. We are all shaped by our experiences and environment, and when you got my early view of life you could not help but appreciate and support the sensible side of socialism.

But despite the disadvantages, there still dawned many a sunlit day when I'd play football until it was dark on the local recreation field – with a tennis ball and two coats for goalposts – or cricket on our lovely village green, using a rough handmade bat and the same tennis ball and the same coats propped up against a stick for the wicket. Those memories, of sunshine summers and footballing winters, will never fade; nor will I forget my time as a choirboy at St George's Church, where I presented an angelic picture in my white ruff, cassock and surplice. I eventually became head choirboy and to this day believe nothing can match the sound of a choir and sacred music, preferably by Henry Purcell, one of the greatest of Englishmen.

My singing, however, was never going to make me rich. We received tuppence for practice on Wednesday nights and a penny for each of the two services on Sunday. But there was another sizeable incentive. Once a year we were taken by charabanc to Hastings for half-a-day by the seaside, and on one afternoon each winter, to nearby Tenterden for a scrumptious tea at the Tudor Tearooms and then to the Embassy Cinema (now, I believe, a supermarket) to thrill to a Tarzan film starring former Olympic swimming star Johnny Weissmuller in the lead role. His Jane, as I recall, was played by Maureen O'Sullivan, later the mother of Mia Farrow. For young country boys in wartime, these outings were considerable treats indeed.

It was during my choirboy days that I received my only severe dressing down from my dad. Before practice on Wednesdays we'd all sneak round the back of the church – daring nine- and ten-year-olds – for a quick pull at a Woodbine or, the cigarette of the time, a Tenner. It was my turn to go and buy the supplies after we had clubbed together to raise the cash. So across the green I went to Mr Baldwin's shop. Now Mr Baldwin, as well as selling sweets and tobacco, repaired bicycles, and, behind a screen, cut the villagers' hair. He was a gentle man of many parts.

'Ten Tenners, please, Mr Baldwin,' I piped up. 'They're for Mr Moore,' I added, quite unnecessarily. Big mistake. Behind the screen at that moment getting his short back and sides was my dad. With the barber's gown flying behind him, he jumped out of the chair and confronted me. I knew the look that he shot at me well enough. Simply translated, it meant, 'I'll see you when you get home.'

Dad never laid a finger on any of us, but I think he came pretty close that night. I certainly never forgot it and made sure I did nothing to upset him quite so much ever again. I should add that it took me another forty years to give up smoking!

At eleven I won a scholarship from Benenden's C of E school to Cranbrook, a public school noted for its sound academic record, its sporting prowess and the fact that Peter West, then a fine and fair commentator for the BBC, was among the old boys.

Now there was some real scrimping and scraping to be done by my parents. School uniform was a must, so were all the bits and pieces of sporting gear – to say nothing of the four pounds they had to find for a second-hand bicycle to get me the five miles between the two villages morning and night. There were no school buses then and certainly no seat belts. Indeed from outlying cottages like ours, my brother and sister and their friends would be transported to and from school on the back of the village coal lorry.

At least I was on the open road and as free as a bird on my bicycle, and even as an eleven-year-old, as I pedalled those country miles, I was dreaming my big dreams. I would listen to Raymond Glendenning, then the doyen of commentators, on our old Bakelite wireless: 'Matthews to Mannion, back to Carter and on to Lawton, and by Jove,' he'd say in that marvellously fruity voice, 'there's a rattling shot from Lawton…' Down those leafy lanes I became, in my imagination, the voice of sport, Raymond

Glendenning. It was a great way to pass the time and the miles – I was years ahead of Fantasy Football. The dream became reality, and when I talk to schools these days, I never fail to stress to the pupils that if you want something badly enough, no matter how unpromising the prospects, you can sometimes make it happen.

My parents knew what I wanted to do with my life and never for a moment did they suggest I was getting ideas above my station. However, towards the end of my schooldays, when I was seventeen, they agreed with the school's careers master that I should be interviewed by a body rejoicing in the title of the National Institute of Industrial Psychology. They were based in the Aldwych in London, and they sent an expert down to Cranbrook to run his eye over a number of us.

I have his report in front of me now and it concludes: 'We are not greatly in favour of his own choice of a career in sports journalism. He is too sensitive and diffident and too easily discouraged. The career, too, is a very precarious one and he seems likely to develop a greater sense of security and confidence in a position which offers greater safety and is less dependent upon personal pushfulness and enterprise.'

The 'expert' came up with several alternative suggestions: a primary school teacher, a probation officer, a job in local government or, and I quote, 'the trading departments such as water supply or gas'. I decided that another sort of gas suited me better. Dad ditched the report and let me get on with my dream.

I'd like to say that my schooldays were deliriously happy, but they were not. For one thing, I never felt fully at ease with boys from well-heeled families. I was a day boy, while most of them were boarders; so I was in one sense an outsider. They had plenty of fun at my expense, not least because my grammar sometimes lurched more towards the village green than the cloistered calm of the library. To this day I remain in awe of authority – of headmasters, lawyers, men of power, doctors, vicars. I have tried so hard to rid myself of a crippling inferiority complex, but all in vain. I'm convinced it all began back in that third form.

23

Sport, however, was my saviour. Almost as soon as I could stand, my father encouraged me to play cricket, his first sporting love. For hours he'd bowl to me – and he wasn't a bad bowler either. We have at home a ball with a silver plate mounted on it showing that he took 93 wickets for our village in 1922 (when he was twenty-one) and another 106 the following year. He was quick, and about that time he had a trial for Kent, but he was slightly built and it was felt that he hadn't the physique to stand up to the daily grind of first-class cricket.

At the age of eleven, I was high in the batting order for the Under-14 Junior Colts and I have great memories of my first game in the summer of 1943 on the county ground at Tunbridge Wells against the local school, Rose Hill. I scored 53 and was pretty full of myself

But cricket came within a solitary second and a few yards of costing me my life a year or so later. This was wartime England, and it had reached the stage where doodlebugs – the V1 rockets – were being fired from France and were raining down on southern England and London. A deep rumbling roar announced their approach, fire spurted out of the single exhaust and when the engine cut out they plunged to the ground and you took rapid cover. Spitfires and Hurricanes intercepted them with the delicate and dangerous job of exploding them in mid-air over less populated countryside before they could cause huge damage in built-up areas later in their journey.

So there we were on a sublime summer day, a dozen or so of us outside our pavilion having fielding practice supervised by our splendid cricket master, Frank Evans, when another doodle-bug droned towards us. This time, about a mile or so away, a Spitfire suddenly got on its tail, guns blazing.

Nearer and nearer it came, and at once Mr Evans saw the danger. 'Down everyone,' he shouted, and down we went. As we did so I had a quick look at the battle overhead. The doodlebug came on and on and the guns continued to stutter. Suddenly it was like a scene from a war movie except that John Wayne and John Mills were nowhere to be seen. The bullets that missed the target were hitting the ground and sending up those little spurts of dust in a lethal line directly towards us at an incredible rate.

There was no time for our short lives to flash before us, no time even to feel frightened. Then it was over. The burst of bullets finished, I swear, no more than ten yards from us. One more second of the pilot's finger on that gun button and it would have been carnage. The doodlebug survived and so, miraculously, did we.

Today I suppose we would be swamped by counselling. In fact we got up, shook ourselves down and calmly got on with the fielding practice! Those of my generation know that that is how it was then. It was not heroic but, more simply, a part of everyday living; and, thank God, on this occasion not quite dying.

For us in Kent it was a time for Spitfires, Hurricanes, Messerschmitts and doodlebugs. Several times on journeys to and from school I'd fling myself into a ditch by the roadside with my bike over me as protection as battles raged overhead. It was over the beautiful countryside of Kent that many of the Luftwaffe squadrons made their approach to their London targets, and waiting to pick them off one by one were the glorious Few. It was like watching a never-ending war film.

I was cycling home once when one pilot bravely attempted to change a V1's course by flying alongside it and flipping its wing with one of his own. The V1 rocket exploded and the Spitfire, with one of its wings blown off, came crashing down, killing the pilot. I later discovered that he was a twenty-four-year-old Frenchman called Captain Jean Pemaridor, and he is remembered in the village church. Some of the sights and sounds of war that we saw and heard as children have stayed with us all our lives. Parents sent their children off to school in those dark and dangerous days never knowing for sure they'd be home again that night. That is no exaggeration. As a parent myself and now a grandfather, I simply don't know how they coped with that.

Getting enough food in the war-time countryside was never a great problem for us. It's true there was stringent rationing of

sugar and butter, for example, and although us youngsters were
allowed, I think, two ounces of sweets a week, in five years we
had never so much as the sight of a banana or an orange. This,
though, was not only the Garden of England but also the
orchard. Apples, pears, plums were there in plenty; and in our
back garden, so were all the vegetables we needed.

And there were rabbits. My father went out catching them at
least once a week in neighbouring woodland, carrying his ferret
in a small wooden box over his shoulder and with nets in plenty
to put over the holes. I often went with him and would watch
fascinated as he put the ferret down a hole. As the poor terrified
rabbits tried to escape, they'd become enmeshed in the nets and
all that was left for them was to await a quick clinical wringing
of the neck to put them out of their misery.

I did it myself as a twelve-year-old, not very efficiently. The
rabbits would squeal their last as I struggled with them and often
my dad would have to finish them off. I'm not proud of that but
it was very much the country way of life – just as I used to shoot
squirrels. I tell this now partly because I can hardly believe it was
me doing it and partly to help cleanse my soul. Today I have
considerable compassion for all animals. I'm not a vegetarian but
I only eat free range chicken and fish and have not touched red
meat in nearly twenty years. But I'll tell you this – my mum's
baked rabbit and her rabbit pies took some beating. They were a
major part of the Moore war effort!

I cannot let my boyhood memories pass without mention of
the hop-pickers of old London town. Each summer, our peaceful
corner of England was invaded by hundreds of London families
making a shilling or two picking hops for the farmers of Kent.
They would treat it like an annual holiday, happily roughing it
in extremely basic living accommodation while spending long,
hot days slaving in the hopfields. It became a matter of local
pride to defend our territory, and on many exciting evenings
there would be stand-offs with the cocky Cockney kids in what
could have been scenes out of 'West Side Story'. It all added spice
to what my memory is convinced were always scorching

summers (yet when I look up old cricket records, I notice there were plenty of days lost to rain, so perhaps I am programmed to have only warm memories!).

Meanwhile at school my work was poor. I stumbled through my school certificate (today's GCSEs) and failed abysmally with higher school certificate (A levels). I tell myself even now that I spent too much time on the sportsfields and not enough in the classrooms. That is partly true, but it is also true that I was never a brainy boy. Today I remain not very well-read or cultured, but I'm still striving, and continue to pursue that side of life.

In winter I played rugby, as a full-back, and in the Easter term, hockey; I was captain of hockey as a left-inner. I itched to get a football team going at the school – I played regularly for our village team – and, against all the odds, and despite a lot of looking down noses at the very idea, I got a splinter football group started. For a few seasons we played a number of local schools.

Cricket, however, remained my main sport and for three years I played in the First XI, captaining it in my last season. I made enough runs as an opening batsman to play two seasons for the Young Amateurs of Kent and for a blissful moment or two even fancied that I might make a career in cricket.

My crowning moment came on 9 and 10 September 1949 when I played for the Young Amateurs against one of Kent's most revered and talented clubs, the Band of Brothers, on the beautiful county ground at Canterbury. We were facing a formidable total of over 300 when I opened the innings. Batting at number five for us was a certain Michael Colin Cowdrey.

The Kent handbook reminds me – as if I needed it – that Colin was bowled for 1 while I went on to make top score of 41 out of a miserable total of 93. I should at once complete the story by saying that normal service was resumed in the second innings. I was out for nought and Colin made a sparkling 66.

He was one of the greatest – if not the greatest – batsman I've ever seen. Certainly the greatest I ever batted with! And to this day I recall his one run when we were partners in that first innings. It was an exquisite late cut – not a customary stroke for schoolboy batsmen – and I can still hear his bat clipping the top of his pad as the ball was despatched firmly past slip. In a sporting lifetime of tumult and shouting, I'm pleased that this enchanted moment remains so vivid.

I was thrilled to get a card from Colin (now Lord Cowdrey of Tonbridge) on my retirement. He wished me well and thanked me generously for my work for sport and for the excitement I had brought into viewers' lives over the seasons. But he didn't mention that innings of 41 all those years ago!

At about this time, I fell in love for the first time. There were moments of high passion, but over the years I've also been guilty of blowing hot and cold in the relationship. Yet Gillingham Football Club has always remained a patient friend and I hope now to draw closer to her again.

My mum was a Gillingham girl and on a visit to my Auntie Mary in Sturdee Avenue in September 1947 I went to Priestfield Stadium for the first time. It was a Southern League match – the Gills were still a couple of seasons away from getting back into the Football League – but 7,225 were in the ground that day to see them beat Bath City 4–1, and that was their average home gate that season!

For a village boy used to a scattered few watching our games on the recreation ground, it was like a trip to another and more exciting world. It was that day, I'm sure, that fired my schoolboy imagination. If I wasn't good enough to play (and I wasn't) I wanted somehow to grab a bit of the action some other way.

I was back there in January 1948 when Gillingham's FA Cup run that season continued with a third-round game against Queens Park Rangers, then leading the old third division (South). The crowd – 23,002 – is still a Gillingham record and I was a part of it, standing just in front of the old Gordon Road stand. With two village pals I was first in the queue shortly before ten o'clock that morning. Early-bird Moore.

It finished in a 1–1 draw, our splendid centre-forward Hughie Russell scoring Gillingham's goal. But Rangers won the replay at Loftus Road 3–1. I can still remember the team: John Burke in goal; George Dorling (soon to be replaced by the inspirational Charlie Marks) and Cyril Poole (also a Notts cricketer) at full-back; Jimmy Boswell, Tommy Kingsnorth and George Piper the half-backs; Wally Akers (or Jimmy Warsap), Tug Wilson (one of my early thrills was to share a seat on a bus with him as he went home after a game), Hughie Russell, Jackie Briggs and George Forrester.

Gillingham have recently celebrated their centenary and they did so with a splendid history of the club called *Home of the Shouting Men*. I earned my place in that history because nobody shouted louder in those days than me.

I commentated a couple of times on Gillingham games although there was some debate in ITV Sport about whether it would be wise for me to cover their matches. How they worried! Would I stray from the line of strict impartiality? Did they really expect me to scream, 'Come on you Gills!' at some crisis point? They need not have worried. A commentator has too many things on his mind during those ninety minutes for any such thoughts to enter his head. There were no complaints.

For ten years I became a director of the club under the caring guidance of chairman Dr Clifford Grossmark. The Doc was on the League's management committee and there wasn't a regulation he didn't know. Equally, as a genuine and knowledgeable football man, there was hardly a player he hadn't filed away for future reference.

He was a fine doctor but a bit impatient on match days. I once heard him chivvy his last patient in the surgery as kick-off drew closer. The man had a severe stammer, and was having problems explaining his ailment to the good doctor.

'For heaven's sake, man, what's wrong?' pleaded Dr Grossmark. 'Spit it out. Don't you know that I've got to get to the football?' In truth he was kindness itself.

A tireless worker for the smaller clubs, he was wise about the sensible running of the club but severely short on optimism. He considered that opponents were always bigger, faster, better, craftier than us – and always likely to beat our boys in blue.

I used to ring him every Saturday night after I had finished my television work to get the Gillingham news of the day. We had made a dreadful start to this particular season and were bottom of the League. Then we beat Chesterfield 4–1.

'That must have been so much better today,' I started.

'We could have been three down in the first twelve minutes,' was his typical reply. But that was the Doc. I was proud to give the eulogy at his memorial service in Rochester Cathedral. The cathedral was packed, which was a measure of the affection in which he was held by football people far beyond the Medway towns.

When Dr Grossmark invited me on to the board, my first away game was in midweek at Blackburn, then languishing, before the days of Jack Walker, in the third division. Our motorway journey from Kent to Lancashire in pouring rain took five hours.

We were warmly welcomed but nonetheless felt like second-class footballing people in Rovers' grand oak-panelled boardroom, still preserved, happily, in a corner of Ewood Park in spite of all the vast redevelopment. The Gills were beaten 4–1 – if there had been any justice it might have been 10–1 – we had our captain sent off, we were verbally assaulted by home fans for most of the night, it rained all the way home, and when I climbed into bed at 4 a.m., Betty turned over and simply said: 'You must be mad.'

That's the other life – rarely publicised – of a football director. I stayed the course for ten years until more live television for me meant that I couldn't give the club the time they deserved. They'll always have a special place in my heart.

I was at Wembley for the 1999 division two play-off final when, agonisingly, they lost to Manchester City. Never for a moment did I dream that I would one day watch the Gills play at Wembley in front of a crowd of 76,000. Still less did I ever expect to look up at the giant scoreboard two minutes from the end and see 'Gillingham 2, Man. City 0'. Sadly, it all turned to ashes in those dramatic remaining moments. City, in a stirring revival, scored twice, and eventually won on a penalty shoot-out. It was so cruel, but the good memories of that day will always sustain me. And my thoughts turned so often to the Doc. He would have loved and hated it in equal proportions, and not been surprised by any of it!

If my early days watching Gillingham kindled something in me that led to my broadcasting life, so too did my first visit to Kent cricket. My first sight of county cricket came at about the same time as my first Gillingham experience. It was at Maidstone, one of several lovely grounds with which Kent is blessed, such as the Mote, the Nevill at Tunbridge Wells and the incomparable St Lawrence Ground at Canterbury.

Lancashire were the visitors that day at Maidstone, and the ground was full to see Washbrook and Place, Ikin and Phillipson – but also the Kent batsmen, Todd and Fagg, Ames and company, who accumulated 400 runs that sunlit day. Leslie Todd was my favourite. I identified with him, perhaps because like him I was a bit stodgy as an opening batsman. I remember he always wore a little cravat when batting and I even considered doing the same. Happily, I never quite summoned up the nerve.

I also saw Denis Compton play at Maidstone during his glorious summer of 1947 when he compiled a record seventeen centuries with his magic wand of a bat. My dad, as a true countryman, was suspicious of all city slickers and Compton, Edrich and all things Middlesex fell into that category. We sat by the boundary ropes with our Tizer and cheese and tomato sandwiches and again the ground was full. We watched Middlesex bat brilliantly all day and Dad couldn't hide his frustration as we shuffled out at the close of play.

'I thought that old Compton scratched around a bit today,' he said as if to console himself.

'Yes, Dad,' I responded. 'He's only scored 129 runs and has probably won the game for them.' I repeated this story to Denis at a tribute dinner for him a year or so before he died. He rocked with laughter. He'd probably heard it all before but he was too polite to dismiss it and he remained, for me, a true star to the very end.

Recently I re-read a signed first volume of an autobiography given to me by the great writer Compton Mackenzie when I interviewed him for radio in 1963 about his love of sport. He wrote that he had resisted writing his autobiography, because 'it amounts to undressing in public, until old age had removed me far enough from the past to be able to regard this youth as somebody for whose behaviour I was no longer responsible'.

My undressing is almost complete, except that now I put on different clothes. My National Service was in the RAF and those two years in uniform certainly did me more good than harm.

I square-bashed at Hednesford at a camp that had only recently been reclaimed after war-time duty. We washed and shaved at 6 a.m. in cold water and in darkness; needless to say, all those rumours abounded about bromide being put in our tea to subdue those manly urges. I was once denied weekend leave because the shine on my boots did not meet with the approval of one particularly nasty drill corporal and I spent two days digging a garden with a bayonet and painting white all the stones round the guard-house. I reached a level of fitness I have never matched since and, above all, learned to stand on my own two feet.

I also took off one Saturday to nearby Wolverhampton to watch Billy Wright (later to become a friend and a great colleague) and his team play Arsenal, who won 1–0. Molineux on a bitter December afternoon was wonderful therapy and as near to heaven as I could get at that time.

I eventually went on an officers' training course at Spitalgate in Lincolnshire, bought my first suit at Burton's for eight pounds to wear in the mess, and eventually became a pilot officer in the RAF Regiment. I was posted to Germany for a year, just south of Hamburg, where I learned a lot about living, played a huge amount of sport, and got hideously drunk one night after some lethal mixing of drinks. I took two days to recover and vowed never to do it again. I've faithfully kept that vow. The red wine that I enjoy nowadays I regard as a necessary measure to keep the heart working well!

But there was one crucial and significant moment for me in Germany. It came when I sprained an ankle and could not compete in a sports gala at the camp at RAF Fassberg.

'You'd better do the announcing on the Tannoy,' the CO said. So I did – and thoroughly enjoyed it. At the end of the afternoon the wife of one of my officer friends came over to me and said: 'You did that really well. And you have such an attractive voice. You should do something about it when you are demobbed.'

It got me thinking.

3

FOLLOWING
EAMONN ANDREWS

THE telephone call that was to give my career a kick-start came from Peter West, then a major player among television cricket commentators and, as I've mentioned, like me, an Old Cranbrookian. I have never been a fan of the old boy network, but here it was working for me.

'Jim Swanton of the Daily Telegraph is looking for someone to drive him around this summer, phone in his copy to the paper and generally make himself useful,' Peter said. 'Thought it might suit you.'

I'd finished my National Service a few months earlier and needed a job. So, having passed my driving test only weeks before among the hazards of Hastings, I now found myself driving the great man's enormous Austin Sheerline to county games and Test matches all over the country.

It was 1953 and what a summer it was to be involved in the world of sport in general, and cricket in particular. This was the year of the Coronation, Hillary and Tensing conquering Everest, Sir Gordon Richards winning his first Derby on Pinza in the week that he was knighted and, wonder of wonders, England beating Lindsay Hassett's Australians to win back the Ashes. Sadly, it was not so wonderful for me, though, because what should have been a glorious summer certainly had its share of dark moments to balance the light.

Mr Swanton proved to be a man easily irritated and hugely

demanding and I was not, truth to tell, the most efficient of dogs-bodies. It was, I suspect, a great relief to both of us when the summer came to an end and our collaboration with it.

He wrote and broadcast with great authority – none more so – and was as shrewd as he was meticulous in his choice of words. So woebetide any of us if his breakfast was spoiled by so much as a solitary word in his *Daily Telegraph* report being wrongly sent over by me or misheard and then missed by the paper's copy-telephonist or sports sub-editor. That always got the day off to a bad start and every day I lived in constant fear of being the culprit.

I was indeed the red-faced culprit one evening during the Trent Bridge Test when, for the first time in my career but certainly not the last, I was outwitted by electronic equipment. The Nottingham ground boasted a new, fully operational electronic scoreboard and very good it looked too, but it resulted in a nightmare moment for me. At the close of play each night, Mr Swanton would deliver a five-minute television report on the day's events. Those were the days when there were no video clips, no captions, just a straightforward and complete round-up of the day's play, and the only notes he had consisted of an up-to-date scorecard. It was my job to keep it up to date.

It was a formidable piece of television at the best of times, but sandwiched between his thousand words or so for his news-paper, it became even more remarkable. He was just going on air this particular evening when I suddenly realised to my horror that I had not put the close-of-play score on the bottom of his card. I glanced quickly towards the all-singing, all-dancing scoreboard – it was blank. They had already switched it off for the night. By now it was too late to get the score from any other source.

Came the end of his broadcast: 'So at the close of play England were…' and he looked down at the blank scorecard and barely blinked as he looked back into the camera lens. 'England were doing very well after that poor start to the day,' he ad-libbed, 'and with that, goodnight from Trent Bridge.' It was a splendid piece of improvisation and I can reveal that he was also by no means lost for words when he confronted me a few moments later. I got a real roasting. It was a lesson learned. In some forty-five years, our paths never crossed again – to my great regret.

It was during that memorable cricket season that I met a splendid, larger-than-life character named Denzil Batchelor, editor of *Picture Post*. He was the son of a High Court judge, educated at Oxford and a constant fount of anecdotes. No press box was quiet when he was around and it was Denzil who set me off on the next step in my career.

'I say, old boy,' he said, 'did you know that the magazine *World Sports* is looking for a young sub-editor. Have you done any subbing?' I said that I hadn't; all I knew was that sub-editors were responsible for the headlines and putting the final polish on articles. Denzil pooh-poohed the fact that I had never subbed in my life.

'Don't let that put you off – go for it,' he said. So I did. Next stop was 184 Fleet Street and the office of Cecil Bear, the editor, a kindly man who taught me plenty, as I began work on the publication that proudly called itself 'the official magazine of the British Olympic Association'.

Certainly I was never going to finish up rich working for them. I started on six pounds a week. I remember we all used to troop down to the Westminster Bank in Fleet Street every Friday lunchtime to get our cheques turned into pound notes (no credit cards then), and line up trying our best to avoid one notorious clerk who always counted out our money boomingly: 'One, two, three, four, five, six pounds...there you are sir, SIX pounds.' Everybody in the bank queue knew I was earning a pittance.

What they didn't know was that also somewhere in that queue was the girl who, I had made up my mind almost on first seeing her, was going to be my wife. Betty was Mr Bear's secretary, but she was shortly leaving for a job close to her home in Leyton. So I had to move quickly – and I did. I asked her out, and within eighteen months we were married. Some forty-four years on we are still happily together. How she has put up with me all these years I'll never know. But I shall be forever grateful to Denzil Batchelor and *World Sports* for bringing us together.

World Sports had a good spread of influential writers, among them Neville Cardus whose descriptions for the old *Manchester Guardian* of a day at the cricket or a night in the concert hall were unsurpassed. He would post his copy to us every month (I just can't imagine him with word processors, modems or fax machines) and every word was written immaculately in a spidery hand and with never a deletion or second thought to scar his manuscript. His mind and his thoughts, even in later years as he continued to write of days gone by, must have been crystal clear.

Each month his copy would be sent off to the Sun Printers in Watford and would be returned with the proofs, and in due course those original handwritten manuscripts, mostly about sunlit days with the gods of cricket such as C.B. Fry, A.C. MacLaren, J.T. Tyldesley, K.S. Duleepsinhji, Sir Jack Hobbs and Sir Donald Bradman, would be ditched in the nearest wastepaper basket. It's not hard to imagine what those collectors' items would be worth today.

That was one of life's little missed chances. When I look back I could add one or two more to the list. For example, I once had a day with the great Joe Louis when he came to London long after his reign as heavyweight champion was over and shortly before his death. I interviewed him at length and we had a good lunch together. Yet, apart from recalling that sometimes his words and his memory became a jumble and that he was truly a gentle man who seemingly had been cruelly ill-used in a cruel sport, I have no specific memory of the day.

Keith Miller, one of cricket's greatest all-rounders, got in touch with me when he was over from Australia simply because he had seen and enjoyed ITV's 'The Big Match'. We also had a good lunch overlooking the Thames and we laughed a lot. I found it hard to believe that one of my greatest schoolboy heroes was just across the table from me, but apart from the laughter my memory has refused to budge.

This is not the case with Neville Cardus. The last time I met him – by then he was Sir Neville – was in the early 1960s when I was working in radio and we needed, for our evening programme, a short obituary on Sydney Barnes, the great old England bowler who had died that day. I went to meet Sir Neville at the National Liberal Club in Whitehall where he had a simple, modest bedsitter. We sat on his bed and I turned on my recording machine. It had a tape-run of seven minutes, more than enough, surely.

'What do you recall of the great Sydney Barnes, who died today?' I asked. Twenty-one minutes later – yes, twenty-one minutes! – he had finished telling me, without pause for breath, without a stumble, with every word in its rightful place. It was a wonderful obituary, and a journalistic masterclass; it was also the longest answer I had ever had to one question. Every seven minutes, when the tape ran out, I would fumble about putting a new one in place and Sir Neville carried on through it all, his mind no doubt drifting back to some splendid cricket ground with Barnes in full flight.

'Thank you, Sir Neville,' was my only other contribution to this amazing interview. That night we used just one and a quarter minutes of it.

Like most young men of any era, I was restless. Soon I was augmenting my *World Sports* wage (on getting married it had gone up to seven pounds ten shillings a week) by doing an evening shift at the Sports Reporting Agency, where Nigel Clarke, now of some eminence at the *Daily Mail*, and Ken Jones, much respected columnist for the *Independent*, were also cutting their journalistic teeth. So I was working from nine thirty in the morning until ten at night and clearly that could not go on for long.

I had a couple of years at the sports-news agency, *Exchange Telegraph*, which certainly taught me all I needed to know about meeting deadlines. I heard on the Fleet Street grapevine that the *Observer* were looking for a sports sub-editor, but their Sports Editor Chris Brasher, an Olympic steeplechase gold medallist in

Melbourne just a year or so earlier, turned me down after an uncomfortable interview.

Then, in 1958, I joined *The Times* as a down-table sub-editor in their sporting room – not sports room you'll notice, as in all other newspaper offices. *The Times* then had a style firmly rooted in the past. No sportsman or sportswoman ever had a Christian name but amateurs were allowed their initials. So it would be Matthews, Lawton and Hutton, but P.B.H. May, T. E. Bailey and Dr R.G. Bannister. Writers had no names either. Readers were, for example, informed about football anonymously with articles from 'Our Association Football Correspondent', who was at that time the eloquent Geoffrey Green, not only the best football writer around but equally at home around the tennis courts of the world. Geoffrey was, if anything, an even bigger character than the aforementioned Denzil Batchelor. As one example of his wonderful eccentricity, I recall him arriving in the Wembley press box for a midweek international on a crutch after damaging a leg. On his shoulder was perched a stuffed parrot!

The Sporting Editor was John Hennessy and he was a good man; his early encouragement played an important part in my career. Soon he let me out of the office to report Saturday football matches for Monday's paper; 400 words, three guineas. He also sent me on my first foreign assignment. It was a European Cup match in Paris between Rheims, the French champions, and Burnley, in the days of Jimmy McIlroy, Jimmy Adamson, Adam Blacklaw and company, who had won the Football League Championship in 1959–60.

It was in the old Parc des Princes on a cold and windy November night, light years away from the Stade de France and the 1998 World Cup. Sitting next to me was Brian James, also on his first working trip abroad but later to become an outstanding sports writer before moving on to general and often more challenging fields for the *Sunday Times* and, mostly, with the *Mail* group. This would be a night that he'd long remember.

We each sat behind small – too small – tip-up desks with barely enough room to balance our notepads, reference books and, in his case, a telephone. *The Times'* budget didn't run to a special phone for me and I had to scurry round immediately on the final whistle to find a public one.

All was going well, even for Burnley who, though losing 3–2 on the night, went through to the quarter-finals 4–3 on aggregate. Brian's trouble started at the final whistle. Two things happened almost at the same instant – first, his phone rang and he lifted an arm to answer it; second, an untimely gust of wind caught fifteen pages of his hastily written masterpiece of a match report. When last seen, most of the pages were disappearing into and decorating the night sky over Paris.

Brian's face was a picture. Then, suddenly, he saw one page fluttering pathetically against the wire fence that surrounded the pitch. He flew down the steps after it, praying that it would be the opening page because, as any journalist will tell you, it's the 'intro' that is the crucial part of any story. Everything else flows from that. But it was not to be. He glanced wildly at his scribbled words and read, 'Then in the eighty-second minute Burnley launched another furious attack but once again the French defence held firm...' It was page thirteen.

There was only one thing for it – he took a deep breath, went back to the phone and ad-libbed the whole story. It probably wasn't as fluent as the original, but he survived and never looked back; a true craftsman with the right words for every occasion.

By now I was a regular football reporter for *The Times*, often covering games in the old FA Amateur Cup – Corinthian Casuals, Leytonstone, Walthamstow Avenue, Kingstonian, Bromley, and Walton and Hersham were all on my beat, to say nothing of Bishop Auckland, Pegasus and Norton Woodseats. I thought that BBC radio should have a slice of this action and so I wrote to Angus Mackay about it.

Angus Mackay *was* BBC radio sport. In those radio-dominated days, he was the all-powerful number one man. 'Sports Report' was his brain-child. The teleprinter results service on television was still some seasons away and so the first time you heard the Saturday results was through the distinctive voice of John

Webster at five o'clock. The programme was essential listening for all football people.

I had no reply to my letter, so I wrote again. Once more there was no reply. This time I telephoned him, which was very unlike me because I'm not by nature a pushy person. This time Angus responded and invited me to go to Broadcasting House for a chat. The upshot was that I started to do one-minute reports on amateur games for a regional programme called 'Sports Session' that went out in the London area at six thirty on Saturday evenings. My broadcasting career began some eighteen years after I imagined myself as Raymond Glendenning!

I needed advice about how to present these reports and I turned to Bryon Butler, who was also on the programme. He later became the BBC's Football Correspondent and now writes with authority and imagination for the *Daily Telegraph*. He said: 'Give it a bright start, because the old man will be listening to that – and, whatever you do, make sure you finish to the second because he'll have a stopwatch on that. The middle bit, well, just do your best.' He was right. It worked.

Eventually Angus engineered a place for me on the BBC staff – at £1,400 a year – and it was the start of a fruitful and enormously happy seven years of my working life; not that Angus was an easy man to work for – quite the reverse. He was a tough, challenging, austere and very punctilious Scot. And that was on his better days! I once arrived seven minutes late for his morning conference – the Old Kent Road traffic had been up to its tricks again – and we went for two months before he uttered a single social word in my direction, not even a good morning. That was better treatment than that handed out to some broadcasters who were much better established than me. They'd inadvertently rubbed him up the wrong way and were never heard of again on any of his programmes.

Even so, Angus shaped my whole broadcasting life. He was a fine producer with a sound news sense, confident enough to change things around during a live programmes, which is akin to changing tactics in a football match when the game is in full flow. He was on top of everything going on in the studio and he had a pretty shrewd idea of what his audience wanted. 'They are always interested in money' was one of his planks. He never failed his listeners.

'Attention to detail' was his constant reminder and they are watchwords I continued to respect right through my career. He used to say, 'Make sure you have at least two pencils sharpened on the studio desk and ready to go,' and, 'Always in a live studio be sure to have some standby material with you, even if it's only "Darlington hope to be unchanged against Chester on Saturday," because it's better that than an ugly silence if you suddenly run out of material.' I used to go to great lengths to be sure that I'd covered all the bases whenever I went live on air, a habit that stayed with me right to the end of my commentating career.

Angus lived for 'Sports Report'. Once, in the crazy way broadcasting executives have, the programme was shifted from the prestigious Light Programme to, in terms of audience size, the relative backwaters of the Third Programme. It was like switching sport today from Radio 5 Live to Radio 3.

It was a daft decision taken by a controller with no interest in sport (and I had my fill of those during my ITV years too, but more of that later). Most of us in the BBC radio sports team felt deflated and defeated – not Angus, though he had every right to feel betrayed. He called us all to his room.

'All we've got to do is make sure that "Sports Report" is better than ever, and then they'll *have* to put us back on the Light,' he said. So we did, and a season later we were transferred back, just as Angus had predicted. What a motivating football manager he would have made.

He didn't believe in flashing the programme's money around or cosseting his contributors with cars to take them to and from assignments. 'Isn't there a train?' he would demand. 'Hasn't he got a car?' Jim Manning, that sharpest of newspaper columnists who always wrote the 'Last Word' in the *Daily Mail*, was a regular part of the discussions towards the end of each 'Sports

Report' show. One particular Saturday he was covering a game at Arsenal and, with a sudden failure on the underground, had no obvious means of getting back to the studio. So he stood outside Highbury holding up a hastily scrawled notice: SPORTS REPORT PLEASE. Such was the stature of the programme that he got a lift within a couple of minutes and arrived back at Broadcasting House with time to spare. No doubt, in true Manning style, he made the most of the story.

And, of course, there was always Eamonn Andrews. The big, amiable Irishman with that slightly lopsided, triangular smile, gave 'Sports Report' its authority and its identity. Strangely, his overall knowledge of sport – boxing apart – was somewhat sketchy; but his preparation was that of a perfectionist. The man had such a presence that sportsmen everywhere confided in him as they would in an old friend.

He was at the time the best sports presenter by some distance, and an excellent interviewer, too. I doubt if there has been a better all-round broadcaster in the history of British radio or tele-vision. He gave me two good tips about the art of interviewing. One was that the best question is the shortest one – why? I'm amazed these days at how often questions ramble over various points and are usually longer than the answers they produce. His other tip was that you should stay silent when you've asked the provocative question.

'The interviewee maybe won't want to answer, but if there's a silence he'll feel the onus is on him to keep things going and most times he'll spill the beans,' Eamonn explained. He was proved right time and time again.

I marvelled at his coolness in a live studio – Angus Mackay's voice in one ear, an interview coming in maybe from New York in the other and his own thoughts and questions somewhere in between. I thought I would never get close to such skills, let alone feel comfortable with them, when taking over the 'Sports Report' anchorman's chair, but experience seems to set up a filter system in the brain so that you hear the words you have to hear and those you don't never get through the filter.

Eamonn, of course, was getting plenty of practice. He was, at that time, the best-known face and voice in the land. He was already hosting 'What's My Line', 'This Is Your Life' and the children's programme 'Crackerjack' on television, to say nothing of the radio comedy show 'Ignorance Is Bliss', and, of course, 'Sports Report'. He was also the BBC's regular boxing ringside commentator in succession to Raymond Glendenning, and somehow he found the time to write a regular labour-of-love column for the *Catholic Herald*. Before making his name in the United Kingdom, Eamonn was an outstanding columnist with the *Irish Independent* and had been All-Ireland middleweight boxing champion. It's difficult to imagine a wider portfolio, but on it all he planted a strong professional imprint.

Eamonn had an apartment in west London but never forgot his Irish roots. He maintained a magnificent home near Dublin with his wife of thirty-six years, Grainne, and he used to write all his script notes in Irish green ink. He took a pride in every programme in which he appeared. His personal favourite was 'This Is Your Life' which he imported from the United States, and he took it to ITV when the BBC tired of it the first time around. Eamonn had a gift for making everybody he hit with the Big Red Book feel special. I appeared as a guest on several shows, and never ceased to be amazed at Eamonn's professionalism and passion for the programme.

It has become part of 'This Is Your Life' legend that right up to his death Eamonn was pouring himself heart and soul into the show. When he died at the age of sixty-five in 1987, he had at his hospital bedside a script for the planned 'This Is Your Life' tribute to rugby and broadcasting master Cliff Morgan. The script pages were covered in Eamonn's green-ink notes. He was giving it one hundred per cent input right up to the end.

I last worked with Eamonn on an ITV series I presented called 'Who's the Greatest?' The basic idea was a simple but good one, yet it never quite worked. Maybe it needed a more up-front presenter, maybe the half-hour time restriction was too great, certainly it needed a better set (accurately described by one critic as looking as if tiled by a council public convenience decorator). The idea was based on the old pub argument of who is the greatest of all time, with the cases for two sporting superstars being argued by celebrity fans and the verdict being given by a twelve-strong jury made up of members of the public. I was The Judge.

We somehow survived a pilot in which Kevin Keegan (represented by comedian Tom O'Connor) was voted eleven to one greater than George Best (with Michael Parkinson as his advocate). That was the night that Parky said: 'If this is British justice, please don't let me ever have to appear in court on any sort of charge!' We later discovered that the jury had been put together by a character who used to help run a Kevin Keegan fan club!

Eamonn appeared on the show representing Rocky Marciano against Muhammad Ali, who had Dennis Waterman arguing his case for him. An hour before we were due to record the programme I was walking past Eamonn's dressing-room at the Thames Television studios at Teddington. What I saw through the open door horrified me. Eamonn was hunched over his dressing table, clearly in great distress and looking desperately ill. At this point I felt it best not to intrude, but went straight to the producer, John D. Taylor, and suggested we might have to call off the programme.

Eamonn had agreed to come on the show as a special favour to his friend Norman Giller, a 'This Is Your Life' scriptwriter and creator of the 'Who's the Greatest?' concept. Norman, summoned to take a large brandy to Eamonn's dressing-room, assured us everything would be all right but I had grave doubts.

I had taken no account of Eamonn's enormous spirit, pride and the adrenalin rush that gets all performers on their toes.

'Now to present the case for Rocky Marciano,' I announced, 'please welcome Eamonn Andrews.' And on he came. He filled the screen, the lopsided grin was in place and his performance was as powerful as it was persuasive. He looked what he was – a broadcasting giant. I shall remember him for that evening above all others. It was one of his very last appearances, and I was proud to have been part of it.

In his later years, as is so often the way, a few clever television critics had gone sniping and tried to pull Eamonn down. Maybe they had grown tired of reporting his successes; maybe they tried to wing the big one in order to increase their own stature. These were the pathetic efforts of men who barely came up to Eamonn's knees. Perhaps, had he noticed them, he would have got comfort from the words of Teddy Roosevelt, as indeed might any performer who believes he's been unfairly judged. The former US President once said: 'It's not the critic who counts. The credit belongs to the one who is actually in the arena; who knows the great enthusiasm, the great devotion; who at best knows in the end the triumph of high achievement; and who, at the worst fails while doing greatly, so that his place shall never be with those cold and timid souls who know neither victory nor defeat.'

Eamonn died just four months after the programme. I joined the huge throng for his memorial service at Westminster Cathedral. There was not a seat to be had. We all wondered if any other broadcaster could have filled so magnificent a place. I doubt it.

When he left 'Sports Report' in the mid-1960s to present ITV's new Saturday afternoon show, 'World of Sport', his radio seat went to Liam Nolan, another Irishman with a similar voice to Eamonn's and a very pleasing manner. It was a clever shot by Angus, but Eamonn was quite simply too huge an act for another of his countrymen to follow and Liam eventually went back to Ireland where he's enjoying a successful career as a broadcaster and writer.

Next up for a few weeks was Robin Marlar. Until recently, he had been captain of the Sussex cricket team and was blossoming as an outspoken correspondent for the *Sunday Times*. He gave it a good stab, but Robin knew – and he still shows it – that he is far more effective answering questions than asking them.

Then I had my turn, and I thoroughly enjoyed it for two or

three seasons, combining 'Sports Report' with Saturday football commentaries. This was an invigorating time and the perfect apprenticeship for much of what was to follow.

I also now attracted my first bit of 'fan' mail. On the Monday after my first commentary I received two postcards. Both were anonymous, and that should have told me something. The first said: 'Why don't you keep your bloody mouth shut!' And the second: 'You'll never be as good as Raymond Glendenning.' Welcome to the world of broadcasting!

One of my first commentaries was in fact with Raymond, the man I had dreamed of becoming all those years ago on the way to school, and it was a match at Fratton Park between Portsmouth and Bolton Wanderers. Even without television exposure, Raymond was as recognisable to the fans as Bob Wilson and Des Lynam are today.

Having been fêted, no doubt, by the Portsmouth directors, he arrived in good time at the commentary box. He was generous in everything he said and not for a moment did he treat me like some clever young upstart with eyes on his job. It was wonderful just to be sitting there with him; I guess Michael Owen must have had much the same feelings the first time he pulled on a shirt alongside Alan Shearer.

The game was nondescript and at the end we quickly went our separate ways. So quickly that I missed the chance to say to him: 'Thank you. You were the man who inspired me to try my hand at this.' I wish I could have done that. I never met him again and, to my surprise, he retired from the BBC aged fifty-five and died ten years later. But he had made his mark.

My commentating career was up and away. Soon I would spread my wings, thanks to Angus Mackay, to commentary boxes around the world.

— 4 —

1966 AND ALL THAT

O NE of the most illuminating memories of my radio days
came, fittingly, at Benfica's majestic Stadium of Light in
Lisbon on a warm March night in 1966. I was in Manchester
United's dressing-room. George Best – then a nineteen-year-old
with hardly a word to say for himself – was sitting alone in a
corner quietly reading, still in his street clothes, while Bobby
Charlton, Denis Law, Pat Crerand, Nobby Stiles and the rest
were just a blur of activity as they prepared for a critical
European Cup quarter-final, only forty-five minutes away.

I had gone to the dressing-room seeking, with some urgency,
a co-commentator. My BBC radio bosses had decided, at the last
minute, to go live with this match, so I needed a summariser,
and Sir Matt Busby, United's manager, invited me in to see if he
could help. That was typical of Sir Matt, and help he did by
offering that spirited, articulate Republic of Ireland full-back
Noel Cantwell, the United club captain who was on the side-
lines with an injury. What a good choice it proved. However, it
was the other Irishman who captured my attention. I was
amazed that night by the nerve and the composure of this slip
of a boy.

Don't for a moment doubt the importance of the night or the
tension being generated. Manchester United had squeezed a
narrow and precarious 3–2 advantage from the first leg and now
faced a difficult examination against the 1965 European Cup

runners-up. Benfica were champions in 1961 and 1962 and unbeaten in eighteen home ties over six years, during which they had scored a phenomenal seventy-eight goals. Five of those came against the superb Real Madrid side the previous season and only once in that time had they conceded more than a single goal at home. Benfica were number one Europe, and few expected Manchester United to hold on, and certainly none of the 71,000 Benfica fanatics who were waiting for the action and the celebrations to start. Yet here was young George giving every appearance of preparing for a casual Sunday morning game in the park.

What followed was unforgettable. United, and George Best in particular, conjured one of the greatest European performances of all time. Noel and I sat in our commentary box unable to believe it all as United scored three times without reply in the opening fifteen minutes; and the young man who had been sitting alone in the corner of the dressing-room had scored two of them. Game over. I remember putting my hand over the microphone, turning to Noel and saying: 'I have got it right, haven't I? It really is three–nil?' It was a night when you simply could not trust your eyes!

George scored the first with a flashing header from a free-kick; the brilliant second came when goalkeeper Harry Gregg's clearance was headed on by David Herd and George spirited his way past three defenders to finish it off. John Connelly, Pat Crerand and Bobby Charlton completed the destruction. A leading Portuguese sports paper declared next day: 'Manchester United were fabulous in all that is most artistic, imaginative and pure in football.'

It was scintillating football that had Matt Busby written all over it, and yet the great man admitted that before the match he had asked his team simply to concentrate on containing Benfica for the first twenty minutes before they started their search for goals.

'George obviously had cotton wool in his ears when we spoke before the game,' said Sir Matt. Clearly George's reading matter had proved more appealing than team tactics and clearly, too, even in those early days, he was a free spirit!

That was the night that the George Best legend really took off. I remember the United players ribbing him at Lisbon Airport on the way home because he had bought a huge sombrero. But they lacked the vision of either George or, perhaps, an alert adviser with an eye for publicity. On arrival in England, George deliberately plonked the sombrero on his head as he walked through customs. The press photographers captured a picture that featured in all of the national newspapers the following day. El Beatle was born. What a great piece of PR; from then on George was known as the fifth Beatle and was never out of the headlines.

In all my time in the broadcasting business, I never came across any sportsman who could begin to match George's attraction for the opposite sex. He really did have pop megastar status. I often wonder whether he would have been an even better player had he been born less attractive and so with fewer distractions! But why should I wish that on him? George's many admirers, myself included, have spent time worrying about his lifestyle, but he assures me that he has enjoyed every moment of his existence. So why should we fret? But I will always have the deep-down feeling that he could have achieved so much more with his God-given talent. That night in Lisbon I thought there were no limits to what he could do in football, and he eventually reached towards most of them.

It was a complete performance by United and Best, and in my commentating career I've been privileged to watch many Manchester United triumphs – that emotional night at Wembley in 1968 against old rivals Benfica in the European Cup final; against Barcelona in the Cup Winners' Cup final of 1991, the Mark Hughes night; that more recent riveting night against Juventus, the Ryan Giggs explosion. But, for me, nothing quite measures up to that ninety minutes of splendour in Lisbon, or to the young Irishman who inspired it.

At least, that is what I thought until that amazing night in Barcelona in the early summer of 1999, when the Champions'

League final was snatched so memorably from Bayern Munich. I was a grateful guest of ITV and UEFA that night, and I took my seat in the VIP enclosure alongside Boris Becker and his wife. He told me that he'd been a Bayern supporter since childhood and the golden days of Beckenbauer and Müller.

So Boris is a genuine football fan, unlike so many luvvies following the latest football fashion. And he proved it to me by knowing all that was worth knowing about every Manchester United player. Also by his obvious passion for the game. What a rollercoaster night we had! He was on his feet when Basler scored with his early free-kick; I was in despair. I was on my feet and cheering myself hoarse in those last unforgettable moments when Sheringham and Solskjaer did their business, and Boris was slumped alongside me.

I commiserated with him as we left our seats. 'In sport there is always another year,' he smiled. 'I should know about that more than most!'

I could not help but feel that this was a night made for commentators – and how I would have relished it! It would be less than honest if I did not admit that the thought flashed through my mind that perhaps my retirement had not been so perfectly timed after all!

After it was all over, I had a drink with ITV commentators Clive Tyldesley and Ron Atkinson, and they were still six feet off the ground more than an hour after the final whistle. It was a great night for them, and from what I saw of the video recording of the match, they captured the moment.

What sheer joy it was going to football in the sixties. If you didn't bump into George Best, you could luxuriate in the work of Bobby Moore and if he wasn't around you could be sure that Jimmy Greaves would be. Jimmy was always one of my favourites from the day that I first saw him play in a youth tournament in Barcelona in 1957. On our five hour flight in a Viking of Eagle Airways – we had to call in at Perpignan to refuel! – he told me of his fear of flying (*à la* Bergkamp) and it is something that has never left him. 'If God had meant us to fly he would have given us wings,' he always says, adding in his no-holds-barred style, 'and also a blankety-blank safety net.'

I always admired Jimmy's football and, in later life, his battle against alcoholism. He freely admits that flying played a part in turning him to drink. 'I would always get stoked up before getting on to a plane,' he says. Indeed, when he flew to Italy in 1960 to start his brief career with AC Milan he was the worse for wear when he arrived after drinking to try to control his nerves before embarking at Heathrow. Drink took him down but he proved he had the character and courage to overcome it. That, he will tell you, was a greater accomplishment than anything he achieved in his glorious footballing career.

His uncomplicated if-you-don't-like-it-you-can-lump-it approach to his new career as a broadcaster was a real eye-opener for those of us who had disciplined ourselves to follow the accepted codes of conduct.

I played golf with him recently. His swing is of his own peculiar design, I must say, but he obviously does something right at the last split-second because he hits the ball for miles! His philosophy of life was revealed in one sentence as we trudged up the 18th: 'When I go to my Maker, Mooro, I shall say "thanks". Do you know, I've not had to work a single day of my life. Playing football was always a pleasure and so was my television life and all that came after it.' How many of us can say that?

Like Best, I remember Jimmy, in particular, for one amazing night of European football. It came in Rotterdam in May 1963. Tottenham destroyed Atletico Madrid 5–1 in the final of the Cup Winners' Cup. Jimmy scored two, Terry Dyson two and John White one, with a scorching shot by Dyson the pick of the bunch. Jimmy was untouchable that night. Anyone who saw him in his greatest days can still see in their mind's eye that lovely skipping, rhythmic run, the slightly left-sided, cheeky control, and goals so often scored by placing the ball so that it scarcely touched the back of the net. There were few belters, practically no headers, but a calculating brain allied to great skill, generating such wonderfully warm memories.

Most of the drama on that Rotterdam occasion had taken place in the two days leading up to the game. We were all staying in a hotel at the nearby seaside resort of Scheveningen where Spurs were doing their best to hide a doubt over the fitness of the incomparable Dave Mackay. His absence would, we thought, be a mortal blow. Mackay was the giant heart of the Spurs team; he had played a major part in their League and Cup double success – the first achieved by any club this century – two years earlier.

Desmond Hackett, of the *Daily Express*, one of the old-school charmers among football writers, immaculately dressed complete with the brown bowler that he so often declared he would eat if a prediction went wrong, got on to the story. Desmond's reporting, it has to be said, often floated above the facts. (It was Desmond who first coined the saying, 'Don't let facts get in the way of a good story.') He revealed exclusively to *Express* readers that, far from being unfit, Mackay had joined the rest of the Tottenham players riding donkeys on the seashore as part of their relaxing preparation!

The rest of the press corps simply shrugged their shoulders, and got on with their factual 'Mackay doubtful' stories. Only at around midnight when the first editions came off the presses did they realise that Desmond, rather than they, was being believed by their sports editors back home. Harassed football writers started getting urgent calls from their offices demanding confirmation of the story – plus pictures, please, of Mackay on the donkey! By then, of course, Des was up and away planning his next venture.

Despite the Hackett story, there was considerable anxiety among all Spurs fans as well as media folk over Mackay's fitness for the match against Atletico at a time, remember, when no British club had ever won a major European trophy. Confidence was sinking, and even their magnificent manager Bill Nicholson was suddenly caught up in the gloomy mood. Then skipper Danny Blanchflower stepped in. Danny, in his quirky way, was a fine leader. 'Perhaps we should stop worrying about who is *not* in the team,' he told his team-mates. 'I know the Spaniards are worried sick about the ones who *will* be playing.' Danny learned so much about leadership, he once told me, from the great Peter Doherty, his Irish team manager, a superb motivator. Danny's words calmed the fears, and confidence had been restored by the time he led out his team, minus Mackay, for what was to be an historic night for British football.

Nobody frightened Atletico more that night than Jimmy Greaves. Sometimes I play a video of his finest goals, and there's one against Manchester United at White Hart Lane in October 1965 when he receives a pass from Dave Mackay, turns close-marking John Fitzpatrick, goes at pace past United defenders Nobby Stiles, Bill Foulkes and Tony Dunne – hard to find three better – glides round the goalkeeper Pat Dunne and, Greaves-fashion, gently strokes the ball into the net. There was no danger for United when he received it – a twinkling later he had dazzled and destroyed them. Every time I see it, even all these years later, I'm on my feet and if I were to choose the ten best goals I've seen in my life this sublime moment certainly would be high among them. Tottenham again won the match 5–1, and Denis Law, a spectator that day because of injury, said he had never seen a better goal. George Best, watching from the halfway line, agreed.

Terry Venables once told me a tale about Jimmy that shows how unconventional he was even then. It happened while they were both at Chelsea, seventeen-year-old Terry just in the side, Jimmy, at twenty, the worldly senior partner. They both lived in Essex and on match days Jimmy would give Terry a lift across London in his little Ford Popular, and they would call in at a restaurant in Gants Hill, Ilford, for their pre-match meal.

'What are you eating?' asked Jimmy the first time they stopped before a crucial home first-division match. Terry decided on a piece of boiled chicken with a side salad; light and sensible, he thought. He looked on with disbelief as Jimmy proceeded to demolish a large plate of roast beef, Yorkshire pudding, roast potatoes and all the trimmings.

'We continued our journey to Stamford Bridge,' recalls Terry. 'We were playing West Brom, and we beat them five–nil. Jimmy scored four!' Yes, James also had a huge appetite for goals!

I had good days with Greavsie during his television life, and one distinctly uncomfortable one at Sunderland's old Roker Park when we commentated live on a game against Arsenal in a ninety-minute rainstorm with no roof over our heads and only a well-worn camera canvas cover for protection. It wasn't such a funny old game that day! The laugh, as well as the rain, was really on Greavsie. When we arrived at Roker Park at noon the sun was shining and there were just a few distant clouds. We decided that we did not want to commentate from a little hut up on the roof because the view of the pitch was not a good one. So riggers were called in to set up our commentary position in the open. We had just taken our seats when the clouds started to gather on the horizon. As the kick-off drew closer, so did the clouds. Just as the referee blew the first whistle, Roker Park was suddenly black and the raindrops started to fall. By the time the final whistle blew, we were soaked to the skin.

Mind you, we finished in profit because Arsenal's vice-chairman, David Dein, took pity on us and presented us with brand new Arsenal tracksuits. I use mine to this day. Greavsie? I can't really imagine him in Arsenal colours!

Television, even on bad days like that one at Roker Park, provided a valuable part of Jimmy's rehabilitation after his struggle with alcohol. Much credit is due to John Bromley, executive producer of sport for London Weekend Television, and later Gary Newbon of Central. Against some opposition, they saw Jimmy's potential, his chirpy, earthy opinions, his humour – the epitome of what Messrs Bromley and Co. were looking for: entertaining and typical pub chat. It was Brommers who came up with the idea of pairing Ian St John and Jimmy for what became a popular and much-loved partnership.

I recall Jimmy being with us as a member of the ITV World Cup panel of 1982 in the early days of his broadcasting career and only a couple of years or so after hitting the headlines by admitting that 'the booze is killing me'. He would come in early every night, make himself coffee, perform well in front of the cameras, then, shunning temptation, be into the basement car park and away before any of us had sipped the first post-programme drink. I don't think his life had ever been all that disciplined, but it most certainly was then.

He was on duty on the last night of that World Cup and, as the presenter, I asked him for his final thoughts. He produced a typical Greaves payoff.

'Well,' he said, 'what a time we've had. For three weeks we've had long balls and short balls, square balls and high balls, good balls and bad balls – and let's face it, Brian, it's been all...' and here he paused for a mischievous moment, '...been all so very enjoyable.' The nation loved him.

Now it seems that television has dumped him. He was dropped for the 1994 World Cup and wasn't even considered for France '98. I think it's a shame, and a serious mistake. Pundits these days are full of authority and credibility. Often what they say is worth listening to, but how many of them have that dash of Greaves humour? And, remember, the man talking used to play the game as well as it has ever been played. With Jimmy you had to be prepared to take risks. At times his humour and his opinions were outrageous, but the fans adored him. He talks (as he flies) without a safety net! In a battle for audiences, his is a voice that was silenced too quickly.

The early sixties were thrilling times to be assigned to Spurs in Europe, even though their manager Bill Nicholson never found it easy making time for, or small talk among, the following media circus. Yet he is a man whose straight-dealing and brusque Yorkshire honesty I came to admire and, as seasons passed, we became friends.

I was at Bill's house, within a goalkick of White Hart Lane – it was as though he dare not be too far from his beloved Spurs – on the sad day in 1964 when poor John White was killed by lightning as he sheltered beneath a tree during a round of golf at

Crews Hill, Middlesex. John was known as 'The Ghost of White Hart Lane' – he drifted almost unseen into positions to pull defences apart with his precise passes. The man from Falkirk looked so frail but his talent as a playmaker was of the highest class; he won twenty-two caps for Scotland and, at twenty-six years of age, was at his absolute peak. He was the hidden ace in the midfield trio (along with Blanchflower and Mackay) that made that great Tottenham double team perform. His tragic death came at a time when, both in life and in his sport, he would have been reaching the golden age.

I had gone to Bill Nick's home with my little BBC tape recorder to get an obituary for broadcasting the following day. He and his ever-welcoming wife, Darkie, invited me to stay for dinner. It was as though Bill needed somebody to talk to, to help him over his grief at the death of one of his players. In spite of his bluff manner and tough discipline, Bill always looked on his players as part of his family and this was a hugely painful night for him.

Looking back, I'm always astonished that nobody from Tottenham was on hand to offer him support and comfort; and even more surprised that I was the only journalist who came knocking on his door. Today, the little street where Bill and Darkie continue to live would be blocked by television vans and nobody would be able to move for camera crews.

There were some stupendous European nights at White Hart Lane. The crowds would be packed in in their thousands, swaying and singing their 'Glory-Glory Hallelujah' song, at least two hours before kick-off. The gates would be closed behind them with 61,000 spectators shoehorned into White Hart Lane. The noise was awesome. All-seater stadiums? They were not even being dreamed about.

I saw the Polish side Gornik demolished by the White Hart Lane atmosphere alone, coupled with a first-minute assault on their goalkeeper by Bobby Smith that softened him up. This was a case of Smith keeping a promise. Jimmy Greaves told me that after the first leg in Poland, Smith, a huge battering-ram of a centre-forward, had quietly approached the Gornik goalkeeper in the players' tunnel, put a fist under his nose and told him: 'Londres, pal...you're going to get it in Londres.' Smith did not disappoint him, frightening the life out of the goalkeeper with his first-minute challenge. Tottenham, 4–2 down from the first leg, ran out 8–1 winners with the goalkeeper quickly waving the white flag of surrender.

Rarely did we cover those big European games live on radio; there were no permanent facilities for radio or television broadcasts at even the major grounds. It was the dark ages as far as television was concerned. At least these days Radio 5 Live have got their act together most impressively, but in my radio reporting days I'd have to leave the action half-a-dozen times during every match. At White Hart Lane, that meant beetling off down the stairs and running through endless corridors to reach a microphone point in a caretaker's store-room close by the dressing-rooms. Tucked in among the brooms and mops I'd wait for my cue and, with the roars still going on overhead, I'd give my 'eye-witness' account. Some consolation was that with no TV coverage my descriptions could never be questioned.

I became quite a Spurs fan, without ever breaking my emotional ties with Gillingham. It got to the point where I was invited to join the Tottenham team as a 'celebrity' guest in a television football quiz show called 'Quizball'. There was a range of questions on all subjects, and even more than twenty years on I cringe in embarrassment at my feeble contribution to the team effort. David Vine, another great broadcasting survivor, was the quizmaster. I recall we went to Glasgow and beat Rangers in the first round but went out in the second round to Everton. I hold my hands up and confess that I was totally out of my depth and I have forever admired those who venture into the dangerous world of panel games.

A 'Quizball' question that I *would* be able to answer is: 'For which major match were you least prepared?' The answer would be the 1967 European Cup final in which Celtic became the first British team to win the premier club trophy.

It was the first time that I had seen Jock Stein's imposing team, and ideally I would have liked forty-eight hours to watch Jock putting his players through their training sessions. That way you get to know the players by their physical characteristics, which is so vital for instant identification.

Because the BBC were keen to keep the costs down, my fellow-commentator, Alan Clarke, and I were flown out to the baking sunshine of Portugal on the morning of the game. It was an after-noon kick-off, and so we had time only to drive quickly from the airport straight to the stadium and into the action with hardly time to breathe, let alone familiarise ourselves with the two teams.

Like me, Alan had not seen Celtic on the way to this final against Inter-Milan, the great architects of defence-dominated football. To make matters worse, those were the days when Celtic played without numbers on their green and white hooped shirts and, of course, no names either. Their one small conces-sion to moving with the commercial times was to have a modest number on their shorts. But you needed the eyes of a hawk to spot that from the commentary box.

The match was played in the marble splendour of Portugal's National Stadium and the glaring sunlight was, to say the least, tough on the eyes. Both of us, if pressed, would have to admit that it was a day when more than a dash of guesswork went into our commentary. In fact, it was a darned sight easier picking out the Italians, who, thank goodness, had large numbers on their shirts. Sometimes I hear snippets of that commentary replayed today and I'm amazed how assured we both sound.

Sandro Mazzola put Inter in front from the penalty spot in the seventh minute, and from then on Inter hid their goal behind a fortress defence. But Tommy Gemmell equalised with a fantastic shot from twenty yards before Steve Chalmers deflected a Bobby Murdoch shot into the net for a winning goal six minutes from the end.

In these sanitised days when players and managers are among the untouchables on occasions like this and every major stadium has an increasing number of no-go areas, I have to report that at the end of the match I was actually on the pitch with the Celtic players and their ecstatic fans, and soon I had my microphone pointing at the beaming and proud Celtic manager Jock Stein.

Jock found the time to tell BBC listeners how thrilled he was to become the first British manager to lift the European Cup (incidentally, with a team of players all born within a thirty-mile radius of Glasgow – I wonder how that reads to today's multi-national teams?). Then he battled his way through the wall of celebrating Celtic supporters to the dressing-room where fellow-Scot Bill Shankly was waiting with open arms. 'John,' the Liverpool manager boomed in that much-imitated voice of his, 'you've just become a bloody legend.'

What a great man Jock Stein was! His generosity with his time, patience and advice is something I shall long remember. It didn't matter that I came from the wrong side of the border. Sadly, I was also a witness when Jock tragically died in harness while managing his beloved Scotland.

I remember warmly and clearly how, as ever, he kindly took time out from a training session to give me team information on the eve of Scotland's crucial World Cup qualifier against Wales at Cardiff's Ninian Park. I sensed that he was not a well man. Indeed, since surviving a bad car smash and a heart attack he had been a shadow of himself. But he was still courteous and his cooperation was boundless just hours from a match of massive proportions.

While the match was going out live on 10 September 1985, Jock collapsed on the Scottish bench. He was carried to the dressing-room and clearly there was a major emergency. Even as I was commentating from the other side of Ninian Park I could see the signs were bad. It was a difficult and delicate time, but it was only later in the strained and hushed dressing-room area that we learned the dreadful truth of his death at the age of sixty-two. My mind went back to the sunshine of Lisbon.

Here in Cardiff, a 1–1 draw was good enough for World Cup finals qualification. Jock Stein's Scotland had triumphed this night just as Celtic had back in 1967.

The game of football said goodbye to a true giant. He had what was, to say the least, a formidable managerial record: twenty-five major titles with Celtic (ten Championships, eight Scottish Cups, six league Cups and the European Cup) plus the Scottish Cup with Dunfermline. John, or Jock, truly was a legend.

During the early sixties, I was also getting the opportunity to branch out and gather up personality interviews for 'Sports Report'. Angus Mackay just loved to sprinkle his programme with showbiz names, so I went to the Palladium dressing-room of Ken Dodd to talk about his Liverpudlian sporting interests. Doddy was, as usual, great fun ('tattifilarious' he called it) and he is still a turn, above all others, I travel miles to enjoy live on stage. He is the last of a kind. Harry Secombe was another at the end of my mike, and at a moment's notice I was once whisked off to Heathrow to catch up with a young golfer who was starting to make a name for himself. Gary Player was still in his twenties, but even though the check-in for his flight to South Africa was going on all around us he gave me a great interview. Gary told me of his developing powers of concentration and of a philosophy that was proving sound even when times got really hard.

'It all comes from a book that I call my second Bible,' he confided. 'It's *The Power of Positive Thinking* by Dr Norman Vincent Peale.'

He was so full of it that I went straight to the Heathrow bookshop and bought myself a copy. I still have it, dog-eared and priced three and sixpence (17.5p). Thanks to Gary Player, I found and still find a lot for me in this book. Another book I find useful is one that Jack Petchey, former West Ham director and owner of Watford, gave me back in 1987, called *How To Stop Worrying and Start Living*. It was written by the great philanthropist Dale Carnegie. You can tell that I'm a born worrier! Jack has written on the fly-leaf, 'I hope this book helps you as much as it has helped me over the last twenty years.' He told me he looked at it most nights before turning out the light. I should perhaps remind you there are few more successful businessmen anywhere than Jack.

In 1964 my broadcasting career spread to the other side of the world, to the Olympic Games in Tokyo. It took some time getting there. Our BOAC aircraft stopped for refuelling at Rome, Teheran, Calcutta, Rangoon and Hong Kong, where we stayed for the night before completing our journey the next day. These days it's one long, exhausting hop, but at least you're there.

I sat next to Frank Bough all the way, me with a sneezing cold to end them all which hardly made me the most welcome of travelling companions. We were based in a slightly seedy, downmarket hotel in Tokyo, rumoured to be the haunt of ladies of the night though suitably cleaned up, it seemed, for the Olympics.

That wasn't the only BBC cost-cutting exercise. We had to share rooms and I was paired with Alun Williams, a wonderful Welshman, full of fun and good stories, as versatile a broadcaster as you could get and very much in the mould of Wynford Vaughan Thomas. The legendary John Snagge of Boat Race fame was there for the rowing and Raymond Brooks-Ward for the equestrian events. One evening, the three of us, greatly daring, went for a Japanese massage. It was, let me say at once, all very proper – but of course we all came out and went on our way feeling we had been proper devils.

I was in Tokyo as a roving reporter for radio and covered the opening ceremony from a local bar, watching it on a colour television. Wow! It might seem pretty ordinary now, but I was excited to be able to tell of the vivid colours of the flags, the uniforms, the crowd, the grass, the sky. Colour TV was still some five or six years away from British audiences, and back home Olympic action was being seen in glorious black and white.

My main beat in Tokyo was the Olympic Village where everything was so relaxed that there was even a media bus to take the newshounds there each day; no special accreditation was required. Now you need a pocketful of passes to get into any training ground, with everything else off-limits. In Tokyo, we wandered around among the stars and the Olympic heroes of days gone by, journalistic gold-dust round every corner; which is how I came to meet and interview the illustrious Jesse Owens. His gold medals in the 100 metres, 200 metres, long jump and sprint relay in the 1936 Games in Berlin were the worthy credentials for being an honoured member of the United States delegation.

I've rarely met anyone with a readier smile or a greater wish to be of help, and some thirty-five years later I can tell you exactly what I coaxed from him in the interview. When researching for this book, I was determined to look up what the great man had told me. I was sure it would still be in the BBC archives, and I was right. Yes, I could have a copy of it, they said, but (probably under the new Birtian regime) it would have to be paid for – thirty-five pounds please, plus VAT. I duly coughed up. But then, what a let-down – and what a blow to my professional pride.

I listened with great anticipation to my interview and heard Jesse Owens telling me about the current crop of American sprinters, his admiration for Lynn Davies, that he was sure the forthcoming marriage of Ann Packer and Robbie Brightwell would be a success and that Mary Rand had one of the finest personalities of any person he had ever met. At last I heard myself getting around to asking him about his memories of the 1936 Games. He said he thought first about the enthusiasm of the crowds and then of his victory in the 100 metres.

'Mr Owens, ' I said, 'thank you very much indeed.'

That was it, the non-interview of our times. I didn't think to mention Adolf Hitler, or the little matter of that racist snub from the Nazi leader for daring to be such a successful black athlete. There had been enormous speculation about his treatment by Hitler through the years and here was the man himself who could have given me his side of the story. Yet when he mentioned the 100 metres all I could find to say was, 'Thank you, Mr Owens. ' But no thanks to you, Mr Moore.

That experience certainly leads the field in 'Interviews I Wish I Could Do Again'. Amazingly, I had the opportunity five years later to make amends when I was in America filming a documentary on the burning issue of black power in US sport. This was in the lead up to the medal ceremony protests at the Mexico Olympics by black American sprinters Tommie Smith and John Carlos, who stunned the world with their clenched black-gloved salute on the rostrum.

I went to Jesse Owens' home in San José, California, and was warmly welcomed, but I was quickly aware that he was a changed and quite confused man. It seemed to me he didn't quite know where he stood on this black power issue. He was revered still in American sport, though the militants had begun to dismiss him as someone who should be doing more for their cause. The worst insult of all, that he was an 'Uncle Tom' puppet of the whites, was being bandied around. It was a damaging accusation that, I know, troubled this good and caring man. This time it was an uncomfortable interview compared with the friendly almost casual conversation in Tokyo. I suppose I should have drawn the thread back to those Berlin Games and talked about his treatment there as a black athlete, but again I failed to get around to it.

The great Jesse Owens provides no landmark in my career as an interviewer, but I'm so proud to have met him. How I wish I could have had a third try. Sadly, he died in March 1980 at the age of sixty-seven.

I had happier experiences with another wonderful black sportsman, Sir Learie Constantine. It was my privilege to bat with Sir Learie in a charity game in Essex. I stood at the non-batting end watching as the local pace-merchant came steaming in to bowl to the cricketing legend from the sunshine island of Trinidad. Sir Learie, then well into his sixties, proceeded to hit his first ball back over the young man's head and it was last seen disappearing deep into the woods beyond long-on. It was a massive hit, sent on its way with a huge chuckle and achieved, it seemed to me, as easily as we might open a door. The ball was lost forever, but not the memory.

I was beginning to do some television work on the local 'Town and Around' programme from the BBC studios at historic

Alexandra Palace no less, where the whole television business began to take root in the late 1930s. I once did a live interview there with Ron 'Chopper' Harris, then captain of Chelsea and not particularly forthcoming with his views at the best of times. It was testimony to Ron's reluctance to deliver and my inability to draw him out that I got through a record fifteen questions in the two-minute item. My technique obviously was not improving.

However, Cliff Morgan, splendid broadcaster and editor of the midweek 'Sportsview', noticed a spark, and he asked me to do a live piece straight to camera on the Beeb's flagship show one Wednesday evening. It was to be on England's apparently faltering steps as they prepared to host the 1966 World Cup. Peter Dimmock, he of the starched collar, distinctive moustache and steeped in television sport, introduced me and I duly completed my two minutes. Next morning our postman said he had seen me.

'If you don't mind me saying so, Mr Moore,' he said, 'you looked like a frightened rabbit caught in the headlights.'

I looked at a recording. Postie was dead right. It had been strictly a second-class delivery. I was still some way from cracking it.

But perhaps it had not been as bad as my postman and I thought. Six months before the 1966 World Cup I received an approach from BBC Television. They were fishing for me to join their team of commentators for the tournament, headed, of course, by Kenneth Wolstenholme. By now I was managed by Teddy Sommerfield, a kind and worldly man who had seen it all before, knew most of the dodges and was not in the least impressed or intimidated by television moguls who came bearing gifts for his clients. He lived in Portman Square, close to Oxford Street, and did all his business from the Connaught Hotel. 'That's my office,' he'd say. In every sense, he was a five-star man.

Eamonn Andrews had put him on to me, and Teddy delivered the pep talk that he gave all his clients: 'Don't get involved in cliques or office politics, put your family on the highest level of private medicine, make good use of your time off and whenever anybody asks you to do a job for them be enthusiastic about it and then refer them to me. You be the nice guy, let me be the tough cookie.' Teddy looked after me well.

I badly wanted to go to television for the World Cup, but Teddy wasn't happy with the money. No deal. They came back again with a slightly improved offer. He still wasn't happy. Still no deal. Again the BBC came back. Same again. Each time the purse strings had been loosened, but not enough. I was getting frantic. 'If they aren't prepared to up the money more than this, they can't want you very badly. Remember that,' was his expert assessment. It's advice I have always remembered.

The BBC had raised their offer to £2,750 a year. Teddy said I would not accept a penny less than £3,000. In truth, I would have snatched their hands off had it been left to me. That explains why I needed – and still need – a manager guided by economics rather than emotions.

Next Peter Dimmock, one of the legends of TV sport, got involved in the talks. Still Teddy was not budging, and the television negotiators decided their patience was exhausted and they'd had enough. Their World Cup would go on without me. I thought my chance of a future in television had gone, and I settled down, with some disappointment I have to confess, to cover the 1966 finals for radio.

Kenneth Wolstenholme, of course, gained lasting fame from that '66 final. 'They think it's all over. It is now,' is a line any commentator would die for. It's not something he could ever have planned in advance (and there *are* some who do compose their 'ad-libs' before the kick-off). It was a moment of brilliantly inspired broadcasting. I hope Ken has been well rewarded by those who have jumped on that particular bandwagon.

I'm often asked what I said at that precise moment in the final when those fans were on the pitch and Geoff Hurst smashed in that glorious fourth goal for England. Nothing is the answer. In those days we were on for fifteen-minute spells – it was felt that our voices needed a rest at that point – and Alan Clarke had the microphone at that stage of the game. I was his silent partner.

The piece of commentary that I often hear replayed, though, is my description of Geoff Hurst's second goal. Did it cross the line or didn't it? I have never had any doubts. I can see it now, as if it had happened today, a sliver of green turf between the ball over the line and the goalline itself. I don't care what anybody says or what interminable television replays and reconstructions try to prove, or even what the Germans say! I was there with the best seat in the house. Take it from me, the Russian linesman Tofik Bakhramov got it absolutely right. 'Da!' It *was* a goal. It is there in black and white in the record books for all time: England 4, West Germany 2, Geoff Hurst three goals.

I have so many memories in my mind of that 1966 World Cup final: Sir Alf Ramsey left stranded on the bench, unblinking and apparently unemotional, as his backroom men leapt to their feet when the Jules Rimet Trophy was won just as he had said it would be months in advance; dear Bobby Moore, who once told me his biggest crisis on that day was when he climbed the thirty-nine Wembley steps to collect the Cup from the Queen, seeing her white gloves and his dirty hands and quickly giving them a rub on the velvet cloth decorating the Royal Box before reaching for the greatest moment of his painfully short life; Nobby's jig and Bobby's tears; big Jack marvelling at the coolness of Moore in the last seconds of extra time, turning a man in his own penalty area and unleashing a forty-yard pass into Hurst's path, and thinking to himself, as he once said to me, 'I'll never be able to play this blankety-blank game.'

More than thirty years on, with football up to its eyes in money, just consider the winning bonus paid to Bobby Moore and his men for their effort on that glorious day for English football. It was £1,000 each, and Bobby had to go to court on behalf of the squad to stop the tax man taking a bite. What a way to treat heroes.

And what about Alf Ramsey? He could be his own worst enemy at times. I recall that three of Fleet Street's finest football writers, Ken Jones (then with the *Daily Mirror*), Clive Toye (*Daily*

Express) and Brian James (*Daily Mail*), had been alone in supporting Alf through thick and thin during an at times unconvincing build-up to the 1966 World Cup finals. Most of the football writers, led I recall by the redoubtable Desmond Hackett, continually poured huge buckets of scorn on Alf for his bold statement that England would win the World Cup. 'Alf,' Des wrote in typical hard-hitting style, 'you give me the World Cup Willies!'

Jones, Toye and James defended Alf to the hilt; and on the eve of the finals even Des Hackett came round to the Ramsey point of view. The day after England's memorable World Cup triumph the three of them tracked Alf down for his comments on what had been the greatest day in English football history. He was in an ITV studio. Alf's reaction? He told them bluntly: 'I don't give interviews on a Sunday. This is my day off.'

Press and public relations were never Alf's strongest point, but he remains, in my book, the finest manager England ever had. I doubt that even Max Clifford would have been able to get him to toe the PR line! When Alf passed on in the spring of 1999, I was saddened, along with many of my colleagues, to miss his memorial service in Ipswich because it had been so poorly publicised. He deserved a hero's farewell, to say nothing of a statue at the entrance to the new Wembley.

Soon after 1966 and all that that I got a phone call from one of football's greatest characters, a master communicator who had no problems with PR – Mr Jimmy Hill. He was about to put forward the most exciting proposition of my working life. Even Teddy was happy with the offer that came my way for a switch to the world of television.

— 5 —

'THERE'S A MR HILL
FOR YOU...'

IT is not often that a telephone call out of the blue entirely alters the course of your life, but that is exactly what happened to me in the late autumn of 1967.

'There's someone name of Hill for you,' I was told. 'He says he wants a quick, private word.'

The call came while I was sitting in the BBC radio sportsroom on the third floor of Broadcasting House. Such is my natural pessimism that I could only believe that I had, somewhere and somehow, dropped a huge clanger and was about to be confronted by the Chairman of the BBC, the redoubtable Dr (later, Lord) Charles Hill. He had become famous in the 1940s as the inimitable Radio Doctor, with a voice as well known and instantly recognisable as anybody's in the broadcasting profession. Now he was controller of the BBC's entire output. Why, I wondered, would he be calling me? All these years later, I realise what a ludicrous notion it was. It speaks volumes for my inbuilt insecurity that my immediate reaction was that I was in trouble with the Big Boss.

It was not the slow and unmistakable burr of Dr Hill in my ear when I picked up the receiver, but the equally familiar Balham tones of Jimmy Hill. The nation had become accustomed to Jimmy's persuasive voice seven years earlier when he had brilliantly led the players' fight for the abolition of the £20-a-week maximum wage. Then he'd moved on, taking over as manager of Coventry City. They were in the old third division when he was offered the job and I remember him telling me he had gone to look them over in an FA Cup-tie against non-leaguers King's Lynn, which they had lost.

'There was only one way to go after that, so I took the job,' he said. Well, he took them on a magic carpet ride to the first division, combining good judgement of players, shrewd tactics, skilful man-management and light-years-ahead-of-its-time public relations. Eventually, he asked for a ten-year contract and when the chairman Derrick Robins turned him down, Jimmy upped and left on the eve of Coventry making their debut in the first division. He never realised his ambition of selecting a team for a first-division match, and instead took on the challenge of a new career in television. Football management's loss was certainly television's considerable gain.

He had made a striking impression as an occasional and strongly opinionated summariser with the BBC team, and jumped at the chance when London Weekend Television, new winners of the London franchise, invited him to become their Head of Sport. It was in this capacity that he was making his unexpected telephone call to me.

'I want you to come and have some lunch,' he said. 'I think we may have something worth talking about.'

That's how I came to be sitting in the sunlit dining-room of the Berkeley Hotel across the table from the most famous chin (and paintbrush beard) in the business. Our paths had only occasionally crossed before this, usually in the hubbub of after-match press conferences and back in those exciting days when he was fighting the maximum wage issue. This was our first real head-to-head meeting.

I've always called Jimmy 'the silver-tongued persuader' and over this memorable lunch he was at his convincing best.

'I want you to come and climb a mountain with me,' he said

as we waited for our appetiser. Can you imagine a more challenging opening?

He outlined how the BBC had just about every sporting
contract worth holding and a fine reputation to go with them;
ITV's portfolio stretched not much further than table tennis from
Haywards Heath, badminton from Milton Keynes and a share of
the football. But why me?

'I've listened to you a lot,' he said. 'I like your voice and, more
than anything, you don't offend anyone.' Talk about damning
with faint praise! He added, 'I can't promise an easy climb, but
one thing's for certain – it'll be an exciting one!'

Jimmy had come to this lunch, by the way, having won an
argument with John Bromley, his number two, who fancied
Barry Davies rather than me as the LWT football commentator.
But Jimmy wanted me, and Jimmy got his way. Now there's a
surprise! Fascinating to think, though, that if Barry had got the
ITV job, I would have been in line for the BBC post and we would
still have been in opposite camps for the past thirty years.

'I can offer you £5,000 a year, a two-year-contract and I'd like
you to be with us in the next two or three months,' was how
Jimmy signed off this lunch date. As I was then earning £1,450 a
year on BBC radio, the money left me wide-eyed and near
speechless. As I headed for home in my little VW Beetle I
wondered what on earth I was going to do with it all.

Needless to say, Jimmy had impressed me enormously and I
duly reported it all to Teddy Sommerfield.

'You go away and think about it, my boy, and leave it to me to
see Jimmy Hill,' he said. Teddy being Teddy, he quickly got the
money upped to £5,500 – that extra £500 paid his commission –
and he negotiated an extra year on the contract. With a wife and
two young sons to think about, I now had to balance the prospect
of a lifetime's security in radio with what could easily prove an
icy plunge into television.

I looked at some of the people Jimmy had already got on
board. There was his right-hand man John Bromley, one of the

finest of all Fleet Street football reporters who had built his reputation with first the *Daily Herald* and then the *Daily Mirror*, where
he had compiled a SportLight column with a youngster called
Michael Grade. Then there was another brilliant journalist,
Michael Parkinson (yes, Parky was there as editor and presenter
of a documentary series called 'Sports Arena'). Signed up as an
anchorman was Dickie Davies, with his boundless enthusiasm
and all the valuable experience he had gained on Southern
Television. Adrian Metcalfe, fresh from his glories as a one-lap
athletics hero, was a member of Jimmy's small band, and signed
from Anglia Television was a wonderfully creative football
director called Bob Gardam. It did not take me long to reach the
conclusion that the Hill climbing team had a chance to go all the
way to the top. I decided to join.

So in April 1968 I left the traditional splendour of Broadcasting
House for a bleak, half-occupied sixties office block, perpetually
windy and impersonal, situated just off the North Circular Road
at unglamorous Stonebridge Park, close by Wembley. Welcome
to Station House! Welcome to ITV – and to the unknown.

There were still several months to go before LWT went on air
when I first arrived at Station House. It was as well that the
make-shift bar there – with Jim the splendid barman – dispensed
excellent champagne at five pounds a bottle. Our creative talents
stretched no further than finding good causes to celebrate and
we cracked a few bottles as we waited for the launch of LWT.

We spent one particular afternoon at Wembley Stadium when
Jimmy had the idea for a press photo-call. We were all dressed
up in football gear for a team photograph, Jimmy's new XI. But
it all backfired. The evening before, the Horse of the Year Show
had been held in the stadium and Wembley's immaculate pitch
looked more like a churned up battlefield. The snappers were
much more interested in that, and it was the ruined Wembley
turf that made the back pages and not Jimmy Hill's All Stars.

In the weeks leading up to going on air in the autumn of 1968,
we were having our honeymoon before the wedding. Those days
were filled with good intentions and long lunches. There was a

particularly fine Chinese restaurant just across the road from the Wembley Studios – 'table for twelve please, maestro, and some of your best Chablis' – where production lunchtime meetings sometimes finished just in time to beat the rush hour but mostly did not.

There was no better host than Michael Parkinson, who assigned me during that long, lazy summer of 1968 to go to America and Mexico for 'Sports Arena' to work on three documentary films: 'Black Power in American Sport', 'Soccer US Style' and 'The Olympics: Can Mexico Cope?' Strange that my first assignments for TV had nothing to do with football and that the first of them, the history-making Black Power story, was way beyond my range or comprehension.

That film, shot mainly in California, was dominated by Dr Harry Edwards, a man of fiery eloquence and with the ability to let rip about the plight of his black brothers the moment a camera was switched on – street corner, car park, athletics stadium, it made no difference where, he was ready with a stream of opinions. Remember that this was in the volatile period in the United States during which the assassinations of Bobby Kennedy and Martin Luther King took place.

They were huge political issues that were a bridge too far for this totally superfluous interviewer. I also spoke to Tommie Smith and Lee Evans, two of the American athletes soon to be seen on the Olympic rostrum with gloved hands raised in black power salutes. We put together a powerful film, superbly directed by Tom Clegg, but my input was negligible.

In those wonderfully naive days at the birth of LWT, the film actually made it on air at 10.30 p.m. on the station's opening night. Needless to say it was a ratings disaster. Today such a film might just struggle to get a showing at midnight, but more than likely would never be commissioned in the first place. Our schedulers had a lot of learning to do.

Incidentally, the film about soccer in America, upbeat and optimistic, hit the buffers when, a week before it was due to go out, the proposed League collapsed and with it our film; and to the best of my knowledge the public were also denied even a glimpse of Mexico's preparations for the Olympics.

It could only get better, and it needed to. London Weekend's ratings and performance in those early months were so pathetically poor that the IBA at one point gave the LWT board just six weeks to get their act together, or else.

This was a very worrying time, and for several days we wondered about the safety of our jobs. Had I made a monumental mistake by leaving BBC radio? It was a worrying thought that more than once crossed my mind.

But then Rupert Murdoch rode into town. He bought a share in the company for a reported £600,000, which helped stabilise LWT's future, as did the arrival of the impressive John Freeman as chairman. But, as I recall it all these years later, can it really mean that my career was rescued by none other than Mr Rupert Murdoch?

Two of his early intrusions stick in my memory. First of all, he picked on the schoolroom sit-com 'Please Sir', starring John Alderton, and saw that it was marked down in the schedules for a twelve-week run. 'Commission fifty-two episodes,' he ordered. Good judgement.

Then he cast his eye over the football schedules, and decided that 'The Big Match' should be switched from mid-afternoon on Sundays to noon. Poor judgement.

Murdoch had a high opinion of 'The Big Match', and wanted its healthy ratings to help lift programmes later in the afternoon. He was only argued out of what would have been a suicidal switch when it was bluntly pointed out to him that all Sunday morning footballers and most football fans would be in the pub at noon. Mr Murdoch was big enough to climb down.

These were turbulent times, with the company lurching from crisis to crisis, but a combination of Murdoch's money and the steady hand of new chairman John Freeman got us moving in the right direction.

My first-ever football commentary for television was at Loftus Road – Queens Park Rangers against Manchester City in the early weeks of the 1968–69 season. Rangers, under the management of Alec Stock and with Rodney Marsh their leading light, had just been promoted to the old first division. Manchester City, with dear old Joe Mercer and Malcolm Allison at the helm and with Francis Lee, Colin Bell and Mike Summerbee in their colours, were marching towards a European peak. But Rangers, I recall, won 2–0 with their goalkeeper Mike Kelly, later an England goalkeeping coach, the game's outstanding player. I commentated on that game from the building site that was QPR's splendid new main stand in the making, and tussled with the change of technique from radio to television. I had to figure it out for myself. In those days Ken Wolstenholme and ITV's Hugh Johns were just about the only regular commentators working on TV, so into the deep end I went.

Commentating, whatever the medium, is no more than finding the right delicate balance between describing the action, imparting the information, and adding that dash of drama and urgency that draws it all towards the realms of entertainment. I always tried to go with the flow of a game, its passion and emotion, and leave everything else as an insurance policy to be brought out only when required. Statistics? No more than a pinch of salt to flavour the dish.

My advice to budding commentators has always been to milk the drama for all it is worth. I used to try to get my audience sitting on the edge of their seats, and to me the greatest compliment was always when a viewer would say, 'I couldn't watch any more. I had to go to the kitchen – the excitement was just too much for me.'

Essentially there is little difference between radio and television commentary; fewer words on TV, that's all. I'm not persuaded by the argument that you should not, as a television commentator, describe what the audience can already see. When I started, one TV old-timer in our production team quietly had a go at me for shouting 'G-O-A-L!' when the ball went into the net. 'Everyone can see it's a goal, they don't need you to tell them,' he figured.

So for a few weeks I reined myself in, with some difficulty, and curbed my triumphant shouting. It didn't seem right. I felt that I was missing out on the most dramatic moments of the whole ninety minutes. I watched the play-backs, and couldn't help noticing that when there was a score the crowd shouted one word: 'G-O-A-L!' They could certainly see what was happening, and that was good enough for me. I went back to doing what came naturally – and did so for the next thirty years!

One sidelight on that shout of 'goal': about a year ago David Wills, an astute lawyer who had taken over from the late Teddy Sommerfield as my manager, rang to say that an advertising agency wanted me to do a voice-over for the electrical giants, Comet.

'But,' said David, 'they say the script is just one word: Goal! Nothing else. They want you at their studio in Soho at one p.m. tomorrow.'

It was a clever production – a man sitting on a sofa is scanning the Comet newspaper ad for a bargain. A football match is going on on the TV in the background. Suddenly, there's a shout of 'Goal!' He looks up only to find his view blocked by the biggest dog in the world and so he goes back, frustrated, to the advertisement. They wanted me for the 'Goal' bit.

So at one o'clock I presented myself at the studio. I bellowed 'Goal!' half-a-dozen times, the producers were satisfied and at seven minutes past one I was back out in the street, job done; and better off to the tune of a wonderful long holiday for Betty and me in a favourite retreat of ours in Majorca.

As one of the production team ushered me out he said: 'We're glad to get that out of the way. You may not believe this but we've had six different actors trying out that script, but none of them sounded quite right.' As I explained, they'd not had the benefit of rehearsing that line for almost thirty years as I had. Nice work if you can get it. G-O-A-L!

When I started commentating for LWT, I realised straight-away that my luck was in. My director was Bob Gardam, raging extrovert, huge enthusiast and soon to be acknowledged as the best in the business. He'd come down from the Norwich studios of Anglia Television where he had pioneered the electronic coverage of football – previously it had been filmed excerpts. We hit it off at once,

Mind you, it took some time getting used to his unending and excited chatter in my headphones. No wonder that these days I suffer from mild tinnitus. Bob was one of those people whose brain was always racing ahead of his tongue, but he was brilliantly sharp when it mattered, had a good eye for the dramatic and, visually, was always on the look-out for the fresh angle. They still call the camera trench dug near the halfway line at Wembley 'Gardam's Pit'.

What I liked more than anything about working with Bob was that he listened to his commentator, and, frankly, there are many who don't. Director–commentator must be a team if a production is going to work for the best. With the massive advance in outside broadcasts, I think that sometimes directors these days have so many cameras and replay machines to consider that their relationship with the commentator is all but lost; and a good deal of the production is lost with it. Bob's best work was probably done with half-a-dozen cameras. My last FACup final in 1998 was covered by twenty-nine.

The best example of good team-work between director and commentator surely came at the end of the 1973 FA Cup final when second division Sunderland completed one of Wembley's greatest upsets by beating Don Revie's mighty Leeds United. Ian Porterfield, you may recall, scored the only goal in the thirty-second minute, and Sunderland were battered for the rest of the match by Revie's men. They surely had to equalise except that Sunderland's defence somehow kept them at bay. When they did manage to force a way through, Leeds found goalkeeper Jim Montgomery in unbeatable form, and a double save from first Trevor Cherry and then Peter Lorimer has gone down in football legend.

Final whistle. Cut to the Sunderland manager Bob Stokoe leaping from the bench and starting to run towards the pitch.

'Where's he going now?' I asked into the mike. Now Bob Gardam would have had a dozen different visual ideas going through his mind and plenty offered to him on his bank of monitors: players celebrating, others in tears, jubilant fans, reaction from the Royal Box, the Cup waiting to be collected, Don Revie's disbelief and so on – and any of them would have made good pictures.

But no, he was listening to his commentator. He, too, was now curious to know where Bob Stokoe was going. So he left the camera on him, and his reward was a memorable sequence of the Sunderland manager – in his perky pork-pie hat and raincoat over his track-suit – running fully eighty yards into the arms of his match-winning goalkeeper. It was a highly emotional moment and a triumphant piece of television direction.

Bob Gardam and I had temperaments that were a world apart and we rarely socialised, but when we were at work he seemed to know instinctively what I was about to say and I often second-guessed where he was going next. I've worked with other first-class directors, such as Ted Ayling, whose pictures were seen world wide when he was honoured as director of the 1994 World Cup final in America, and superbly he did it, and John Watts, whose current work for ITV on the Champions League in particular is the best in Europe by a distance. But it was unquestionably Bob Gardam who set the pace.

'The Big Match' was a programme that, without argument, transformed the coverage of football on television. In a few short years it became a part of Sunday afternoon tradition. Middle-aged men still come up to me – making me feel quite ancient – to say: 'I grew up with you. Sundays in the seventies meant a game of football in the morning, Mum's roast beef and Yorkshire pudding, and then Jimmy Hill and Brian Moore on the television in the afternoon.' Just recently a taxi driver put it another way.

'I used to get such whacks from my mum,' he said, 'for wolfing down my Sunday dinner too quick so I could watch you on "The Big Match".'

For so long sport on television – particularly football – had been earnest, worthy and always a bit po-faced. We changed all that. As well as outstanding football pictures, we offered a rich mixture of crazy clips from around the world, viewers' letters, fun spots, and a Golden Goal competition (this was the original goal competition, incidentally, later copied shamelessly by the BBC, and this tired old nag is still being urged on thirty years later). It was an imaginative, full-throttle programme that drew our audience in to enjoy it all with us. And then there was always Jimmy's analysis.

Younger readers will no doubt respond with a 'so what?' to that. They may not realise that back in those late sixties and early seventies, Jimmy's weekly analytical talk-ins opened new horizons for our audience. It had never been done before. It was just as though a curtain had been pulled back on our great national game. 'Just see here how Alan Hudson makes that little dash to the right...there's room now for Peter Osgood – and as Liverpool try to cover that gap, just notice how Charlie Cooke is given space to work. See how he looks up to catch John Hollins' run...and that's such a well-worked goal – started way back by Hudson.' And so on every Sunday afternoon.

It was a real eye-opener for our viewers. In a few weeks 'The Big Match' had opened up a whole new dimension of the game for them, and spawned a whole new generation of football experts! Suddenly there were budding Jimmy Hills everywhere. Not for the first time – and doubtless not the last – Jimmy had spotted a gap in the market and exploited it brilliantly.

Over recent years, he's become something of an Aunt Sally for fans and critics alike. 'He pontificates too much,' or they may say, 'He's too much the schoolmaster,' or simply, 'He's a pain in the neck.' They don't realise what a pioneer he has been, and they just don't know the real Jimmy Hill.

I've never worked for a better boss and he's always been wonderful company. When I was invited to contribute to his 'This Is Your Life' programme a couple of years back, I was glad to have the chance to say that if we had a dozen more Jimmy Hills in this country the game of football would be in a healthier and more wholesome state, and probably the nation, too! Sadly the blazer-wearers in the Football Association and Football League were frightened of him. The affair of the maximum wage was too recent, his television appearances too frequent, and they feared he'd be too big a threat to their comfortable sporting world.

Those who watched Jimmy in his peak years at ITV will recall that he was a major player every Sunday afternoon. Today the clever graphics and myriad camera angles have made the analysis of decisive football moments more exciting to the eye, but there was a freshness to the words and the concept in those far-off days that has never been bettered. Frankly, I'm bored by much of today's picking over the bones of a game. It's usually my cue to go off and make the tea. Television simply hasn't moved it forward.

I enjoy 'Match of the Day' on BBC but rarely get excited by what is revealed in the studio; on ITV Bob Wilson does a great job in what I well know is the suffocating straitjacket between commercial breaks, but again it is almost impossible to find anything fresh to reveal about key moments that have, in any case, been seen from various angles and speeds and debated and analysed by commentator and co-commentator when they happened in the body of the game.

Surely there is a challenge here for the new wave of sports producers to lift match analysis out of the predictable 'So what about United's second goal, Terry?' or, 'Did that look offside to you, Alan?' and into bright, fresh avenues. At the moment all it appears to be is a slightly glitzier rehash of the way it was thirty years ago. What is needed is a modern-day Jimmy Hill to kick the coverage into the next millennium with some innovative thoughts, fresh opinions and instructive comments aided by all the new technology. Andy Gray, assisted by an expensive computer, is on the right path in his role as Sky analyst. Jimmy Hill in those early days never made the mistake of going over the heads of his viewers. But at least Sky are trying to push out the frontiers.

Live games require something to fill the half-time slot. Talking heads should be the last resort. Why not action from other games being played that night and a thorough, visual round-up of the rest of the day's football news? I would use the studio experts only when an incident or a fantastic moment of individual skill demands a further comment. And for those late-night recorded highlights, I would dispense with all experts except one as a standby. Give the viewers what they most surely want – more action and less talk.

Far be it from me to send Trevor Brooking, Alan Hansen, Barry Venison and company to the dole queue, but the time has surely come for a huge shake-up in the way football is presented on television. The mould needs to be smashed, just as it was by 'The Big Match' more than thirty years ago.

Working with Jimmy Hill was a joy. I cannot recall a single serious argument with him. The nearest Bob Gardam and I came to it was the day Jimmy wanted to appear on 'The Big Match' as a sheikh. He had been to Saudi Arabia to play in a charity football match. Jimmy Greaves, I remember, was among the gathered stars and we had a few snippets of action from the game for the programme. These included pictures of a whole grandstand full of men in flowing white robes and matching headgear. It was without doubt one of the most amazing crowd shots of all time. It was Jimmy's idea that, without any comment from me, I should introduce his analysis spot with him sitting there in similar robes and headgear.

Bob, quite correctly, decided against it. Jimmy argued the point fiercely for a few minutes, but eventually gave in to his producer. In truth he would have looked magnificent! In the end, disappointed, he had to make do with collar and tie. It was one of the few arguments Jimmy has ever lost in his life.

When Arsenal reached the 1971 FA Cup final against Liverpool, 'The Big Match', as a London programme, naturally adopted the Gunners. We had no fears that Frank McLintock's men would match Liverpool skill for skill, but we worried that the decibel level of Liverpool's exuberant Kopites would comfortably outshout Arsenal's fans. Jimmy got on the case.

'Liverpool have "You'll Never Walk Alone",' he said. 'We must find a song for the Arsenal fans to sing.' His first idea was 'Land of Hope and Glory' and we duly wrote suitable North London words to go with it, and announced it with a great flourish on the programme. Major snag. A letter from the Elgar Society came whistling our way. Quite rightly, they are protective of all such things and, informing us that the music was not yet out of copyright, threatened serious legal action if we went ahead. So, as the final drew closer, we had to forget about Edward Elgar making a Wembley appearance in Arsenal's colours. Meantime the Arsenal players, led by Frank McLintock, had plumped for Sinatra's 'My Way', with suitably altered lyrics. More legal letters!

Jimmy called another meeting. The idea of getting an Arsenal song had grabbed the imagination of the public and he was determined to come up with the right (and legally acceptable) tune.

'We want something rousing and, like Arsenal, very traditional,' he said. 'What about "Rule, Britannia"? That must be out of copyright by now.' So in his office and on the back of the proverbial envelope, we combined to write these words:

Good old Arsenal, we're proud to say that name,
While we sing this song, you'll win the game.

All right, so they are not lyrics for which Cole Porter or Tim Rice would have expected Ivor Novello awards, but they proved just what the North Bank wanted. We had time for one rehearsal at Highbury a week before the final; then the Arsenal fans belted it out superbly at Wembley. Arsenal won the Cup and completed the double on that glorious sunlit day – 'Charlie George, he can hit 'em' – and that song has been with the club ever since. Today when Arsenal fans let rip with 'Good Old Arsenal', I wonder how many of them know who dreamed it up? It was Jimmy Hill.

His ideas were mostly good, and there was nothing mealy-mouthed about him either. Once, in 1972, when Manchester United had been humiliated in a five-goal débâcle by Crystal

Mum and Dad, who had little yet gave so much.

The Sporting Moore: I was captain of both the cricket and hockey teams at Cranbrook in 1950 – that's me in the centre of the front row – but football was always my first love.

Pilot Officer Moore. It was while I was doing my National Service in Germany that someone suggested I had a good voice and should make use of it. This triggered my commentating career.

Radio days: here's Tommy Docherty, Chelsea manager in those early 1960s, on the receiving end of the microphone. Judging by the look on his face, it wasn't the usual laugh-a-second interview with the Doc.

It snowed on our wedding day and the three-tier cake collapsed. Yet Betty and I are still together and just as much in love more than forty-four years on.

The Jimmy Hill XI getting ready to score for LWT, back row: myself, Mike Archer, David Scott, John P. Hamilton, Bob Gardam, John Scriminger, Tom Clegg; sitting, from the left: Ian Marshall, John Bromley, Jimmy Hill, Dickie Davies, Adrian Metcalfe. As a production team, we were the champions.

The four men who revolutionised football talk on television, goaded by Jimmy Hill and myself in the background, from the left: Bob McNab, Pat Crerand, Derek Dougan and Malcolm Allison. They provided passions and opinions that made the 1970 World Cup the breakthrough for ITV Sport.

'Sit me next to Cruyff and some of the magic may rub off on me,' said Cloughie before the kick-off to the 1978 World Cup finals. So I did, and did it?

Yes, it was a funny old game when Greavsie was together with Cloughie on World Cup duty. Two of the greatest goalscorers in the game's history. That's not funny, that's fact.

Our line-up for the 1982 World Cup included John Bond, the slim and immaculate George Best and, away from the horses, Mike Channon. It was a mix 'n' match that really worked.

Bobby Moore and his men. It's a familiar 1966 image of an historic football day. Indeed, it deserves to be cast in stone to grace the new Wembley.

Colin Cowdrey at the wicket. One of my proudest sporting moments came – on a rather more modest occasion – when I was batting as a Kent schoolboy at the other end.

Sundays in the 'Big Match' studio were very special. Jimmy Hill's influence did more than anything in those days to push TV football programmes towards new frontiers. Here I'm simply waiting for him to finish his make-up!

'Niki, you've just no idea how difficult it is driving down the Old Kent Road!' In fact, Niki Lauda is the most inspiring sportsman I've ever met and I look back on my documentary on his life as one of the highest points of my broadcasting career.

'Brian Moore Meets. . .' Princess Anne and Captain Mark Phillips – a relaxed moment during the making of the documentary. They forgave me for managing to lose them on the way to one of our shoot locations.

Following Bjorn Borg around for the *'Brian Moore Meets. . .'* series was a great pleasure, not least because he was based in Marbella and the next stop was Monte Carlo!

When you interview Bobby Robson, it's very hard to get a word in. His passion for the game is such that he launches himself at every question and every topic.

Going back to our roots – Bob Wilson in a Chesterfield jersey, Jim Rosenthal in Oxford United's colours and I'm proudly supporting Gillingham.

Palace – and Don Rogers in particular – he launched a verbal attack, over a shot of the visiting directors' box, on the men in charge at United, including the venerable Sir Matt Busby. Jimmy stuck his chin out even further than usual that day and won no friends in Old Trafford circles. The thrust of his argument was that they were not giving enough boardroom support to the manager Frank O'Farrell and that a great club was being allowed to slide. His attack also caught the eye of the decision-makers in the BBC sports department, uppermost the dynamic football chief Sam Leitch, and that strident two-minute piece of television did more than anything to win for Jimmy a long and distinguished career with the BBC.

One Hill afterthought: his good luck at this time was legendary. If there was one free parking meter in London, he'd find it. He tells the tale of driving around Hammersmith Broadway on a filthy, wintry Friday night in the rush-hour. The traffic was appalling, and he suddenly realised that he had got a flat tyre. For you or me this would mean writing off the next couple of hours, but not for Jimmy. As he trundled to the side of the road, already late for an appointment and cursing the circumstances, he pulled in right behind an AA van. What is more, the AA man was just finishing with his previous breakdown.

'Hello, Jim,' he said. 'I'm a great Fulham fan and I used to watch you at Craven Cottage. Can I sort you out, pal?' Within ten minutes the bearded wonder was on his way again.

Lucky Jim, a very special man.

All this was very much the era of the sheepskin coats. They were required winter warmers for all TV commentators. Funny how that has stuck with so many cartoonists and critics. It must be all of twenty years since I last wore one! It was also the era of basic technology. The games were covered on just three cameras, two up aloft on the gantry and one on the touchline for the close-ups. In these high-tech days it's still hard to believe that we went along to games without a single slow-motion machine.

Nowadays the slo-mo is there at the touch of a button (and so convenient that it is, in my opinion, often over-used). Back in the sixties and seventies the one machine with slo-mo facilities was kept back at base, so when a goal was scored I would have to memorise the whole build-up and then repeat it as if talking over the action – 'The move started by Peters, out to Sissons on the wing and his perfect cross met at the near post by the head of Geoff Hurst. What a goal!' and so on.

Then back to the studios we would go that evening to fit the slow-motion pictures to my words before 'The Big Match' went out the next day. It's moved on a bit since then, but it was London Weekend who broke new ground when John Bromley persuaded the board to invest £60,000 – 'serious dosh then' as Brommers now points out – in something called an HS-100, the first slow-motion machine of its type. It proved to be a vital investment and a piece of hardware that helped put ITV's coverage ahead of the field.

As many of my old colleagues will testify, moaning about the proliferation of slow-motion replays in modern sporting television is an old hobbyhorse of mine. It was brought into sharp focus for me recently when I was asked to commentate again on the replay of the 1970 FA Cup final, a dramatic night at Old Trafford. Dave Sexton's young Chelsea side beat Don Revie's ultra-professional Leeds United excitingly in extra time when Ian Hutchinson's long throw to the far post was charged into the net by David Webb. A technical blip in the archives had wiped off my original commentary. It gave me the opportunity for a fascinating trip back in time to an era when there wasn't a single replica shirt in the crowd, only scarves and bobble hats. People went to cup finals in those days in a collar and tie. In 120 minutes of football there were only twelve slow-motion replays and the first was not used until the game was twenty-five minutes old. The replay, with Osgood, Cooke, Hollins, Bremner, Big Jack, Lorimer, Clarke and Co., did not suffer as a spectacle. Indeed it came across as a true and exciting reminder of a memorable night.

Today sport is in danger of being strangled by the technology around it. In a match like that 1970 classic we would most likely have replays, from all angles, at the rate of one a minute – not twelve in the night, but 120. I find this hard to take. I also find cricket, my other passion, almost unwatchable because of replays that come up, it seems, after almost every ball. Golf, with sparse use of the replay, has become the model for all sports to follow.

I've sat with TV directors, including Ted Ayling and John Watts, at big games and know something of the pressure they are under when a huge bank of pictures from so many cameras gives them so many options. The temptation to put in just one more replay is enormous, but I beg them to be more selective.

A couple of years back, I was invited to speak at a commentators' workshop run by UEFA in Switzerland and I made the same point there. Directors from all around Europe wisely shook their heads and agreed they must in future have more respect for the overall view of the game. They all went home and did absolutely nothing about it. In fact, they doubled the slo-mo output!

There are times, golden times, when the super slo-mos greatly enhance the service to the viewer. The unforgettable Roberto Carlos free kick slips easily into that category. His effort from thirty-five yards for Brazil against France during the 1997 Tournoi ranks among the most graphic sporting images of all time. With the camera behind Carlos, to see the ball apparently swerving wildly outside the goal (the ball-boy behind it even began to duck) and then swinging majestically just inside the post was a magical television moment; and from so many different angles, too. It was way beyond the range of those brave early days on 'The Big Match'.

But this was for something very special. Too often, we are bombarded with slo-mo replays of ordinary events that barely warrant a second look, and certainly not a third and fourth one. I know from my postbag that a lot of viewers got irritated by the procession of action-replays that were dropped into the France

'98 World Cup matches. I have to point out that this was the work of French directors, and I think it highlighted how they trail behind their leading British counterparts. It was just as irritating for the commentator to find an action replay of an unremarkable incident on the screen while the only action that mattered was continuing out on the pitch.

And another thing – I would put almost a total ban on cut-away shots of the crowd!

My commentaries from those early days fill me with embarrassment, mostly because I had the foot too hard down on the accelerator. I concede that I shouted far too much. Over the years I relaxed enough to come down a gear or two and my commentaries became a lot more acceptable to me and, I suspect, to the poor viewer, too. Mind you, there was plenty worth shouting about all those years ago – Best, Law and Charlton; Bill Nicholson's Tottenham, with Greaves and Chivers peppering the opposing goals; Moore, Hurst and Peters at West Ham; Bertie Mee and Don Howe piecing together a double-winning side at Arsenal; Dave Sexton and his wonderful Chelsea team; Bill Shankly at Anfield; and, to top it all, England holders of the World Cup. If that wasn't worth a good bellow, then I don't know what was!

Sometimes we got it wrong. There was, for instance, the occasion when a large dog came bounding on to the pitch during a game between Colchester and Brentford at Layer Road. It proceeded to chase the ball as it was passed back to the Brentford goalkeeper Chic Brodle. Chic gathered the ball safely, but the dog kept running and crashed straight into the unfortunate 'keeper who collapsed in a heap. It looked hilarious to us and to the fans on the terraces. What fun we had with that for a couple of weeks, with replays requested by viewers. But the laughter stopped when we were informed, very curtly, by the Brentford club, that, far from being a fun item, the collision had so seriously injured Chic Brodle's knee that his career was all but over.

An annual feature of 'The Big Match' was a special Christmas number when we'd invite footballers – and famous football people – to take over the show for the day. What frantic coaching and rehearsals we had on those Sunday mornings! John Hollins, Mick Channon, Kevin Keegan and David Webb all took their turn; and Bobby Moore was a natural when he made a memorable appearance in my presenter's chair.

I recall that there was a moment in the studio that would have wrong-footed even the most seasoned television professionals. An item finished ahead of schedule, and Bobby was caught on camera with a glass of water to his lips. Most people would have reacted with a gulp and a sheepish grin before moving on. But not Bobby. 'Cheers,' he said, raising his glass to the camera as if it was all rehearsed. This was the Bobby Moore brain at work; the sort of quick thinking also made him one of the greatest defenders of all time. I remember how when a volleyed clearance had knocked out a referee during a league match at West Ham, he calmly picked up the ref's whistle and blew to stop the action and summon the trainer. Manager Ron Greenwood said afterwards, 'I cannot think of anybody else who would have had the presence of mind to do that.'

Bobby was always a thought and a deed ahead of everybody, and all of us in television and in football stand guilty of sadly under-using this talented man after he had retired from playing. The Football Association could surely have used him in an ambassadorial role, and either BBC or ITV should have found a place for him in their teams. He was a man who had done it all, seen it all and had a million memories that were never satisfactorily drawn from him in front of a TV camera.

When Kevin Keegan filled the presenter's chair on the Christmas show, he gave us all a laugh with a great Norman Wisdom take-off (which I have to say was later bettered by Peter Taylor, who became one of Glenn Hoddle's England backroom team). Keegan's great friend Mick Channon was another who was always good for a laugh.

Mick was incredibly laid-back. He used to say in that warm Wiltshire, country burr: 'Oi gets up when it's loight, oi eats when oi'm hungry and oi goes to bed when it's dark.' It's a great philosophy, and I don't doubt that he continues to live by it as one of England's outstanding racehorse trainers. He once told me, 'Mooro, your trouble is you worry too much. Don't forget, live every day as though it's your last – because, as sure as eggs is eggs, one day it will be!'

He gave a great freshness to his television appearances with a unique delivery (even today, Gary Lineker is known as 'the boy Lyne-a-ker'), and he was a richly talented footballer with Southampton, Manchester City and England. But even in those days I knew that horse racing was his first love.

I remember the day we were covering a Southampton game at Tottenham, and he told me that he'd had a bet on the 3.15 at Newbury.

'Do me a favour, Mooro,' he said. 'Give me a thumbs up or down when you know the result. I'll look up to the commentary box when I reckon the race is over.'

His horse duly won, and I gave the thumbs up from the television gantry. To the astonishment of a 30,000 crowd the Southampton number eight suddenly proceeded to gallop all round the White Hart Lane pitch whipping himself jockey-style with an imaginary whip. What a delightful character! It is hard to think of anybody who has had a more perfect life: a local footballing hero grows into a star with the England team and then becomes a trainer of major race winners.

We had a great coup on one of our 'Big Match' Christmas Specials when Elton John agreed to host the show. Not only did Watford's chairman show himself to be a master of the autocue but, with a grand piano pushed into place, played and sang for us, too. He was meticulous in his preparations with the placing of microphones, quality of the sound and so on. It was just perfect. He told me that only a week earlier he had been reduced to tears as he sat on his stairs at home because the quality and balance of the sound on a recorded TV spectacular of his had not been up to the standards that he had set himself. We marvelled at his professionalism and his massive attention to detail. It is something I have seen and admired in all the great champions of sport, and here it was being underlined by a champion of music.

In those days we had a common bond – he chairman of Watford, me a director of Gillingham, both in the old third division. We knew a lot about life in football's lower reaches. With his financial clout he was able to find a way clear for his beloved Watford to reach football's sunlit uplands. Sadly that was always more than I could do for the Gills.

For a few years Elton and I worked together – with Jimmy Hill – for the Goaldiggers charity which was committed to providing hard-surfaced pitches for children in deprived areas. At the end of one of our meetings at the headquarters of the National Playing Fields Association close to Harrods, Elton asked: 'And where are you taking the family for a holiday this year?' I said we hadn't decided. 'Why not borrow my house in Beverly Hills?' he said. He insisted, and so we did!

Elton's generosity was overwhelming. I'd heard tell of it before, but now we experienced it first-hand. There was a stretch limousine to meet us at Los Angeles Airport, tinted glass and all, to say nothing of a cocktail bar and TV. It took us to his splendid house in Tower Road with its amazing views over Los Angeles, where Alice, his wonderfully welcoming housekeeper, was on hand to look after us.

For Betty, myself and our sons, Chris and Simon, it was a holiday we'll never forget. Elton made sure there was a car to ferry us to all the sights – Disneyland, a Dodgers baseball game, the Universal Studios tour, Chinatown – and of course there was also the complete run of the house that was one of Beverly Hills' finest.

It had a special golden age of Hollywood feel about it. It didn't take much imagination to see the likes of Clark Gable, Claudette Colbert, James Stewart, voluptuous Jane Russell, those two hell-raisers Errol Flynn and David Niven and the rest partying around the massive pool. Niven, in fact, refers to parties at the house in his autobiography, *The Moon is a Balloon*.

It had once been the home of the legendary Greta Garbo, and there was still a reminder of the time the enigmatic 'I want to be alone' movie star was in residence. On the lawn between the pool and the two tennis courts stood a lovely little summerhouse. Apparently Miss Garbo, who had just about everything and the dazzling Californian climate to go with it, felt she lacked only one thing. It was the sound of Scandinavian rain in the midst of all that sunshine. So she had a summerhouse built and over the top of it she had a showerhead installed. Placed inside within easy reach was a switch. When she felt the slightest bit homesick for Sweden, she would go to the summerhouse, flick the switch and at once hear the sounds of her homeland as the water tumbled down outside. It presents an enchanting picture.

A few years later, I was back in Los Angeles on an assignment. By then Elton had sold his home. I took a cab to Tower Road, but the house had gone and another was going up in its place. I couldn't see if the little summerhouse was still there. Maybe it had gone as well – but our memories of Garbo-land will stay with us forever.

6

MISBEHAVING AT
WEMBLEY

M Y first FA Cup final for television was the 1969 match
between Manchester City and Leicester City, won 1–0 by
Manchester City with a left-footed strike from their local hero
Neil Young. It was the most brutal encounter seen at Wembley
for many a long year; not on the pitch but off it and surrounding
it, between the rival forces of ITV and BBC, who went head-to-
head with their live coverage.

It was, looking back, a shameful episode and it deservedly got
a quick red card from the Football Association, outraged that
while the players largely behaved, the Wembley spectators were
subjected to the unseemly sight of TV crews literally fighting
among themselves.

The background to it was that ITV – driven by London
Weekend Television – were the new kids on the block, seeking
to storm the Wembley fortress built over the years by the BBC;
they, in turn, were pouring boiling oil over us from their
ramparts. We were aiming to make a dynamic impact on the
viewers; they were determined to stop us. The main point at
issue was the battle to see who would be first to get the game's
star players in front of their cameras for those interviews before
the match and, more importantly, after it.

ITV had a valuable ally in Malcolm Allison, a good friend then working alongside Joe Mercer in that superbly balanced, good-guy bad-guy partnership that was bringing glory to Maine Road. Thanks to Big Mal, a team of ITV backroom hustlers was kitted out in Manchester City tracksuits with the sole object of beating the formidable Wembley security system and infiltrating the pitch to get the first grab at the headline-makers.

So it was that bewildered players were hustled in half-Nelsons to our waiting cameras by ITV workers looking for all the world like Man City substitutes. The BBC crew were, naturally, not going to stand for it, and they responded vigorously. For a while it was mayhem around the pitch.

I could hear the arguments, including expletives, on my head-phones as I looked on from the Wembley commentary box, trying to pretend all was sweetness and light. 'He's ours!'…'No, we got him first'…'You try and get him then.' We had sent our burliest men into the fray and, no doubt suspecting foul play, so too had the BBC. Fists began to fly. One of our floor managers, David Yallop, now a successful author, had a tooth knocked out and men on both sides went away badly bruised. To this day, survivors of that wild afternoon talk about the events like old soldiers looking back on a war-time campaign.

It was madness. It was also childish, unsavoury and in the context of a full afternoon of football, totally without conse-quence. There were more tackles off the pitch than on it that afternoon, and it was all played out in front of guest of honour Princess Anne.

It didn't stop there. Malcolm Allison had been banned from the Manchester City bench because of his touchline coaching when his tongue ran out of control against match officials. We found him a seat in the stand alongside his close pal, Paul Doherty, a brilliant reporter and later the innovative head of Granada TV Sport. Paul had a microphone up his sleeve – yes, I do mean up his sleeve – and we were given regular, graphic Big Mal insights into the progress of the game. The FA were furious about that, and their anger was further fuelled when it was revealed that another excellent reporter, Peter Lorenzo (late father of Sky's Matthew Lorenzo), had apprently been hidden under a carpet with his microphone close to the touchline benches where he was getting his updates from Leicester City manager Frank O'Farrell.

All this came over to the nation in black and white (colour coverage came along in time for the next final), but the blood still showed vividly on a day best forgotten by both broadcasting organisations. There could be only one outcome, and the FA, for once, acted swiftly. Their secretary then was Sir Denis Follows, knighted for his part in organising the 1966 World Cup finals. He was one of the proud but slightly pompous old school who believed in meticulous behaviour whatever the circumstances, and he called both sides to Lancaster Gate.

He made it quite clear that football's greatest day was not to be scarred in future by such squabbling. 'A shameful exhibition', he called it. Thereafter on the eve of every final the two television sides would get together, each with their list of preferred players in order of merit, and they would solemnly toss a coin for the right to have first choice for the interviews the following afternoon; no more fisticuffs, no more tracksuits, and certainly no more hiding under carpets. Sanity returned to the Cup final.

One of our features for that 1969 final was on referee George McCabe who created history at the toss-up. He used the first ever 50p piece, put into circulation six months before decimalisation; black and white television, pounds, shillings and pence, yet in my memory it all seems like just the day before yesterday.

Although everything calmed down after those pitchside punch-ups, there was still plenty of rivalry between BBC and ITV to see who could produce the more imaginative show on Cup final day and editorial minds were fully exercised and stretched on both sides.

The BBC came up with 'Cup Final It's A Knockout', and we had a celebrity bar where anyone from Sir John Mills to Freddie Starr might pop up. They brought in 'Cup Final Snooker' and we responded with 'Cup Final Wrestling' and we had Alf Garnett (created by Johnny Speight for the BBC) in the crowd down

Wembley Way for good measure. They opened up at 11.30 a.m., so we started at 11.15; next year we started at 11.15, and they came forward to 11 o'clock; next year they'd move the start time to 10.45 – and we'd beat them by having Dickie Davies smiling into the cameras at 10.30. The way it was going, there was a real danger of us delivering Cup Final Cornflakes.

We would sit for hours – about a dozen of us – in meeting after meeting looking for something to trump all the BBC aces. In one such meeting before the 1973 Leeds–Sunderland final we delivered the master-stroke, and it came from a totally unexpected source; not from all the clever journalistic types sitting round the table, but from a technical whiz-kid named Roger Philcox. Even then, Roger was a highly gifted boffin, but his reputation over the years has grown into the world league. There is nobody on his side of the technology business more highly respected.

'Would you like a camera on the team coach on its ride to Wembley?' he casually asked. Our jaws dropped. It had never been done before and nobody, until Roger, had even thought of it. Don't forget that this was in the days when miniaturised cameras were just a dream, and the technical challenge of bringing live television pictures from a moving bus was something that lived only in the imagination of sports-loving boffins.

Roger could take care of the technicalities, no problem; but there was the little matter of persuading the clubs that it was a good idea. First there was Don Revie and his Leeds United side. They were so wrapped up in superstition that there was not a chance that they would change any of their match-day routine that had got them this far along the Wembley trail. Perhaps Sunderland's Bob Stokoe might go along with the revolutionary idea. But he wasn't sure. 'Give me a day or two to think about it,' was as far as he would go.

Bob came back, and his answer was, 'Sorry, but no.' We discovered that he had gone to Arsenal manager Bertie Mee for advice. I admired all that Bertie had done, in harness with Don Howe, in turning Arsenal into a double-winning team two years earlier, but I knew him to be a cautious and very conservative man. I was not surprised that he advised Bob, 'Don't touch it with a barge pole.' We decided to have another go at Bob Stokoe.

'Look,' we said, 'nobody gives you a chance. You are rank outsiders, you have nothing to lose. Just consider that the presence of cameras and the interviews might just help your lads to relax and take away some of their anxiety.'

There was silence. He thought about it for a minute. Finally he said with that beaming smile of his, 'Okay, let's go for it!'

Now the technicians had to get to work. A coach was found with a kitchen at the back that could be stripped to take our generator and other technical equipment. 'No,' said Sunderland firmly. 'We will not go to Wembley in anything other than our usual coach. Our players are superstitious about the coach and the driver. They've been with us right the way through our Cup run and that is how we are going to Wembley.'

Back to Roger and his team. They inspected the Sunderland coach, and decided that the generator could be fitted into the luggage compartment. That meant we had to hire a second coach to ferry the kit and the players' personal luggage to Wembley.

But it was worth all the trouble. In the end it worked magnificently. It's true the reception was sometimes patchy but it really came good in that last half-mile up Wembley Way and into the stadium. This is where it really counted. For the first time television was able to tap into the true emotions of Cup final day, with Sunderland's fanatical fans cheering their team on the drive up Wembley Way, and the on-board camera capturing the stirring response from the players. It again put ITV in the lead, and I am convinced it helped the Sunderland players by taking their minds off the pre-match pressures. Their 1–0 victory over Leeds was one of the all-time great upsets in FA Cup history.

For years afterwards there was a race to do a deal with one or other of the finalists for a camera on their coach. It was a great idea at the time, but the novelty wore off, and it has now quite rightly been dropped. It's fascinating to think that today it could all be done with one miniature camera sending pictures digitally for transmission right round the world. But that 1973 excitement at being first will never be recaptured.

This was still an exciting and innovative time in television, before the invasion and advance of those faceless, bean-counting men in grey suits, before the day of accountants, of account-ability and the dreaded 'bottom line'. The cost, then, was often secondary to the quality of the programme but, deep down, I think we all knew it couldn't last. We were living in something of a fools' paradise – and we loved every minute of it. Now, sadly, television programme quality is often shackled and at the mercy of 'the suits'.

They were indeed exhilarating times and none more so than in the summer of 1969 when ITV bought the rights for a live England game against Mexico in the Azteca Stadium in Mexico City, a game that was a vital part of Sir Alf Ramsey's high alti-tude preparations for the defence of the World Cup the following year. Off we went, Jimmy Hill, the producer Graham Turner, extrovert and big-time player in those early ITV days, his PA (who happened to be his wife), an engineer and me. We left on the Monday, six days before the game was to be played, and flew first-class with Qantas, calling in at Bermuda along the way. We lived it up that week in the exclusive Parc des Princes complex, with a magnificent pool, on the edge of Mexico City. I shared a luxury bungalow with Jimmy, and in the neigh-bouring one was the French singer Charles Aznavour, who was working in one of the city's glitziest night spots. It was that sort of place.

On the second morning after the maid had cleaned the room, our toothpaste and toothbrushes were missing, so we bought another set. Next day, the same thing happened. This went on for five days. Neither Jimmy nor I really wanted to challenge the maid, but on the last morning the mystery was solved when I discovered a little catch on the bathroom mirror. It opened out into a small cabinet – and there, neatly lined up, were ten tubes of toothpaste and ten toothbrushes! We thought she was light-fingered. She must have thought we were lightheaded.

I would like to report that, after all those days of preparation, the programme was a great success. It wasn't. Jimmy was there to introduce it from the touchline and we got to the stadium in very good time for the scorching midday kick-off (8 p.m. peak time at home). Rehearsals were perfect. Jimmy was ready to go live to the nation in about five minutes. Suddenly the biggest Mexican army band that you are ever likely to see marched into position on the far side of the ground. Nobody had told us about this (perhaps we should have asked!), but at least the band was striking up on the opposite side of the ground. It would not, we hoped, interfere too much with Jimmy's opening words.

Four minutes to go, and to our horror the band started moving round the touchline towards Jimmy's microphone point. Their blaring brass instruments gleamed in the midday sun, their drums boomed, and their cymbals clashed as they belted out their marching tunes as if their lives depended on it. The closer Jimmy's opening cue came, the closer came the band. They duly arrived and, still playing at full volume, came to a halt just ten yards from him as he attempted his, 'Good day to you from Mexico City...' introduction to the audience back home. The viewers hardly heard a thing!

Drowned-out, Jimmy handed over to me, and my nightmare began. I was in a little glass cubicle, which all commentators hate. We feel shut off from the action and the atmosphere, and in scorching-hot Mexico City it was simply suffocating. My microphone was not of the conventional lip variety either, but one of those thin, steely ones that arched up towards the face. Monsieur Aznavour would have felt at home with it, but it was hopeless for a football commentary. To make matters worse my little cabin was pitched so low that every time there was an exciting build-up in the game hundreds of animated Mexicans stood up in front of the window and completely blocked my view of the action. In fact, it would have been better for me to have stayed in London and done the commentary off a television monitor. It would have saved ITV thousands of pounds, and me a lot of toothpaste! In keeping with it all, the match finished in a desperate 0–0 draw.

Overall, I have mixed memories of Mexico City. Things never seemed quite to work out as you would think. I was there again in 1985 for a pre-World Cup tournament, and the key game live on ITV was England's meeting with Franz Beckenbauer's West Germany. This time the commentary position was a good one and my co-commentator was our old friend Mick Channon. Though the pictures were good, the sound wasn't. In fact London could hear nothing in the build-up to the match. In desperation, Mick and I commentated for the full ninety minutes on a public telephone at the back of the commentary box.

'I hope you've been able to reverse the charges, Mooro,' Mick grinned. It turned out that a dozy technician in El Paso had pulled the wrong switch. On such detail can huge TV operations flounder. For the record, down those phone lines Mick and I were able to describe a fine England performance – a 3–0 victory, with a goal from skipper Bryan Robson and two from Kerry Dixon, marking his first full game for England.

Mick was amazingly easygoing as a workmate. I doubt if he has been changed much by the racing world, but his language in those days was in the heavy industrial category. When he was excited every sentence needed a regular bleeper, yet such was his smiling manner that nobody took offence. I used to worry frantically that in the intense heat of a thrilling live match he might pepper his commentary with descriptions and language that would go straight to the next day's front pages, but he never did. Somewhere in that nimble brain of his there was a safety catch that never let him down.

A year after that telephone commentary, I was back in Mexico City again for the 1986 World Cup final and the victory for Argentina over Germany. Two days before the final I went shopping with Kevin Keegan. This was only a few months after an appalling earthquake and a by-product of that disaster was that junk shops in the city were filled with many sad, but appealing pieces. We were passing one such shop when I spotted in the window a lovely piece of Lladro, a beautiful figurine of two terrier dogs remarkably like the ones we had at home at the time, Tommy and Daisy.

'I must have those dogs,' I said to Kevin, so in we went.

'They are sixty-four thousand million pesos,' said the shop-keeper, clearly giving the first figure that came into his head. I did a quick calculation. It worked out at about £65. I was happy to pay it, but Kevin told me not to be so quick.

'Walk away,' he said. 'He's certain to come after us with a far better price than that.' So we started to walk and walk and walk until we were back out in the street. The shopkeeper hadn't budged. I glanced back to see that he was now putting the dogs back in the window.

The Keegan tactics had been a disaster. We walked round the block again, but whichever way you looked at it our bargaining power had been shot to ribbons. I still wanted those dogs. So we went in again. I paid the full price.

There is a footnote to this shaggy dog story. In the summer of 1997 I was walking along Piccadilly past a Lladro shop. I went in and an assistant showed me their catalogue; I pointed out a picture of the dogs. I wish Kevin had been alongside me as I read the caption explaining that it was a piece with a limited run, and it was now valued at just over £1,000. Moral: if you are looking for a bargain and Mr Keegan offers his advice, think again. He may be a good judge of a footballer but when it comes to Lladro dogs...

That 1969 débâcle in Mexico City may have been a broad-casting nightmare but it was rewarded with excellent viewing figures. The success in the ratings set off another chain of bizarre events that could have happened only in those television days before the greysuits grabbed command.

While I came back to London, Alf Ramsey's men flew on to matches in Uruguay and Brazil, both to be covered by the BBC. However, within two days of getting home I was summoned to the office of an ITV executive, John McMillan, who said that he had done a deal with a Brazilian TV company for us to share the rights for the Brazil game with the BBC. So off I went again, this time first class with Air France by way of Paris. I was accompanied by Gerry Loftus, ITV's excellent chief negotiator, and an engineer, Bill Sutton.

It was a long, champagne flight, and I was excited by the spectacular sight of Sugar Loaf Mountain and the prospect of commentating at the famous Maracana Stadium. But within a couple of hours of landing in Rio, it was perfectly clear that we had wasted our time. ITV had no chance of getting pictures of the game. There was no contract for us. Generously, our bosses told us to stay out there to see the game, which was still three days away. So I spent much of the time on Copacabana Beach just across the road from our hotel. While I relaxed in the sun, poor old Gerry was left waiting for a visit from the Brazilians with a reimbursement of ITV's money. They finally turned up just in time for us to go to the game in the Maracana where Pele and company won 2–1. And then we flew home again. Such was the life of a football commentator in those crazy early days of ITV sport.

During all those years at Wembley Cup finals, I was head-to-head at the microphone with three different BBC commentators – Kenneth Wolstenholme, David Coleman and John Motson (my pal Barry Davies had a crack at the FA Cup final only after ITV had for a time lost the contract). We commentators were never in the market for kicking verbal lumps out of each other, though I sometimes think Mr Coleman would have relished that sort of relationship! So while the rivalry simmered and sometimes exploded around us, we managed to stay above it all. The darned job was difficult enough as it was.

Ken Wolstenholme was coming towards the end of his commentating career when I arrived in the late sixties. He was an avuncular figure out of the old school, a former war-time pilot who had seen it all and done it all as a football commentator since the middle fifties. I sensed he was a likeable man but I was of little consequence to him so our paths rarely crossed. His great commentary line that has brought him enduring fame – and rightly so – is, of course, 'They think it's all over. It is now!' as Geoff Hurst crashed home England's fourth goal in the 1966 World Cup final. As I have acknowledged, it is a line all commentators would die for – and one we would all be proud of as an epitaph. Indeed, I wonder if Ken has even thought about having it on his own tombstone. It was a piece of natural commentating genius.

On his own admission, Ken was never a man for statistics.

'Far too many of them in commentaries these days,' he growled at me during a recent lunch. 'I remember,' he went on, 'doing Leicester City against Manchester United. Leicester had all the play and must have gained something like forty corners. But United won the game five–nil – and that was the only statistic that mattered.' That figures.

David Coleman was quite a different proposition when he took over from Ken in 1972. Nobody is more competitive and I had the feeling that he had a pretty high opinion of himself and of the BBC. There's no doubt that at his peak he was an outstanding broadcaster. I had no contact with him on those Wembley days which was probably to my advantage since he would doubtless have set out to denigrate ITV and probably me with it. That's his way. I once went to watch a game in Cardiff where he was broadcasting. 'You here looking for an audience?' he said as an introduction with that mixture of smile and sneer. I had no answer. Now I could point to the 27 million who switched on to ITV for the England–Argentina game in the World Cup, certainly larger than any audience in his career. That's me – twenty years too late with the answer. What an ad-libber! I never sought David's company and he didn't seek mine. We preferred to keep our distance.

In 1977, Motty took his place (though David came back for one more final in 1978), and this was the start of a good and valued friendship. We had both come out of the radio school, and were similar in our approach to our job. I remember I left a note of welcome on his commentary seat in 1977, and he made a point of reciprocating before my last final and at the World Cup final in Paris. Motty's preparation runs well into the leave-no-stone-unturned category that puts me in awe and it often made me feel just a little vulnerable.

Motty and I agree that the biggest Wembley upset in our time together was Wimbledon's victory over Liverpool in 1988, featuring Lawrie Sanchez's goal and Dave Beasant's history-making save from the John Aldridge penalty. But perhaps the most exciting and open game was the 3–2 victory for Coventry against Tottenham the year before. I shall long remember Keith Houchen's flying header for Coventry, by my reckoning one of Wembley's finest-ever Cup final goals.

I remember, too, something else from that game and how Motty calmed my fears the day after that Coventry triumph. There was a developing story that some of the Spurs players had worn shirts without the advertisement for sponsors Holsten on them. It had come about because Spurs had taken delivery of a new set of shirts just before the final. Mixed up with the Wembley kit were some short-sleeved shirts without an adver-tising logo that were meant for the youth squad. Five of the players had pulled these on as they were leaving the dressing-room, preferring short-sleeves on what was a sweltering afternoon. This was the twist, but I had no inkling of it at the time; angry sponsors, shame-faced Spurs, player power – it had all the ingredients of a front-page story that might run and run.

To my embarrassment, I had commentated for ninety minutes that day and simply had not detected the Great Shirt Mystery. First I heard of it was from a ten-year-old on the way home. I had given a lift to near-neighbours and good friends Lord Ted Willis, his wife Audrey and their grandson Tom – all great Spurs fans.

'Tell me, Mr Moore,' said young Tom, as we drove round Trafalgar Square. 'Why did some Spurs players have advertising on their shirts and some didn't?' It's a wonder I didn't drive into the fountain! I had no answer. It was the first mention of it, and I went cold. It cost me a night's sleep.

I tossed and turned, imagining the inquests. 'Mooro, what a

cock-up…what were you thinking of? You didn't even mention that the Tottenham players had snubbed their sponsors.' I could also imagine the cutting words of those oh-so-smart television critics, particularly as I was convinced that Motty would have swept up the whole business with his customary efficiency for the BBC. I rang John early that Sunday morning – he hadn't even got out of bed – and feared the worst.

'No, I didn't spot it either,' he said to my huge relief. So at least the damage was somewhat reduced. But to this day I still cannot fathom how two experienced broadcasters could have such a big story staring them in the face – much of it in huge close-up – and completely miss it. David Pleat, then Tottenham's manager, told me years later that, even from his place on the touchline bench close to the action, he'd missed it too. Perhaps we all needed the innocent eyes of a ten-year-old.

The one constant factor through all those Cup final years on ITV was Dickie Davies, for so long the face of 'World of Sport'. He had a priceless broadcasting quality. The camera and the viewers loved him. 'Good old Dickie,' they'd say. 'Our Saturdays wouldn't be the same without you.' They felt comfortable in his friendly, assured company. He had the gift of being able to talk to the camera as though it was a friend.

I first met Dickie in those early days when he was Richard Davies, a former purser and entertainments officer with the *Queen Mary* and the original *Queen Elizabeth*. There was an actor with the same name, so to avoid any confusion it was Jimmy Hill who suggested to him that Richard should become Dickie – and how much better that suited his whole image. The makeover was complete when he arrived back from a summer holiday sprouting a moustache – he told viewers without directly referring to it, 'Amazing the things that grow in the sunshine.' Then along came that distinctive white badger-like quiff in his hair that became his trademark. Some critics said it looked as if he had been painting the ceiling at home, others that he must have been the target for a passing pigeon. The important thing was that he was being noticed.

Dickie had come originally from the old Southern Television, where among other things he was occasionally a continuity announcer – the on-screen personality who used to guide viewers through a night's television. So he was well used to handling any little crisis of the sort that can so often and so quickly hit you between the eyes on live TV. He told many a tale, like the time he was on duty at midnight close-down and his last task was to run through the weather forecast for the following day. There were no clever graphics in those days. Everywhere in television, we used what we called 'fish and chip boards', as seen in all the best chippies. Individual white plastic letters were pressed into grooves on a board to make up the words. This particular night Dickie was just referring to the weather caption when the letter 'F' dropped off and it became 'Mist and og'. By now Dickie was well into reading the forecast, and heard himself say, 'Tomorrow plenty of sunshine, but only after early mist and fog. By the way, I am sorry about the F in fog.' I invite you to dwell on his words.

At Wembley he would be asked to introduce Cup final day from all manner of places, once from a huge crane platform some 200 feet above the stadium with the wind playing havoc with his carefully groomed hair. It was a formidable test of his television skills.

'Only one cup of coffee at breakfast this morning,' he told me. 'There's nowhere to go up there.' That was his only anxiety. He had to be a quality act to get through such a complicated opening sequence from that sort of position, without anything or anyone to prod him back on the rails if he lost the script.

It was at Hampden Park that Dickie had perhaps his most frightening television experience. We were coming to the end of a five-hour programme, the Scotland–England match was over, the interviews done and Dickie was coming to his closing link. The powerful lights in a little temporary studio behind one of the goals had produced an afternoon of sweltering Sahara heat and it was quite airless, too. Dickie was about to pass out and his last half-minute was pure gobbledegook. But great trouper that he is, Dickie stayed with it just long enough to say his goodbyes and cue the music. No sooner had the camera light gone off than he collapsed. Thankfully he made a quick recovery.

Yes, Dickie was and is a great trouper. All of us in broadcasting are lost in admiration for the way he overcame the handicap of a slight facial stroke to appear once again on camera, presenting eminently watchable nostalgia programmes on Sky. He quickly proved that he had lost none of that communications skill with his audience.

They were great days with Dickie and the 'World of Sport' gang; and I was about to have fun with another gang as ITV launched another new phenomenon – the World Cup panel.

7

FRED, FREDA – AND BIG MAL

THE first inkling that ITV had a World Cup hit on their hands in 1970 was when, early in the tournament, our hand-picked panellists went shopping together close to the studios at Wembley. It was a Saturday morning, and they completely stopped the traffic as men and boys – but mostly excited women of all ages – mobbed them. It was as though the Beatles were arriving back at Heathrow. We suddenly realised we had hit the jackpot with what was a revolutionary approach to discussing and dissecting the World Cup action in far-off Mexico.

The Four Musketeers who generated all the interest and attention were Malcolm Allison, Pat Crerand, Derek Dougan and Bob McNab, attractive men with a knowledgeable, knockabout style. They gave football punditry a fresh, intoxicating sparkle that has never quite been matched since. The nation loved every minute of it.

It was my first World Cup in charge of a panel, with Jimmy Hill alongside to help pepper the proceedings with his biting opinions. But in truth it was Messrs Allison, Crerand, Dougan and McNab, with their wide lapels, their kipper ties, seventies hairstyles, their flares and their flair, who drove the show for the three weeks of that World Cup. Letters of acclaim came flooding in and the critics were falling over themselves to herald the new dawn of sporting television. 'The talk is even better than the football,' they were saying, and the viewers deserted the BBC in droves. Our ratings were stunning.

For the first time during the coverage of sport on television, we had passionate, controversial, confrontational discussion, sometimes outrageous, even bigoted. It was the essence of 'pub talk', so much sought after by our innovative executive producer John Bromley. But the difference between what was said at the bar and what was being said on the screen was that the panellists were men of stature and credibility. Each show buzzed and bristled with strong opinions and argument, each panellist being encouraged to chip in when the mood took him – all of it totally unrehearsed, totally natural and sparkling in its spontaneity.

It would be convenient to say that the success of the panel was born out of long hours of ice-packs and head-banging around a darkened executive table, but that was not so. Plenty of thought went into it, of course, as the search was conducted for men who looked good on the screen, who knew what they were talking about and were not afraid to voice their opinions; fence-sitting was not part of the brief. But not until the camera started to roll could anyone be sure whether it was going to work or not. Chemistry and charisma are capricious qualities. These four gentlemen had them by the bucketful.

Often the panel were at work into the early hours, and the nation stayed up with them. They were dubbed the Midnight Cowboys by the press.

Malcolm was the key player. A big, handsome man who might have just strolled in from some film set having played a tough, lovable rogue – expensively dressed, large cigar, an easy, everyday South London accent and a passion for the game of football that was second to none. He had made his name as the coach and driving force of the exceptional Manchester City team of the late 1960s after his playing career with Charlton and West Ham had been cruelly cut short by tuberculosis.

Of all the men I have met in my football travels, none was bigger, brasher, brighter or more likeable than Big Mal. He looked striking enough on our panel to fit the James Bond image, and in no time he had captured every female heart – well, almost. The only time I saw him come off second best was when, in our hotel one lunchtime, he tried to chat up that stunning actress Diana Rigg who was passing through. She gave him a haughty once-over and in five seconds turned on her delectable heel and left him for dead. Malcolm's presence in our team, however, meant nearly as many women as men were tuned in to the ITV World Cup coverage. Ladies who did not know an overlap from an underpass were hooked. There's no question that Allison was the magnet.

Derek Dougan was a fascinating character, and an ideal foil for Big Mal. The towering Northern Ireland international centre-forward had something of a scallywag image with Wolves, and over the years had garnered a reputation for being a footballing renegade and rebel. But the poacher had turned gamekeeper, and he now played the serious statesman part, which sat comfortably with his role as chairman of the Professional Footballers' Association. This new image fitted perfectly into our jigsaw, and his occasional high and mighty stance at times irritated Malcolm and company to the point where they sometimes fed the Doog false World Cup information which, to their obvious glee, he sometimes innocently passed on to the watching millions. But, to give him credit, Derek had carefully weighed up his worth to our panel and had twigged that in the midst of so much shouting there had to be a sane voice. He provided it to perfection.

Pat Crerand was a jewel. He was just coming to the end of a distinguished playing career with Manchester United, he gave us a respected Scottish voice and, more than anything, he was a genuine heart-on-the-sleeve performer who spoke with an honesty and a passion that could burn you at five paces. Paddy talked like he played the game – with commitment and precision. He also had a nice line in dry humour, and often wound up other members of the panel with poker-faced comments that were said purely out of a sense of mischief.

To complete the jigsaw, we needed a current England international, and Alf Ramsey unconsciously supplied him when he axed Bob McNab from the World Cup squad when making his final twenty-two-player selection. Bob was one of those rare animals, a quiet, retiring Yorkshireman! We invited him on to the panel to bring some balance to the proceedings, and at first the Arsenal left-back seemed completely overawed by his more boisterous and extrovert fellow panellists. He hardly got a word in during the first few transmissions, but we solved that by giving him a bell to ring every time he wanted to make himself heard. It was that sort of irreverent, lively and imaginative show.

Bob and I swapped memories of those gloriously mad panel days when we both appeared as guests on Bob Wilson's 'This Is Your Life' tribute in the autumn of 1998. He had flown in specially for the show from his adopted home in Los Angeles, and I noticed that life in America had given him an extra dimension. I could hardly get a word in, and he no longer needed a bell to make himself heard. He talked fondly of those raucous, exhilarating days and the part Big Mal played.

'He was at that time an absolute football genius, years ahead of everyone,' Bob told me. 'But he had a problem. He had the answer to everything, but then he couldn't stop looking for an alternative answer!' In life, it seems to me, Malcolm so often was three goals up only to throw the game away. But I loved being in his company and there's no denying the man had that indefinable quality called style.

'Malcolm taught me to drink excellent Rhine wine,' Bob recalled, 'and to eat wild strawberries for lunch in a five-star hotel. He introduced me to a world that most people probably think exists only in Hollywood.' No doubt Big Mal also taught him how to make spectacular claims on his ITV expenses!

Malcolm had a big appetite for all the good things in life, and one day during the World Cup the manager of our hotel, the Hendon Hall, went to John Bromley with Big Mal's running hotel bill in his hand; boy, was it running. There were not only fine Rhine wines and wild strawberries to account for, but the very finest champagne and the best cigars. Brommers ran his experienced eye down the bill, and even this veteran of Fleet Street expenses had not seen anything quite like it. But he shrugged, handed the bill back to the hotel manager and said in typical style, 'Don't worry about it, master. It's no problem.'

He knew that ITV's biggest hit in years, Big Mal and the boys, was also the biggest bargain. For their month of high-profile work, Big Mal and the rest of the panellists were on contracts that brought them just £500 each.

There were two other important and unheralded members of the ITV team that year: Fred and Freda. They were our imaginary, average ITV viewers – Fred just home with the fish and chips for supper, to be eaten out of the paper naturally, and with Freda settling down for some good fun and entertainment to go alongside the football on the telly. At every editorial conference they were there. Every idea was put before them. 'Should we do a piece on Germany's defensive strategy?' John Bromley, miming Fred taking a hot chip from the paper, would shake his head. '"No, boring," says Fred.'

'How about a discussion on whether Gordon Banks is the world's number one goalkeeper?' Brommers would take another imaginary chip and nod approvingly. 'That's more like it,' he'd say in his Fred voice. 'That won't send Freda to sleep. Everybody loves Banksie.'

It no doubt sounds daft, but Fred and Freda provided the perfect test pad for all our ideas. They helped to keep us in touch with our audience, kept the programmes down to earth and gave them a tabloid feel that truly hit the spot. There is always a danger that you can get too close to your subject, and disappear up your own slipstream. Fred and Freda kept our eyes on the ball.

Soon there were spin-offs. A jeweller delivered handsome Breitling watches for us all, Pringle weighed in with a selection of cashmere sweaters, Slazenger with casual shirts, and a tie manufacturer, impressed by our undiluted patriotism, ran up Union Jack ties for us to wear when England played.

It was Pele and the magical Brazilians, of course, who took our eye. Jairzinho, Gerson, Tostao, Pele and Rivelino became household names, each of them revered by the panellists. The Brazilian ambassador was so impressed by our support for his team that he invited us all to a party at his embassy.

One particular night we came on the air immediately following Shaw Taylor's 'Police Five' programme in which the main story had centred on the theft of a consignment of distinctive designer shirts. Unwittingly Bob McNab, a fashion dandy, had that very day bought a number of these same shirts at a pound each – and now each member of the panel was wearing one for all the world, but not apparently the boys in blue, to see!

It was all great fun, but there was the occasional downside. For example, Malcolm once referred to the Russians and Romanian players as 'peasants', and protests practically jammed the switchboard.

There was more angry response from viewers when our panellists, in despair, threw their Union Jack ties to the studio floor after England had allowed a two-goal lead to slip and were beaten 3–2 by West Germany in that unforgettable quarter-final in Leon. They poured oil on Alf Ramsey for substituting Bobby Charlton when, for the only time in his life, with England two ahead, Alf seemed to take it for granted that England had the game won. He was saving Bobby for future battles; sadly, this turned out to be Bobby's then record 106th and final game for England.

A spicy twist followed that England defeat. Most people looked in the direction of Peter Bonetti, the Chelsea goalkeeper, for a convenient scapegoat. Peter had replaced the suddenly and mysteriously sick Gordon Banks just hours before the game (to this day Gordon is convinced he was 'nobbled' by a doctored drink). Bonetti, the most reliable of goalkeepers for years with Chelsea, had played only one game since the end of the previous season and understandably looked less than his old sharp self when conceding the three goals. But Big Mal did not join in the condemnation of Bonetti. Instead he chose this moment of

England's devastating defeat to launch into a violent verbal attack on the performance of Alan Mullery, who had scored the first of England's two goals against Germany.

The main thrust of Malcolm's assault was that Colin Bell, the 'heart and lungs' of his Manchester City team, would have been a better bet than Mullery in England's midfield. He went on to castigate Mullery, and point up his shortcomings. It was powerful stuff and riveting television. But, as you can imagine, it did not go down at all well in the Mullery household.

Even before he flew home from Mexico the day after the elimination by Germany, Alan knew that Allison had been attacking him. His brother reported in full on what Malcolm had been saying when he met Alan at Heathrow. Like the true pro that he is, Alan first of all shrugged it off, saying that Allison was entitled to his opinion. 'We all know Malcolm...' he said.

But it didn't end there. Letters began pouring in to us, taking up the argument for and against the Allison view. It provided the perfect platform for what we knew would make a great television confrontation, and we invited Alan to our studio so that he could have the right to reply.

'I'll do it but only if it goes out live,' Alan said. Surely, this was our first whiff of grapeshot.

I contacted Alan when writing this chapter to make sure I got my facts right. He remembered arriving at our hospitality room only for Malcolm to turn his back on him.

'He didn't say a word to me,' he recalled. 'Our first words to each other went out live in the studio.'

By then the atmosphere was pretty warm and things began to get even hotter when Malcolm started by criticising Alf Ramsey. Such was Alf's bond with his players that none of them would ever tolerate that, and Alan came back with both barrels in Alf's defence.

Then Malcolm switched the point of attack to Alan's own performances and that's when things erupted.

'How many England caps have you won?' challenged Alan in

a voice that boomed around the studio. 'Come on, put them on the table.'

He had hit Malcolm where it hurt and Big Mal had to admit he was never capped. At this point Alan pulled out an old Marks and Spencer bag and from it fished out a velvet England international cap.

'There you are,' he snapped. 'I've got thirty of them, and this one's spare. You have it because it's the only way you'll ever get one.'

He thrust the cap in Malcolm's direction. As dear old Eric Morecambe might have said, 'There's no answer to that!'

I sat open-mouthed in the middle of it all. In its way it was all pretty unpleasant. This was not contrived for the cameras. This was out and out animosity. But our producers were rubbing their hands. It was raw, enthralling television. Nobody could possibly switch it off. I've never known anything on sporting television to generate more heat or hostility.

The World Cup programmes went a little flat after England's departure and Mullery's fireworks. But we still had the stunningly gifted Brazilians to watch and wonder at, and we supported them all the way to their historic third World Cup triumph. For the final we all wore dinner jackets and bow ties and got invited back to the Brazilian embassy for another great party.

I have often been asked if I would have preferred to have been in Mexico commentating rather than back in London. It was my choice to be studio bound, and I can truthfully say I have not known more rewarding or challenging days in all my time in television.

Our 1970 coverage set the standard for all future World Cup panels, though none have had remotely the same impact. It was more or less the same ITV team in 1974 for the tournament in Germany, with the major difference that Jimmy Hill had switched to the 'enemy' BBC camp. A lot of the juice was squeezed out of the finals by England's failure to qualify, and it was left to Scotland to give us just a little to shout about. Poland were the surprise package. They somehow got past England in the qualifying rounds, but then proved they were worth their place by taking a richly merited third place.

The tournament was won by Franz Beckenbauer's functional Germans, lacking the flair and finesse of the 1970 Brazilians. The final in Munich made a memorable television event because of the one Englishman involved. Referee Jack Taylor had the courage to award Holland a penalty in the first minute.

'That's the bravest decision I've ever seen,' said Derek Dougan. And he was right.

'Bet he cancels it out,' said Big Mal.

In the twenty-fifth minute, Taylor pointed to the penalty spot again, this time in favour of the Germans.

'What did I tell you?' said Big Mal, a satisfied smile spreading round his ever-present cigar.

England were missing again from the 1978 finals, which, from a parochial point of view, led to a pretty flat tournament. The television pictures that stay in the memory are of the anguish of Scotland's Ally McLeod as he died a thousand deaths on the touchline watching his team under-perform. There are times when the television camera can be extremely intrusive on private grief.

Brian Clough had now talked his way on to our panel. We also had Johan Cruyff in the studio for that World Cup. I recall Brian sidling up to me one night as we were going into the studio.

'Could you sit me next to Johan tonight?' he asked. 'I'd like a little of his magic to rub off on me.'

Was Cloughie really star-struck? I'm not sure, but it won't have escaped your notice, I'm certain, that his Nottingham Forest team went on to win the European Cup for the next two seasons! Maybe some of that Cruyff magic did rub off, but I'm enough of a Clough fan to believe he really didn't need it. He was a footballing magician in his own right.

Jimmy Greaves, his rehabilitation complete, was the star for us in the 1982 World Cup. It was like musical chairs in the studio as a procession of pundits took turns on the panel. As well as

FRED, FREDA - AND BIG MAL

Greavsie, the impressive line-up included George Best, Jack Charlton, Mick Channon, Denis Law and Cloughie. We were not exactly short of opinions. We also saw the first teaming of Ian St John and Jimmy Greaves, and the Saint and Greavsie partnership was not far behind.

Mick Channon brought fresh vigour to the screens in 1986, particularly during one spat with Cloughie. Brian had got on his high-horse and told his audience in a very sniffy way that he wasn't in the habit of discussing football matters with players. He said that he had never done it at his club and he wasn't going to start now. This was something of a problem because Mick, then playing with Southampton, was an important part of the panel that night. I started to protest, but before I had got very far Mick jumped in with both feet.

'What you have to learn, Mr Clough,' he said, his eyes blazing, 'is that football is all about players – not managers. It's all about players.'

It was a tense and scary moment, but Brian took the point. It was about the only time in all the years that I've known him that I saw Cloughie come off second best in any argument.

By the time the 1990 World Cup in Italy came around, studio panels based in London had become a thing of the past. I believe that is a mistake. If the balance and chemistry are right, panels really work brilliantly and I feel strongly there is still room for them.

However, as television technology has advanced so too has the desire to control everything from the scene of the action. As the main ITV presenter, I fought hard and successfully to keep the studio in London for the 1982 and 1986 World Cups in Spain and Mexico, but by 1990 too many voices were ranged against me. Elton Welsby presented all the programmes that year – and presented them very well – from the grounds in Italy.

I always argued in favour of a London base and for a small band of regular contributors, choosing each day from no more than five or six. If you have a small team it encourages a relaxed rapport between the panellists. In London they also have a better

115

chance to respond to what the audience is thinking, and to react to their excitement or anger. Most important of all, there's nothing like having everything technological under your own control. The decision, however, was to take the programmes to the edge and to do them from the grounds.

For the 1994 World Cup in the United States, ITV made a dog's breakfast of it by doing neither one thing nor the other. The programmes came from a dungeon-like studio in Dallas that had neither the visual, vibrant excitement of the stadium nor the comforts of home. The panel were far removed from the action and looked (and probably were) bored. The presenting was now in the hands of young Matthew Lorenzo, who had been unfairly saddled with the label of 'the new Des Lynam' at the World Cup press launch. But his engaging, easy style of presenting had no chance here. The BBC stayed at home and cleaned up. These truly were ITV's darkest sporting days.

Things brightened up in France in 1998 thanks in no small measure to the massive audiences for ITV's live England games against Romania and Argentina, but also to Bob Wilson's assured handling of affairs at all the grounds and Jim Rosenthal's late-night debates with Messrs Atkinson, Venables, Ferguson, Robson and Co. that produced some of the most imaginative television of the whole tournament. Studio based, you see. I rest my case.

When I arrived home from France after a successful ITV World Cup, all I could hear was how entertaining the likes of Martin O'Neill, Alan Hansen and Ally McCoist had been on the BBC. They had opted from the start to put Des Lynam in a safer, less adventurous environment of a studio overlooking Paris. They made their mark with the words around the games; we made ours with the games around the words. The key is to get it all together and get the balance right. I think that both BBC and ITV achieved their targets in France.

The 2002 World Cup in South Korea and Japan will be a major headache for all European broadcasters. The time difference will be huge. All the matches will be played outside peak television time, thus making it much harder to draw huge audiences.

The sheer scale of the travelling for commentators and pre-senters will be daunting. The commentators must be up with the action, of course, but could there be a better time to turn the clock back, with all the advantages, and do everything else from a London base? The search should now be on to find the men to step out of the shadows cast all those years ago by Big Mal and his friends.

One man who was never ever overshadowed was Brian Clough.

I consider him worth a chapter all to himself.

8

THERE'S ONLY ONE BRIAN CLOUGH

EVERYONE who has ever met him has his own memories and stories – often exaggerated with excruciating mimicry – of Brian Clough. Mine, based on a friendship of more than thirty years, are a mixture of the exciting and the challenging. Just to watch any of his teams play was exciting enough, and to have him alongside me in the commentary box and in the studio was certainly challenging; and then there are the darker memories as his life went into extra time and was filled with a piercing pain from the knee injury that sliced into his playing career. With it came his long and fearsome battle with alcohol. It is a battle he has tried so hard and so often to win, and it's one victory all his friends want him most to be able to enjoy.

I think back to all those years when, often wearing that famous green rugby shirt, he called the odds so compellingly. There were his fearless tilts at authority, those battles in all his board-rooms, his command and influence over all his players, no matter how bright their stardom or sinister their past; his amazing record of success, his winning style with everyone, the humbler the better; and his incredibly strong family ties with his wife Barbara and his children Simon, Nigel and Elizabeth.

Sometimes, even through those glory years, I sensed there was indeed another, more retiring man lurking somewhere behind all the bombast, one who found the daily grind and the unwavering spotlight increasingly difficult to bear; and always there was the record of past achievements that anybody would have found impossible to live up to. Indeed, he once shook his head wearily as he told me: 'It's a damned sight harder hanging on to success than it is to get it.' Therein lies a clue, perhaps, to the demons working deep inside him. He gave another indication that the increasing burden was getting too much when he confided to me: 'It's such a lonely job. We work in front of tens of thousands yet when the job is done we have nobody to talk to and say, "Do you think I've done the right thing?" Yes, it's a damn lonely job.'

I would always start our telephone conversations by asking, 'How are you doing, commander?'

He would always respond, 'Surviving.'

I used to think he was joking, but on reflection there might have been a hidden truth there too.

So before I get carried away with tales of Cloughie it would be fairest to remember the pain and problems of his later years and recognise the lofty platform which gave all those stories about him that extra vibrancy. He was a big man in football – for a time none bigger – for forty years, and nothing should be allowed to detract from that.

As a manager he was a giant, standing in my estimation alongside greats of the game like Ramsey, Busby, Shankly, Paisley, Revie, Nicholson, Stein, Graham, Dalglish and Ferguson.

Cloughie has, of course, left behind his own testimony. As a player there was no more prolific goalscorer. Even Jimmy Greaves could not match an output that produced 251 goals in 275 league games for his hometown club Middlesbrough and then Sunderland before, at twenty eight, a knee injury forced him painfully into premature retirement.

All that he accomplished as a player was dwarfed by his achievements as a manager. In terms of trophies, he won a League Championship with Derby County and another with Nottingham Forest, where he twice in successive seasons brought home the European Cup, and four times the League

Cup. It was the way he achieved this success that lifted him into the land of footballing legend. All his teams played the game the way it should be played; they got spectators off their seats and put beauty into the beautiful game.

I once asked him on television to define the Clough style.

'On the floor, quick, neat, decisive and above all clean,' he said in those much-impersonated Yorkshire tones. 'Referees give lectures on the way we play.'

It pleased him no end that the redoubtable Jim Smith, who followed him on the managerial trail to Derby, told him once that when he felt down and depressed about results, he always sent for a Forest tape of those Clough days to remind him of the better things in football.

Yet as a manager and a colleague he was an extraordinary enigma. He could dazzle you with his generosity one moment and then hurt or anger you with a piece of boorish behaviour the next. 'Come and have some champagne with me tomorrow,' he once said to a journalist friend when he heard it was his birthday the following day. Delighted with the invitation, he duly arrived at the City Ground for his bubbly. Cloughie, through his secretary, denied all knowledge of the arrangement and refused to talk to him or to let him into the office block. When he in his confusion persisted, Cloughie threatened to call the police unless he left the premises at once. That was typical of Cloughie, but he mended bridges with my pal and they remained friends.

Joe Melling, who has broken so many stories for the *Mail on Sunday*, tells of his time as ghostwriter for Cloughie's weekly column in the days when he was working for the *Daily Express*. One week Joe spent two frustrating and fruitless days trailing Cloughie at the Nottingham Forest ground trying to catch the great man's attention, but he was much more interested in playing squash with his goalkeeper Chris Woods.

The third day was also the birthday of Joe's wife and he'd promised to do all the things a busy man hopefully promises his wife on such a day. Instead Joe was back at the City Ground once more. This time he caught Cloughie and between them they wrote, as Joe recalls, a compelling column.

Two days later Mrs Melling had a huge delivery from the local florist shop and a note from Cloughie. 'Sorry, love,' he'd written, 'but we've been working.'

It is no secret that many in the media, and also in the game itself, found him too hard to take and enjoyed seeing him cut down to size. Many more, though, were fascinated and captivated by him. 'What was Brian Clough *really* like?' remains one of the questions I am most frequently asked, long after Cloughie's retirement. The answer is easy. He was one of the most invigorating, stimulating men I've ever met. 'And what was the secret of all his success as a manager?' is always the follow-up question. Frankly, I am no nearer the answer to that than when I first met him in those far-off days when, as Hartlepool manager, he drove the team bus to cut costs. Perhaps some of the following tales may give us a clue.

As Joe Melling and scores of others found, he delights in wrong-footing people. Stephen Potter's *One-Upmanship* had nothing on Brian. I travelled from London to see him while in the foothills of preparing this book to talk over old times. We had been chatting for no more than a couple of minutes in his stylish sitting-room with its stunning views over the Derbyshire countryside when his doorbell rang.

'That'll be the postman,' he said. 'His name is Alan, and he wants to meet you so I told him he could join us.' A minute later the dear old postie was sitting with us, and here we were talking about the postman's problems and listening to his views and opinions on football and television. Brian asked the whereabouts of the driver who had brought me from the station.

'He's in his car in your driveway,' I explained.

'Can't have that,' said Brian. 'Bring him in.'

So now the driver was sitting with the postman and we were discussing *his* problems and listening to *his* opinions, too.

It was all very laudable, very democratic, very Cloughie and very interesting, too, but not what I had travelled miles to do. We had our afternoon tea, the four of us, and said our goodbyes. I left without a single moment of quiet conversation with my old friend, though I certainly knew all I needed to know about the Derbyshire postal and taxi services!

Brian was the same with his players. They never knew quite what to expect from him. He'd often change the time of the next day's training without any warning.

'It means they can never plan in advance to have an afternoon of snooker,' he reasoned, 'or go shopping with the missus. Their first thoughts always have to be for Nottingham Forest.'

Did it work? The answers are in those handsome trophy cabinets on display in the inner sanctum at Nottingham Forest.

He was always hot on homespun psychology. I remember the Dutchman Johnny Metgod telling me he learned more about running a club and managing players under Brian at Nottingham Forest than he did in all his time at those majestic clubs Ajax and Real Madrid.

I was privileged – with my bosses at ITV, John Bromley and Michael Grade – to travel on the Forest team coach from their hotel to the Olympic stadium in Munich for their European Cup final against Malmö in 1979. This was the biggest night in the club's history and certainly in the careers of those Forest players, but here were three outsiders being allowed to share this special journey. No other manager would even have considered it. More than that, there on the back seat we were amazed to see two large crates of lager. Halfway to the stadium the coach was dead quiet and tense as each player withdrew into his own thoughts when, from the front seat, Cloughie suddenly piped up: 'Go on, lads – help yourself to a beer, but try to finish it before we get to the stadium.' And this was a European Cup final! It was more like a works outing to the seaside than a date with the greatest match of their lives.

I am sure, also, that this was Brian's way of saying to his players that the game must be approached with no greater fear or anxiety than any other night's football work. This was a date for a relaxed performance and not for knotted nerves. As it happened the beer remained untouched. Nobody had a drop of it – until the trophy had been lifted.

Forest won that match, beating Malmö's unashamed smothering defensive tactics with a brilliant thrust down the left by John Robertson before he released one of his perfect crosses that was dramatically headed in by a stooping Trevor Francis, his first game and goal in Europe after Cloughie had boldly made him the first million pound player.

'Mind you, our Elizabeth could have scored it,' said Brian afterwards. But as someone who scored all those goals for Middlesbrough and Sunderland, he knew better than that. There's a wonderful picture hanging in the Forest hospitality room that shows the Robertson cross the moment before Francis gets his head to it. It's called 'One Second From Glory'. Belittle it he may have done, but Brian can still savour that glittering moment every single day. He's got the same picture hanging in the study at his home.

My personal souvenir of that night, incidentally, is a splendid crystal replica of the European Cup which Brian thoughtfully gave to Betty and me on one of our trips to Derbyshire. It's here now in the room where I am writing, and resting inside it is a champagne cork from the bottle we cracked together at Elland Road on the night he was sacked after forty-four days in charge at Leeds United. There's no better illustration, surely, of the ups and downs in the life of a football manager.

By keeping his players on their toes, he also tightened up their discipline. He took the view that you could not expect players to show discipline and do the right things for ninety minutes on Saturday afternoon if they didn't do them at, say, ten o'clock on Tuesday morning. As a manager he abhorred bad manners (though he would admit that he never always set the best example), he loathed long hair and said he would never allow a Forest player to wear an earring. He once delayed the team coach's departure for a European game by ordering Garry Birtles back to his hotel room to shave, and there was a famous occasion when he fined Larry Lloyd for not wearing a club blazer on the return from another European match.

Cloughie had a running battle with another of his defenders at that time, Terry Wilson, about his penchant for garish modern fashions, and demanded that he follow the Forest dress code of club blazer and tie on match days. I once saw him slap a fifty-pound fine on Archie Gemmill, who had committed the crime of passing across his goalmouth at a crucial time in the previous night's game – and he once employed Peter Shilton as a drinks waiter! This happened soon after Shilton had become the League's most expensive goalkeeper when moving from Stoke City to Forest, a master deal, incidentally, that turned Forest into a championship team.

I was a witness to Peter being made to serve the drinks. John Bromley and I had gone to Nottingham to talk to Brian about appearing as a panellist for ITV in the forthcoming 1978 World Cup finals. These were always harum-scarum days at the City Ground and this was no exception. We were shown into the Forest boardroom – we thought for a private discussion about a contract – only to be joined round the boardroom table by the entire Forest first team, just back from a morning's training, still sweating and still in their kit.

'Drinks all round,' announced Brian. Then, pointing to England goalkeeper Shilton, he ordered: 'Peter, you serve the drinks. You've done nothing else today.' Shilton was getting his first lesson that no player was bigger than another in the world of Brian Clough. So Peter started to take the orders.

'No,' said Cloughie, 'it's lagers for everyone.' One of Forest's centre-backs at this time was Dave Needham.

'Could I have a soft drink, boss?' he said. 'I don't like lager.'

'David,' said Cloughie, as always using the player's full chris-tian name (it was Cloughie who insisted on calling Teddy Sheringham Edward!), 'listen to me. You are a good-looking man, you have a lovely wife and bairns, you live in a good house, you have a brilliant contract here. Life is wonderful for you. But you also have to learn that sometimes you must put up with things you don't like. Peter, give him a lager.' There was no further discussion.

Neither was there any further discussion about a contract with ITV. Brommers and I left empty-handed with the distinct feeling that he'd had us playing to his captivating tune as well.

Brian invited me to join him for a pre-match lunch one Saturday at the Kensington Hilton when Forest were due to play Queens Park Rangers. It was a three o'clock kick-off on what was then that notorious artificial surface at Loftus Road. Once we had finished our lunch, I was prepared for Brian to hurry off to the ground for the pre-match preparations. As we sipped our brandies, the clock ticked past one thirty and then one forty-five and the players, who had long since left the dining-room, were waiting in the coach and, understandably, getting distinctly agitated.

It was two o'clock before he made his move. It would have been about a ten-minute journey to the ground if it had not been for the heavy match traffic, and the team-sheet had to be in by two fifteen in those days. In the end, it was a breathless hustle with one of his training staff running through the crowds for the last quarter-mile to meet that deadline. I asked him later why he had dallied so long over our lunch and cut things so fine, causing such anxiety among his players.

'Simple,' he said. 'While they were worrying about getting to the ground on time, they weren't worrying about playing on that bloody awful pitch.' You'll not be surprised to know that Forest won the game.

Forest players have told me of how a hush would always descend on the dressing-room on his arrival, and of one occasion when after a poor first-half performance, he just sat there at half-time glaring at them for ten minutes without uttering a single word. It was also common for him not to go near the dressing-room at half-time, leaving the players to stew and worry about what he might have said!

Indeed, before extra-time in one of his League Cup finals at Wembley, he remained seated on the bench while his players looked anxiously towards him for guidance. His assistant, Ronnie Fenton, urged him to get out on to the pitch, but he refused to budge. Forest still took home the Cup.

I remember Cloughie being most upset when I suggested in a television conversation with Lawrie McMenemy before a Forest–Southampton final that Brian was dictatorial and that, to some extent, he ruled by fear. Cloughie preferred to think it was respect. He did not want to be liked, but he did want to be listened to and obeyed.

I was once in his office before a night game against Sheffield Wednesday with the deputy Labour leader Roy Hattersley, a passionate Owls fan. Twenty minutes before the kick-off Brian was on the phone to the dressing-room.

'Send my son and young Carr to my office,' he ordered. Nigel Clough and Franz Carr duly arrived, having walked past the arriving crowds, fully kitted-up and ready to play. They looked puzzled, as they had every right to be.

'It's all right,' said Cloughie, waving a hand in the direction of Roy and myself. 'You know who these two gentlemen are. I just wanted you to meet them before you went out to play.' Just that. We spoke about nothing much for a couple of minutes and the two perplexed (and, I'm sure, far from impressed) youngsters were then sent back to continue their preparation for the game. Where else could that have happened? Incidentally, Brian was still entertaining Roy and myself with just ten minutes to go to the kick-off when he at last got out of his chair and headed for the dressing-room.

'Now I must go and put a bit of colour in their cheeks,' were his parting words.

He believed that the foundation of all great sides was the defence. 'They are built on clean sheets,' he would say. 'You can only deliver goals from a solid background.'

In Forest's prime, he had exactly that solid background with Peter Shilton guarding the goal behind exceptional defenders of the calibre of Viv Anderson, Larry Lloyd, Kenny Burns and Frank Clark. 'They won the championship for Forest,' he has often said. 'We had a firm belief that if we ever scored we'd win, because the others would never have scored against us.'

He once told me he would only buy players who were good, but still hungry; players without medals on their chests but with huge ambition in their hearts. Trevor Francis filled that bill. He had won nothing at club level with Birmingham City; similarly Peter Shilton, Kenny Burns (Cloughie tells hair-raising tales of rescuing him from the blandishments of Midlands dog tracks), Garry Birtles, Ian Bowyer, Martin O'Neill, Larry Lloyd (out of Coventry's reserve team), Tony Woodcock – for all of them there was a huge appetite for success that had not been satisfied, until they sat down to what proved to be a banquet at Cloughie's table.

It was in spotting players that Brian and Peter Taylor, for so many great seasons his right-hand man, dove-tailed so effectively. This was a mould-breaking partnership. A manager was always on his own until they proved it was a two-man job at Hartlepool, Derby and then Forest. Taylor was the spotter and Brian knew that was the important part.

Cloughie idolised Frank Sinatra and never tired of telling of a conversation when Ol' Blue Eyes said to him that in his business it was the written words that came first, the music later. 'It's the same in football,' Brian would say. 'The one who picks the players comes first, the rest is just bullshit.'

That was as close as he got to a good word for Taylor in their last acrimonious years. Peter, then manager at Derby County, had snaffled John Robertson, who was out of contract at Forest, without telling Brian. Brian never forgave him.

'All it needed was one tuppeny phone call,' he said.

Peter, I thought, was a splendid man, and I understand he tried to bridge that unhappy gap in his last years but Brian would have none of it. When Peter died Brian went to the funeral, and I sense that he had time then to contemplate and regret those wasted years. At their peak together, Cloughie and Taylor were an untouchable partnership.

Just about everybody who played for Cloughie would have been richer for the experience. I was with him once on a late winter afternoon in the car park at the City Ground when a young apprentice was walking towards us trying, with head down, not to be noticed.

'Head up, son,' yelled Brian. 'Down there, there's only mud. Up there [pointing to the skies] are the stars.' It's a small point, perhaps, but of all the clubs I visited it was at Forest where the apprentices would always look you in the eye and say 'good morning'. That would certainly have been a part of the Clough master-class.

As a television pundit or a co-commentator he had one priceless gift. Sometimes he'd be difficult, sometimes downright cantankerous, sometimes he'd not be particularly well informed about the foreign players. But at some point during those ninety minutes he would say something that would have people rushing into work next day to repeat. In that respect, too, he was out on his own.

Even in my world of television he was full of surprises. We worked together on the second leg of the 1984 UEFA Cup final between Tottenham and Anderlecht at White Hart Lane. It was a night of raw drama at the end of which Spurs won on a penalty shoot-out with reserve goalkeeper Tony Parks the Tottenham hero. But there had been an even bigger drama for us off the screen. Brian arrived for his co-commentary role in the company of a friend, Mike Keeling, only to find forty-five minutes before the kick-off that an observant Spurs official had spotted one too many people on the gantry. This, we were told, meant we were exceeding the weight restriction. He announced quite firmly that someone would have to leave. Naturally, it had to be the non-working Mike Keeling. So away he went and, to my amazement, Cloughie went with him.

With Cloughie, you never knew what that might mean. Twenty minutes to kick-off and still he had not reappeared. We feared he may have taken umbrage and left the ground altogether and by now we were urgently trying to find a replacement co-commentator. Ten minutes to go – still no Cloughie. Just as the teams came out on to the pitch, I caught sight of him climbing down the steps on to the gantry carrying two steaming plastic cups of tea.

'Thought you might want something to whet your whistle,' he said. Then he tripped and spilled both cups all over my notes. They were totally ruined. Fortunately the game was such a good one that the notes were almost superfluous; in any case Brian was in magnificent form.

He has always been loyal to his friends. I remember when Jimmy Hill left ITV for the BBC in 1973, we were desperately worried about how Jimmy's absence might hit the credibility of 'The Big Match' at the start of the new season. I told Brian we were in trouble and wondered if he would make a guest appearance for us on the opening day; not only did he drive down from Derby at dawn that Sunday morning and return after the recording in the early afternoon, but he did it for the next three months as well. And this was while he was coming to grips with all the problems of that brief but explosive stay at Leeds United.

As an extra bonus, he was at his most outspoken on those Sundays and provided back-page story after back-page story for the grateful football reporters. We could not have had more positive publicity, thanks to Brian, and it completely disguised the considerable absence of Jimmy Hill.

The only spat I can remember us having was when I went to see him soon after attending a press conference at Downing Street during which I asked a couple of questions of Margaret Thatcher.

'I saw you there,' he said, 'loving every minute of it. You gave it big licks and lapped up everything Thatcher told you. I don't know how you've got the nerve to come near me.'

It took him quite a while to come round and calm down and it got quite unpleasant before he did. He'd quite overlooked the fact that, like him, I'm also a supporter of the Labour Party – though without quite his passion. He once told me that his socialism comes from the heart.

'I've been lucky,' he said. 'I've made a few bob and everybody should have that. Everybody should have a book, everybody should have a nice classroom and everybody should have the same opportunity.'

Fine principles, I can hear people say, for someone who has a fine house and more than a few bob in the bank. But his critics should know, too, that he went marching with the best of them when the cause was a just one. I felt tortured for him when his name was dragged through football's mud with allegations of bungs and back-handers. He is without question the most unforgettable character to cross my path, and I feel privileged to have had him as a friend, warts and all.

Along with many of his other friends, I have quietly done my best to help him in his battle with the bottle. He deserved nothing less. Brian is lucky to have a loving and supportive family. Even in his lowest moments, he commands the love and respect of those fortunate enough to have known the *real* Brian Clough.

It was the inimitable Cloughie who provided me with one of my more unusual moments on television. I interviewed him for a 1993 ITV programme called 'Over the Moon, Brian' in which I looked back on my twenty-five years as a television commentator. Unbeknown to me, the producers had arranged for Brian to make a presentation to me on camera at the end of the interview.

I was winding up the programme in the garden of Brian's house when he came from behind a hedge carrying a huge framed cartoon caricature of myself. It had been signed by just about every great England footballer alive, as well as many of my colleagues on both ITV and BBC. Only Cloughie could have handed it over while singing one of his Sinatra favourites, 'S'Wonderful, S'Marvellous…'

It was a major disappointment to me when he rang to say that he was not well enough to join all my friends for an ITV retirement dinner in my honour at the Café Royal in the autumn of 1998. A couple of weeks later I went back to Derbyshire to visit him. He was in quite good shape, but suffering acute pain in both his knees.

'You can have them,' he said.

Our lunchtime conversation, incidentally, was accompanied in the background by his favourite tape of the 1940s harmony group The Ink Spots. So it was that Brian broke off from chatting to join in the choruses of 'Whispering Grass' and 'I Like Coffee, I Like Tea'. It would not have been the same old Cloughie, of course, without a little eccentricity. His singing was as suspect as ever, but his memory for the words was perfect.

I asked him once more if there was a single secret to his magical career. 'I remember how before a game at Derby or Forest,' he reminisced, 'I would put down a towel on the dressing-room floor and place a football on it. My players would gather around and I'd say, "Now I know you don't like me a lot, and to be honest I am not exactly enamoured by you..."' The smile on Cloughie's face betrayed that deep down he knew he and his players generally had an unbreakable, mutual bond of respect. He continued: '"But listen to what I am going to say because it will make you better players. I want you to treat this football like your friend. Stroke it, caress it, love it, respect it, be comfortable in its company. Yes, treat it as if it's your best pal. That's your first and most important job this afternoon. The rest will be easy, provided you treat the ball properly."'

Football has moved on so far since those Clough days, but good passing and skill on the ball remain the essence of the game. Brian lost himself in his thoughts for a moment, and then added almost to himself: 'When I walked down the corridor to the dressing-room I knew I was good. I *knew* I was good.'

Later that day I met Dave Mackay, whom Brian had described as his greatest-ever signing 'just ahead of Roy McFarland'. Dave's parting words to me, typically understated, said it all about Cloughie.

'He certainly was,' said Mackay, 'a wee bit different.'

9

'ON THE BALL'

I HAVE no greater friend in television than Bob Wilson, but there was a time when, frankly, I could hardly bear the sight or sound of the man! That was back in the early seventies when we were head-to-head in the fiercest possible rivalry for viewers for our Saturday lunchtime shows – Bob fronting 'Football Focus' on BBC and me presenting 'On the Ball' for ITV.

Bob felt that they always had the edge, but, of course, I *knew* that we had it! He insists their ratings were superior; I know better! The pair of us have laughed long and loud about those duelling days since he came over to the ITV camp in 1994.

Following his arrival as a greatly respected team-mate, we shared many a meal (and confidential thoughts and anxieties), and many a flight to distant parts, to say nothing of late-night motorway journeys after big nights of European football, dividing up our last Kit-Kat as we reflected on the glamorous life of TV people while the clock ticked on towards dawn.

'On the Ball' got its title in typical TV fashion. A meeting was called to consider what we could name this new magazine and news football programme that was to be a self-contained package within the hugely popular 'World of Sport'. Our Editor, Michael Archer, came up with 'On the Ball'. He thought that it was concise, had a nice double meaning and would be easily remembered. Our boss John Bromley was not so sure. In the end the meeting broke up without a decision.

A few days later, a *TV Times* schedules man rang for the name of the programme. He was chasing a deadline. Panic! Brommers looked to the ceiling for inspiration in the hope that a better title would come to mind. Nothing. So he shrugged and said, 'Let it be "On the Ball."' Thus was born the title of a show that has run and run in various shapes and sizes, but always under the 'On the Ball' banner.

I presented the programme for the best part of ten years, at first from the commentary gantry at the ground where I would be working later that afternoon. What fun and games that provided.

In those days we were not allowed by the Football League to give even the slightest hint of where our cameras were operating for the Sunday afternoon highlights show. It was considered that any sharp-eyed viewers identifying the ground at lunchtime would not bother to go to the match because they knew they could watch it the next afternoon. So much for the Football League's faith in their own product.

So every Saturday it used to be operation cover-up. The cameras to which I worked would be strategically placed so that the background would be totally anonymous. Even in the depths of winter, I would sit through the morning rehearsals with my sheepskin coat buttoned to the neck, risking double pneumonia, as we put the finishing touches to the show. I am sure that our viewers were at times more interested in my nose getting redder by the minute than in anything I might be saying.

After a few seasons battling with the elements, it was, thankfully, decided to bring me in from the cold. I moved into the comfort and warmth of the 'World of Sport' studio with Dickie Davies. That was a big step forward for 'On the Ball', and the show was not only given a much glossier look, but we stiffened it up editorially and gave it a sharper, more hard-nosed style.

Regular appearances from the inimitable Mr Clough, Kevin Keegan and Mick Channon helped give us muscle and authority.

Cloughie used to come down to our Thames-side London studio after his Friday training sessions to record his strident opinions. He was never comfortable working with an autocue, the on-camera prompter that carries a revolving script, so I would volunteer to kneel beneath the camera lens holding large sheets of card on which would be written keynote words to jog his memory. They are called 'idiot boards' but Cloughie, of course, was anything but an idiot. Doing it his way meant that he retained a natural approach that set him apart from most tele-vision performers.

We prided ourselves on digging out our own stories and features, rather than holding a sheet of tracing paper lightly over the week's back pages. It is something that bugs me about much of today's television and radio sports broadcasts, and news broadcasters, too. So often their so-called news is no more than a follow-up (and then, sometimes, a contemptuous, smirking put-down) of something that has been unearthed in the first place by newspaper journalists. I think many of the modern broadcasters could have done with a year or two under the scrutiny of my old radio boss Angus Mackay. He would have knocked them into shape and insisted that they gather up their own stories.

Among our innovations was the idea of holding the draw for the Football League Cup ties live in 'On the Ball'. Oh dear, I almost blush at the memory of the first time we did it. Into the studio trooped the Football League top brass led by their very strongly opinionated secretary Alan Hardaker, who had dreamed up the idea of the competition.

Two other league officials sat either side of Mr Hardaker, one with the responsibility for drawing a numbered ball from the traditional velvet bag for the home team; the other for the away team. Mr Hardaker's job was to translate the numbers into teams and Cup ties. With five minutes to go, we were nicely tensed and waiting. Suddenly one of our intrepid Football League officials managed to drop the bag – and all the balls spilled out right across the studio floor, under desks, under cameras, into the

folds of curtains, in among the cables, everywhere. It was pan-
demonium. The dignified old gentlemen, more used to sitting
importantly in directors' boxes, were scrabbling around on their
knees retrieving those numbered balls, helped by Dickie Davies,
me and all the production team.

'Here's number 12...', 'I've found 23...', 'We're still missing
17...' and so on. The last ball was rounded up as the familiar
'World of Sport' music struck up, and Dickie went into action.
Amazingly, the draw went ahead on schedule.

However, we decided that we could never take that sort of risk
again with the draw, so for the next round the gentlemen of the
Football League came down half-an-hour earlier, and this time
we safely recorded the whole sequence. That was fine – until we
went on air. I introduced the item.

'Next we come to the draw for the fifth round of the Football
League Cup. Let's just remind ourselves of the teams still left in
the competition at this stage.' Still no problem, except at this
point the 'World of Sport' director David Scott, a good pro and
usually so meticulous, was obviously side-tracked by something, and he cut to a picture of the completed draw instead of
the surviving teams!

Our cover was blown. I quickly blustered something about
having recorded the draw just a couple of minutes earlier, and
the original caption was hurriedly put up. We decided after that
that there was something of a jinx surrounding 'On the Ball' and
Cup draws, and we never tried it again. A pity.

Ours was a small, enthusiastic team, led by Michael Archer,
who is now one of Mark McCormack's valued producers. He
was superbly supported by Mike Murphy and Jeff Foulser, who
were picked originally as office juniors by Jimmy Hill. Jimmy has
always prided himself on being able to select winners, and he
was spot on with these two creative characters. Both are now TV
moguls in their own right.

Linda King, who was my secretary for eighteen years and
comes from a family of Arsenal fanatics, completed the team.
Linda is one of those amazing ladies who always gets everything

done superbly, no matter how demanding, but somehow you never catch her doing it. When her little son, Jack, arrived I knew at once that the world of Brian Moore and television would slip a long way down her list of priorities. She went off with my grateful thanks for helping guide me through the minefield of organisation that goes into every television operation. Bringing up baby could only be child's play after that experience!

Putting a lot of thought into 'On the Ball' in those early days, of course, was Jimmy Hill. He was anxious to forge a strong link between the programme and its predominantly young audience. He has always been in the market for making dreams come true, and now he served up an ace. While it was impossible for youngsters to play alongside their heroes, he came up with the next best thing. His idea was to have boys, and sometimes girls, in the under-fourteen age group taking penalties against the League's leading goalkeepers.

So it was that 'On the Ball' launched a penalty-taking competition, now a common part of half-time entertainment on many grounds to say nothing of every summer fête. It was fresh and novel when we introduced it, and it was all down to Jimmy. It was he who insisted that to make the idea work we had to stage the competition right at the heart of the game, on grounds of leading clubs and before major matches. Penalty Prize we called it, and it was an instant hit. The 'On the Ball' ratings took a massive upward leap. The more angelic the youngster and the greater the goalkeeping embarrassment, the greater our viewing figures.

Each week from a selection of six successful applicants we produced a winner to go forward to a grand final. But where would we stage that final?

'It's got to be Wembley,' argued Jimmy. 'The ideal time will be as an appetiser just before the League Cup final.'

ITV had exclusive rights to the final, but would the Football League hierarchy play ball? Our preliminary talks with Alan Hardaker offered little promise. He and Jimmy had locked horns many times before, notably, of course, when Jimmy was leading the players' fight against the maximum wage. However, through all their battles they had learned to respect each other.

I liked Hardaker, who was just as controversial as Jimmy in his own world and highly regarded as a negotiator. Hardaker always shot from the hip, and had an acid wit. Author Simon Inglis, in his *History of the Football League*, captured him perfectly when he described him as a cross between Cagney and Caligula. Certainly he had Caligula's cunning, and he really did have more than a passing resemblance to screen idol James Cagney. He had been a senior naval officer and became League secretary back in 1957. He knew all the angles. We also knew that he liked a good laugh, so Jimmy and I tried a charm offensive, and invited both him and his wife to join us for an evening out at a West End theatre.

For our entertainment we selected one of the funniest comedies around at the time, *No Sex Please, We're British*, which starred a young Michael Crawford. Afterwards, we took them across the road for supper at the Savoy. By the end of the night, the Wembley stage was ours for the Penalty Prize.

The thought still lingers, though, that Alan could always see that the idea was a good one and just played Jimmy and me along to get a good night out. Anyway, we got what we wanted and had a good laugh and a splendid meal in the process.

For several seasons, Penalty Prize became a valuable segment of the League Cup final day, and, try as they might, no sporting television programme has yet come along with an idea to match it for its across-the-board appeal and for putting the fan and his or her hero together on the same pitch.

All the leading goalkeepers, including Ray Clemence, Pat Jennings, Alex Stepney and Bob Wilson, stood in the firing line against the young hopefuls. On one memorable occasion we even flew the great Eusebio over from Portugal to show everyone how it should be done in a special shoot-out at Loftus Road against Gordon Banks. Eusebio beat our Gordon with nine out of ten penalty kicks with that deadly right foot of his. That's what you call shooting.

They were wonderfully happy days with 'On the Ball', yet my leaving of it was less so. I had gone on holiday with my family to the United States at the end of the 1978 World Cup in Argentina. They do say in our business that you are at your most vulnerable when you are away from your desk and that you go on holiday at your peril. Sure enough, while I was enjoying the Californian sunshine there was some crafty work going on in the London Weekend sportsroom.

When I returned after a two-week break, I found that there was a move being made to kick out 'On the Ball'. The curious thinking, following immediately after a successful ITV World Cup, was that the British public were getting fed up with too much football on television. 'On the Ball', they said, had run its course.

The plan was for 'On the Ball' to be replaced with an all-sports programme called 'Headline'.

'You have got to be crazy,' I protested, unable to believe what they were doing. 'There is still a great demand for "On the Ball", and there always will be while football remains the nation's number one attraction. I'm telling you that general-sport magazine programmes never work in a world where specialist fans abound.' My protests hit deaf ears.

All my working life, I have been haunted by a persecution complex. It has been a constant, pestering companion, and so you can imagine my innermost feelings when I was told that I would not be presenting 'Headline' alone, but in harness with my friend Dickie Davies.

Rightly or wrongly, I saw it as a demotion. I'd loved working with Dickie, both comfortable in our own territory and not crowding each other in any way, but I was sure that appearing as joint presenters and on such a limp idea could only lead to problems. I was learning that you must always stand your ground or risk being trampled on. I jumped up and down and shouted louder than I ever did at the mike! It was out of character, but I wanted to make my feelings known. Then I put the matter in the hands of my agent Teddy Sommerfield.

'I cannot allow you to be under-valued,' he said, licking his lips at the prospect of a contract war. 'You have built your reputation as a sole presenter, and making you a joint presenter is a backward step that I will not tolerate under any circumstances.' Teddy loved a good fight, particularly when he felt he held all the cards. 'I'll tell you something,' he said ominously, 'they will be made to pay for this.'

Several at first tough and then quite spiky letters were exchanged by my fired-up agent and Michael Grade at London Weekend. To be fair, I think there was a hidden agenda in Teddy's campaign. I'd heard that somewhere in the past he had swapped verbal punches on behalf of a client with Michael's father Leslie and his Uncle Lew, two of the most powerful men in showbusiness. Now he saw the chance to draw blood from the latest in the Grade dynasty.

I was caught in the middle of it all. Teddy was a splendid guiding angel through the early steps in my television life; Michael as a boss was as good and supportive as they come and, indeed, I still have the letters he sent me from his Controller's office giving me backing when it was most needed. Now two of my most respected supporters were scrapping with each other over me.

There was a real storm brewing, and then Fleet Street got in on the act. The *Sunday People* ran a story headlined, 'Moore in row with ITV'. I was annoyed that the argument had become public property, but looking back I realise that the story worked in my favour. Triumphant Teddy was later able to say, 'That story was a generous Godfather to us because within twenty-four hours of it appearing in the paper I had a call from the BBC.'

Now Teddy had a powerfully strengthened negotiating hand. The BBC call came from Mike Murphy, the same young man who had been in at the ground floor of 'On the Ball'. He was now forging ahead in the BBC sports department, and he invited me to join him and the BBC's Head of Sport Alan Hart for lunch. It was a very cordial affair, conducted in a private room at the

Carlton Tower. They saved the best for last, offering me a job as we drank our coffee.

'We want you to come over to us,' Alan Hart said, but adding with the honesty that made him respected throughout the business that he would not dislodge John Motson and Barry Davies from their 'Match of the Day' commentary jobs.

I fully understood and appreciated the situation, and I warmed to him for being honourable enough to make the point. Mike Murphy, who was editing 'Match of the Day', added: 'We would still like to find a role for you in "Match of the Day", and we will offer you a set number of Saturday night games.'

He paused before tossing in specially prepared bait. 'There's something else we would like you to consider,' he said. 'On top of the football, we would like you to help present our cricket coverage.'

That really struck a chord with me, as Mike realised it would. He knew that I had a passionate love of the game, and he saw me in a Peter West type role, anchoring match coverage from grounds around the country.

As I drove home to Kent my mind was already made up that I would accept the offer. The cricket had been the icing on the cake, and suddenly the move back to the BBC where I had started my career really appealed to me. There was so much enthusiasm coming my way across the lunch table from the BBC men that I realised they really did want me as part of their team, while after twelve years at London Weekend I felt that I was in danger of being taken for granted by those who should have known better.

Teddy Sommerfield, as usual, saw a broader picture. He tugged me back from leaping across to the BBC, and made the point that my long association with LWT should not be lightly broken.

He fired off a hand-delivered letter to Michael Grade, confirming the BBC's approach and offer of a highly desirable position with them. Michael responded immediately with a note that was quick and to the point: 'What does he want to stay with us?'

For a long time I had been trying to persuade ITV to let me have a crack at a series of sporting documentaries. It seemed illogical to me that for years television had trained its cameras with ever-increasing vigilance on sportsmen and sportswomen in the field of play, but had never seriously looked at them once the shouting had stopped. What were they like away from the heat of the action, how did they live, what were their hobbies and their habits, their likes and dislikes? What were they like under the skin? This was my chance to make the ITV hierarchy listen to me.

'He wants to do a sports documentary series called "Brian Moore Meets..."' Teddy told Michael Grade.

'Done,' said Michael at once, 'and I'd like him to start with a film on Brian Clough. What's more, I'll put fifty thousand pounds into the budget to get it off the ground.' Teddy smiled a winning smile.

'And, of course,' he pointed out, 'we would want a considerably improved contract.'

So peace was restored, and I was soon back presenting 'On the Ball' for a couple more seasons before Ian St John took it on with a refreshing authority. Then he teamed up with Jimmy Greaves for several years of fun and great acclaim on the irreverent but highly entertaining 'Saint and Greavsie Show' that grew out of 'On the Ball'. The show has resurfaced yet again under the on-screen partnership of Gabby Yorath and Barry Venison.

'Whatever happened to "Headline"?' you may well ask. Well, the magazine programme got an airing but very quickly found itself back on the subs bench. It was never a starter for me, or for the audience, it seems.

The proposed move to the BBC was the closest I came to leaving ITV during my thirty-one years in their team, but there was a false alarm about a mooted switch to Sky in the early 1990s, just after Rupert Murdoch's satellite giant had planted a huge footprint on sport. I was chatting away to Tottenham owner Alan Sugar during a half-time break in the Crystal Palace boardroom when he started quizzing me about my position at ITV. His link, of course, was as the provider of Sky dishes that had helped launch the satellite revolution, and it was no secret that he carried a lot of muscle at the Isleworth headquarters of the Murdoch TV empire.

Alan confided that Sky wanted to beef up their Monday evening football coverage and to make it an extension of the footballing weekend. He wanted to know whether I was a fixture at ITV.

I was flattered by his interest, but when my manager, by this time David Wills, followed it up with a call to the Sky Head of Sport David Hill, he got a lukewarm response.

'Commentators don't boost ratings,' he was told by the blunt Australian, who later moved on to launch Murdoch's sporting TV interests in the United States.

Oh well, I had plenty to hold my interest at ITV. Some time later, that fine all-rounder Alan Parry transferred from our team to Sky to take over as their Monday night voice of football, and a fine job he does for them, too.

As for the Brian Clough documentary that was so attractive to Michael Grade, it never got off the ground. I had been paired with an excellent producer for the 'Brian Moore Meets...' series in Richard Drewitt, respected throughout the broadcasting world for his work on the 'Michael Parkinson Show' on BBC.

He and I went together to see Brian at Brighton the night before a Forest match at the old Goldstone Ground. It was one of those crazy Cloughie nights. We sat in the New Courtlands Hotel discussing the documentary, while enjoying a superb fish dinner and a couple of bottles of expensive French wine. Brian sat alongside Peter Taylor and the pair of them teased us, amused us and amazed us with their string of stories. Richard, meeting them for the first time, was growing more wide-eyed by the minute.

'We're on a surefire winner if we can pull this off,' he whispered to me during a lull in the entertainment.

But come midnight, Cloughie suddenly announced that he did not want to do the documentary.

'I don't think I've got an hour of television in me,' he said, leaving Richard and me speechless. I knew that once Brian had made up his mind there was no changing it. It was a closed book.

I had to wait another twelve years before he finally relented, and together we made a video on his life and times for Grant Bovey's Watershed Films. I look back on the experience with great pleasure and satisfaction because I got Cloughie at his sparkling best. But I just wish it could have been part of my 'Brian Moore Meets...' series. For the football episode, I turned from Cloughie to Kevin Keegan, and he did not disappoint me.

— 10 —

'BRIAN MOORE MEETS...'

Michael Grade was as good as his word and the 'Brian Moore Meets...' series was up and running. Teddy Sommerfield was also as good as his word and negotiated a contract for me that, at that time, could not have been bettered anywhere in British sporting television. He always said that he wanted to get me to the six-figure mark, and now he had lifted me to the threshold of it. This was enormous money in those late 1970s, and for a country bumpkin it was truly harvest time.

All I had to do was deliver some decent programmes. For that I needed to meet some distinguished and newsworthy people to make the series work. I went to Hamburg to catch up with the number one European footballer of the time, Kevin Keegan; to Monte Carlo for off-court chats with the Swedish tennis champion Bjorn Borg; to Austria and Silverstone with Niki Lauda, still the most single-minded as well as most inspiring sportsman I've ever met; to Spain where I chatted with – and caddied for – the golfing superstar Seve Ballesteros; then, closer to home, to Doncaster racecourse for a laugh-a-minute (or rather a cackle-a-minute) meeting with wee Willie Carson, as well as a surprise interview with a racing legend; and for four months of a glorious summer to Gatcombe to enjoy the company of Captain Mark Phillips and Princess Anne and their horses.

During the series I discovered the key to the success of all my celebrated subjects, and, no doubt, to the success of all world-class sportsmen and women. The clear link between them all was a driving, insatiable desire, above almost everything else in their lives, to be victorious and to be, quite simply, the best.

Borg and Ballesteros might easily have been wearing blinkers. Both practised for six or seven hours every day, without complaint. When I asked Ballesteros what he wanted to do with his life outside golf, he said he hadn't even given it a second's thought. Golf *was* his life.

Keegan, I learned, was sometimes so wrapped up in his football and exhausting ancillary work that sometimes it wasn't until he had gone to bed that he realised he had not eaten all day.

We captured on film how the remarkable Lauda battled back after receiving the last rites following a horrifying crash that would have put most people off motoring down gently to the local Tesco.

Carson, his constant laughter masking his inner toughness, was back in the saddle after a near-death experience in a terrifying race fall. Captain Phillips often worked twelve hours a day to fit farming in with his horsemanship. The point is that they all regarded this as quite normal. It was this almost obsessive dedication that set them apart from the rest of us.

My aim was to produce a portrait of each of these great sporting idols away from the shouting, to investigate their triumphs, their foibles, their fears and to find the real people who for years television had banished to the background once the sporting action had stopped. Looking back, I was pleased with the films about Keegan and Captain Phillips. Lauda's was probably the best; I just about got away with Carson's, but probably not with Borg or Ballesteros.

The Royals' programme created most interest, although it got off to a less-than-promising start. My producer Richard Drewitt and I had arranged a preliminary talk about the film with Captain Phillips at a farm in North Devon where he and the Princess were staying with friends. We flew, bumpily, in a small plane to Exeter, hired a car and, after a good deal of searching, eventually found the isolated farmhouse. You can imagine our disappointment and frustration when, on our arrival, we were told that Mark had forgotten the appointment and had gone off for a day with the horses.

A heated voice – very recognisable! – could be heard clearly from the kitchen: Her Royal Highness sent out her apologies for Mark's absence and we left for the long journey home.

Richard and I had been around the interviewing business long enough to know that such a setback often works in your favour, and so it did now. Captain Phillips probably felt he owed us something and, at the second meeting, the deal was quickly closed and he agreed to all our filming requests. Over the following months there was never, remotely, another hiccup.

I got on well with Mark, possibly because we shared a love of football (he is a passionate Tottenham supporter). I knew little about the workings of the equestrian world, but this is not necessarily a handicap when you are trying to dig out background facts. You can be too close to your subject.

It was impossible not to be impressed by the work that Mark put into farming the several hundred acres at Gatcombe. If they were long days for him, they were, too, for those who followed him with questions and cameras!

At the time that I was interviewing him he was having a bad press. 'Fog' was the unkind nickname that had been hung on him, apparently because of his reputation for being at times a little vague. I saw none of it. Sometimes, it is true, he took forever to answer a question, but that was his way of carefully weighing up his answers because he knew full well the pitfalls of a Royal word out of place.

In all our time together, he was as sure-footed as he and his horses had been gathering up three titles at Badminton as well as that gold medal at the 1972 Olympics. Even with my limited knowledge, I knew that without any argument he was a master horseman. Perhaps, like so many in that world, he was more comfortable and at ease in the company of horses, but he managed to relax in front of our cameras and to give a good account of himself.

Here's the latest light of my life, grandson Calum, who I hope will one day learn that his granddad did more than just watch television.

A gathering of the Moores – Simon, Betty and Chris.

Not just my sons but my two best pals – Chris (*bottom left*) who is a surveyor and partner in a company in Harrogate, and Simon (*right*) who has followed me into the broadcasting business as a sports producer with ITV.

There was no more inspirational captain in the 1980s than Graeme Souness – as he proved on this night in 1984 when Liverpool beat Roma in the European Cup final in Rome. But it still required a canny word from manager Joe Fagan to tip the scales.

For ninety minutes my eyes deceived me in the 1987 Cup final when some Spurs players wore advertising on their shirts and some didn't. But at least I got it right when Keith Houchen scored this stunning goal in the Coventry victory.

Wimbledon proved once more that underdogs have their day at Wembley – however it still needed a penalty save by Dave Beasant from John Aldridge's kick to make it happen in 1988.

'It's up for grabs now,' I croaked as Michael Thomas swept through to score for Arsenal at Anfield with almost the last kick of the 1989 season to win the Championship and silence Liverpool. Arsenal fans still greet me a decade later with those fateful words!

It was a sweltering afternoon in New Jersey – Ray Houghton had scored early for the Republic of Ireland against Italy and Jack Charlton's men held on superbly for a famous victory. It was my favourite memory of the 1994 World Cup.

Some nights everything goes right. It did for Terry Venables and his England team when they thrashed the Dutch 4–1 in Euro '96. Outside that very special occasion in July 1966, I have never seen a better performance by England at Wembley. Here, Alan Shearer celebrates.

Michael Owen scores for England against Argentina in the 1998 World Cup – and a nation is on its feet.

David Beckham gets the red card in the same match – now a nation begins to fear the worst.

Brian Clough said, 'Always treat the ball as your friend.' He produced teams and television comments that were second to none.

Trevor Francis – and a plane-load of Brazilian supporters – were my fellow-sufferers on a journey from hell between Detroit and New York.

Kevin Keegan was the co–commentator for my last-ever commentary at the World Cup final in Paris. He presented me with a very special case of wine – a few months later I raised a glass to him as the new England manager.

This is the 1994 World Cup final in Pasadena. No, that's not J.R. Ewing alongside me but my great old pal Ron Atkinson. He arrived, as usual, with my favourite throat lozenges and the latest quiz questions.

The ITV team for France '98 – back row, from left: Clive Tyldelsey, Gary Newbon, a soon to retire commentator, Ruud Gullit, Bob Wilson, Jim Rosenthal, Gabriel Clarke, Peter Drury; sitting, from left: Barry Venison, Alex Ferguson, Bobby Robson, Terry Venables, Kevin Keegan, John Barnes. Like France, a winning team.

One of my passions is cricket, and one of my greatest nights was hosting a dinner honouring Denis Compton. Here, he certainly wouldn't be telling me about his record seventeen centuries in a single season, more likely to be discussing the quality of the wine, old boy!

Captured by Snowdon for an LWT brochure. His professionalism and attention to detail was overwhelming.

My retirement dinner at the Café Royal. From the smiles on the faces of my best friends, they've just heard that ITV are generously footing the bill!

He was just determined not to be caught out. Once, I remember, he left behind some of his riding gear when competing in a jumping event in the Cotswolds. He sent home for it, but where to change?

'Why not behind that barn?' I suggested.

'Can't do that,' he replied. 'Press cameramen are everywhere, and wouldn't they just love to get a long-range lens on me changing clothes. "Mark Phillips caught with his pants down!" would make quite a headline for them.'

He was further ahead of the game than most people realised, and certainly not lost in any fog.

Princess Anne, a born horsewoman who twice represented Great Britain in the Olympics, was just as impressive. True there were mornings when one look at her told you to keep your distance, just as there were others when she warmly invited conversation.

My worst and most embarrassing moment was when we were driving to an event at Eglinton in Scotland, me with Mark in his horsebox and Princess Anne driving the one behind. I was supposed to be the navigator. We were close to the Scottish borders when my concentration was captured by the radio commentary of a Coe v Ovett race from the Moscow Olympics. I had taken my eye off the road and my attention off the map, and I got us completely lost!

I contrived to take these two huge vehicles and their royal drivers round a shopping precinct, through a large housing estate and then off in what quickly became apparent was quite the wrong direction. The only solution was for the whole procession to complete a rather hazardous U-turn on a dual carriageway to get us back on course.

Mark's mouth tightened, a sign of tension I had seen once or twice before when things had gone wrong. I just dared not think about the steam that was surely coming from the driver's cab behind.

Camera crews have seen and done it all, of course, and most of it hasn't impressed them greatly. But every member of our

147

team came away with great admiration for the poise and professionalism of Princess Anne; not least when she sat down with
me to do the film's major interview alongside Mark at
Gatcombe. She had a heavy cold, bordering on flu, but refused
to give in to it. For an hour she talked entertainingly, fluently,
and – true to form – often waspishly about a whole range of
subjects; about her riding and Mark's, about working on the
farm ('I'm just slave labour – and of the two tractors I never get
the better one'), about the press, the Civil List and, significantly,
raising a family.

Stories were circulating that summer, confirmed just a few
days before we began interviewing, that she was pregnant again
(with Zara). Richard Drewitt, conscious that our agreement with
the Palace was for a film on royal horses and not royal family life,
was not at all happy about me raising the subject of babies. But
I couldn't stop my journalistic nose from twitching and I knew
it had to be tackled. I led into the subject gently by suggesting
that the following spring would be a particularly exciting time,
though it would also mean a temporary halt to riding and
helping out on the farm.

'A *boring* six months,' she said with a dazzling smile.

'Boring?' I inquired.

'Well, I don't suppose that I'm particularly maternal in
outlook,' she added, 'an occupational hazard of being a wife.'

How the newspapers loved this! Here were front-page quotes
that quickly buzzed around the world. 'Anne Puts Her Hoof In
It Again' roared the *Sun*. 'Honestly, Anne, You've Got It Just
Right' argued the *Daily Mail*. Also in the *Mail*, Esther Rantzen,
no less, weighed in with her advice. 'Dear Anne,' she wrote,
'relax and think beautiful.'

The speculation over the next few days was intense indeed.
Everybody who rang all those radio phone-ins had a view. The
columnists had a field day. The lady herself? She was perfectly
happy with the film and said as much when she and Mark came
to a private showing over tea one afternoon at the Savoy.

Indeed it *was* a good film, with some stunning pictures from the camera of Mike Humphries, who worked on most of the series with me. He got in among flying hooves, racing cars and football action as only top-class cameramen do, but he also framed up and shot the interviews with the sort of flair and attention to detail that is too often taken for granted in our business.

Over the following years I continued to meet Mark Phillips occasionally, mostly at football matches and notably when he came along with me to watch his Spurs favourites beat Anderlecht in the 1984 UEFA Cup final. Tottenham manager Keith Burkinshaw invited Mark into the victorious dressing room (he loved it when the players referred to him as 'mate'), and in the boardroom the ladies were agog (and for years afterwards asked me when I was next bringing Mark to a game).

We finished off a memorable night with a nightcap in his private quarters at Buckingham Palace. Now that doesn't happen very often to your genial match commentator after a game!

The 'Brian Moore Meets...' series had been launched by my film focusing on Kevin Keegan, without doubt the most competitive of all the superstars I interviewed. That really is saying something when you consider the line-up, and my assessment has not changed with the passing years. Indeed, I remember strolling with Kevin through Paris some seventeen years after the programme – it was during the 1997 Le Tournoi in pre-World Cup year – at a time when his life had been thrown into great turmoil by his acrimonious exit from Newcastle United. He was steaming over the way his departure had been misrepresented. It rankled then and, knowing him, it probably still does. You cross Mr Keegan at your peril.

However, turmoil and head-above-the-parapet living are no strangers to Kevin.

'You know, Mooro,' he told me during our stroll through Paris, 'I had two slogans put up on the dressing-room walls at Newcastle. One was "Anyone can take the helm when the sea is calm" and the other "There are two ways to get the biggest house in town – build on your own or knock down all the others".'

Now that, I assure you, says everything you need to know about Kevin's view on anything that provides a challenge. They are words that certainly served as inspirational sentiments to help bring a new era of glory to Newcastle United.

I do not go along with those who say he spent a fortune but produced no silverware for the Newcastle trophy cabinet. What he did was to pump new and vibrant life into one of football's greatest institutions. You just have to ask anyone swarming to St James's Park these days in their proudly worn black and white striped shirts what they believe Kevin Keegan left behind and their smiles will tell you all you need to know. No trophies, perhaps, but he put the pride back into the place. That deafening welcome when he returned to St James's Park for Peter Beardsley's testimonial match said it all.

I find it sad that the wounds remain so deep. But I have seen that look in his eye before and that set of his jaw, and I believe that those wounds are unlikely ever to be healed.

At the time of my filming with him he had become a huge star playing for Hamburg. Thousands of Germans would go to the games wearing replicas of his famous No. 7 shirt and chanting 'We love you, Kevin'. He was on his way to helping his team to the German championship, was about to be named European Footballer of the Year for the second time and, like some knight on a white charger, would return to England from time to time to captain his country with distinction.

They were days of amazing and undiluted success, unmatched I would say by any British footballer in the history of the game. Other British players had gone to play abroad before and many have done so since, but none have enjoyed greater eminence.

Anyone who plays abroad and applies himself to the challenge mentally as well as physically goes back to his home country a more rounded individual. Kevin's first objective was to learn the language. He and his wife, Jean, often had team-mates back to the house, with the rule that only German could be spoken that night.

Kevin told me that only six weeks after arriving at Hamburg he did his first live TV interview in German. It was halting and not very revealing for the audience but the result was that the Germans warmed to him and came more than halfway to meet him.

We had chosen the perfect time to make the film. Kevin and Jean could not have been more welcoming. I made several trips to their lovely home at Itzstedt, just outside Hamburg, to capture not only the moments of high acclaim on the football field but on the domestic front as well. Happily they had just come successfully through a crisis in the life of their one-year-old daughter Laura Jane, who had recently recovered from bronchial pneumonia.

'That's when I knew you could keep all my football medals,' Kevin told me. 'It was a frightening experience that got the priorities right in my life.'

Their old English sheepdog Heidi had produced eight pups just in time for our cameras, and Kevin had made his first record, 'Head Over Heels in Love'.

There is a story behind the record. Several months after its release, Kevin was over from Germany and driving up from Dover with Jean when he heard on the car radio a local disc-jockey announcing their 'Smash Hit of the Week'. Kevin was delighted when it was announced as 'Kevin Keegan's "Head Over Heels in Love"'.

'You see,' Kevin said to the doubting Jean, 'the record's doing better than you thought.'

They listened to the record being played, and then heard the disc-jockey announce, 'So now you can understand why that is our *smash hit* of the week,' and he proceeded to smash the record to pieces with all the appropriate sound effects to go with it! 'So now we don't have to play that one ever again,' he added. Kevin and Jean laughed all the way home.

The record was, in fact, a huge hit in Germany, but Kevin

hardly made a penny out of it. It was the idea of two Eastern Europeans, and Kevin was so convinced it would not sell that he agreed an upfront payment deal without royalties.

'Last time I saw those two gentlemen they were each driving a top-of-the-range Mercedes from their earnings from the record,' Kevin told me. 'But good luck to them. They could just as easily have lost a lot of money on the project.'

Kevin led a lung-busting life in those days. Apart from playing and training, he was heavily involved in promotional work, school visits, supermarket openings (once he even travelled right across Germany to open a bank), and he was flying here, there and just about everywhere. Young fans were forever knocking on his front door, and in the end he put a pile of auto-graphed photographs in a box at the front gate to satisfy them. It was the only way that he and Jean could get a little peace.

I once voiced my anxiety about Kevin's crazy schedule to Gunter Netzer, the distinguished former German international and at that time an executive at the Hamburg club.

'He's twenty-nine,' I said. 'At this rate he's going to burn himself out in a couple of years.' Netzer shook his head.

'If we stopped him doing all these things we would also kill something that makes him so successful,' he said.

It was Kevin's restlessness that brought all the right results; and, clearly, he is still a long way from being burned out.

One Sunday morning, the camera crew and I accompanied Kevin in a private jet from Heathrow to Nantes in Brittany for a promotional day with Patrick Boots, his boot sponsors. They had a factory close to the airport. I was so impressed by him that day. He had eaten a dodgy sausage for breakfast at an airport hotel that morning and spent the flight to France either throwing up or groaning in agony between hasty visits to the back of the aircraft.

I was certain we would have to write off the rest of the day or at the very least curtail it severely. But no. Somehow he managed to conjure up that warming smile as he charmed the factory workers and found all the right things to say to the executives,

even to dally with a forkful or two and a glass of wine at a typically sumptuous French Sunday lunch in a stunning château.
His PR work done, he collapsed back on board for the flight
home. It was a superb winning performance that captured the
sheer determination and professionalism of the man.

He went beyond the call of duty during the flight home, giving
me an on-camera interview during which he revealed something
of his hopes and plans for the future. Football management was
not a part of them!

'I have no wish to stay in football when I finish playing,' he
said. 'What I would like to do is to go into politics – but not the
bits and bobs of politics. I'd like to be Prime Minister.'

Again a front-page story – and not even the smartest and
cleverest critics were moved to ridicule the idea. People simply
felt then – and many still do – that with Kevin Keegan all things
are possible.

His return to football with Fulham after that controversial exit
from Newcastle was what he and the game needed. Bill Shankly,
his manager at Liverpool, has always been his guiding light. You
can see Shankly's passion and his unshakeable principles in
everything that Kevin does. He often says that when faced with
a problem, the solution frequently arrives when he asks himself,
'What would Shanks have done?'

Kevin Keegan could, I believe, profitably be used as a role
model for anyone – in or out of sport – in the often difficult art
of handling public acclaim. His tolerance and generosity with his
time are legendary.

I was with him once in Dusseldorf Airport – it was the
morning after a Manchester United Champions League defeat in
Dortmund – when he was spotted and engulfed by hundreds of
United fans waiting for the departure of their delayed charter
flight. Their disappointment with the result of the night before,
his earlier Liverpool connection, the fact that Newcastle had
quite recently pulverised United 5–0, to say nothing of his
undoubted and recognisable celebrity had set an early, hostile
agenda.

Indeed one man, by no means a youngster, who had obviously spent quite a part of that flight delay, and plenty of marks with it, at the departure lounge bar, thrust his face into Kevin's and demanded to know not only if he thought he was worth the money he was getting at Newcastle, 'but how f****** much is it, anyway?'

Kevin remained calm, gently punctured the loud-mouth and discovered good support from the more reasonable fans. He patiently signed all their autographs and provided enough winning one-liners to turn what promised to be an ugly confrontation into an entertaining encounter. 'There's only one Kevin Keegan,' they chanted as they disappeared through their departure gate bound for Manchester with tales of what a great bloke Kevin Keegan is.

Kevin once told me he'd had a word with Andy Cole on this general PR theme when Andy wore the black and white of Newcastle. He'd noticed that this high-profile striker – like many sportsmen, it must be said – was long-faced and uninterested when signing a string of autographs. Kevin offered excellent advice.

'Give them a smile,' he suggested to Andy. 'Tap the youngsters on the head and say you hope they enjoy the game. It costs nothing, takes no time, and you have a friend for life.'

As we sat among the summer crowds in France during the World Cup, I could never have guessed that within months he would become England's manager, but then neither could he.

As a friend, I still have doubts about his decision to take the England job, and I just hope he doesn't get scorched by his experience. He deserves better than to be pilloried by the press, who collectively pushed so hard for him to be given the 'impossible job' in the first place. It seemed that the honeymoon was over almost before it started.

I remember playing golf with him in France a few years ago. It was a motley fourball completed by Clive Allen, now an astute television pundit and one to watch, and my boss Jeff Farmer. As we sipped our beers in the Brittany evening, Kevin, still wound up by his recent departure from Newcastle, said that he was glad of the rest away from football and was now looking for other things to do with his life. Some rest!

Over the years, I've always known him as a man of impulse, so nobody can possibly guess what stands ahead of him. Probably even Kevin himself doesn't know which route his life will take.

What I do know is that anyone who has the stamina should hang on to his coat-tails. They are in for one heck of a ride.

Niki Lauda did not graduate from the Kevin Keegan school of public relations; far from it. When we were filming in his splendid modern home just outside Salzburg, a couple of ordinary, inoffensive families – two fathers, their wives and half-a-dozen young children – wandered up his lane obviously trying to get a sighting of this famous Austrian hero. He flung open the window.

'Get away!' he yelled. 'You have no right to be here. Get off my land at once.'

He slammed the window shut and the shocked and unwelcome visitors turned and trudged away in a mixture of embarrassment and disappointment. Certainly, they would not be his friends for life!

'I know that I'm public property,' he explained, 'but that ends at my own private property.'

He added, with a note of triumph in his voice, that he had given short shrift to a press photographer a few days earlier, who had wanted to take a picture of Niki's baby son Lucas.

'That's OK,' Lauda told the cameraman, 'but first you must ask my boy for permission to take the picture.'

'But he's only three months old,' replied the photographer.

'Tough shit,' Lauda told him. 'So you'll just have to wait until he is old enough to understand.'

That was Niki Lauda. I knew of his short-fuse outlook and that he suffered fools not at all, so it was with considerable trepidation that I went off to Luton Airport for our first meeting. He was arriving in his private jet in the week of the British Grand Prix, in which he was driving for Brabham. I remembered a tip Eamonn Andrews had given me years earlier in our radio days together when about to embark on what could be a difficult assignment. 'Show your subject that you've done your research,' he advised. 'Let them see you know plenty about them – and always include one or two personal, domestic facts.'

So, as we left Luton Airport in our hire car, I broke the ice by saying, 'And how are those two Great Danes of yours, Baloo and Bagheera?' (Obviously the family had enjoyed the *Jungle Book*.) He smiled.

'You've certainly done your homework on me,' he said. It was the start of one of the most successful and amazing few days of my career. We got on well together from that moment and the film was the most dramatic of the series.

Lauda was an extraordinary and mesmerising man. Pragmatic in all things, meticulous too, as brave as they come, a risk-taker (while we were filming he was also personally negotiating the purchase of a first DC10 aircraft for his fledgling airline, Lauda-Air) and, as a great bonus for us, he proved to be someone who put words together so graphically in that clipped, positive Austrian accent that he was an interviewer's dream.

During my career, I was privileged to ask a few thousand questions of a few thousand sportsmen, but never did I get an answer so vivid as when I questioned him about the horrific accident at the 1976 German Grand Prix that came so close to costing him his life.

To this day, nobody – least of all Lauda himself – knows exactly what happened when his Ferrari, without another car involved, swerved off the track at high speed and crashed in a huge ball of flames. The terrifying inferno left him hideously burned and horribly injured. He was at death's door. Talking to me movingly on camera, he recalled those early hours in the hospital as he battled for his life.

'I remember at one stage thinking, "Now it's the end coming" because you just feel that everything is getting so weak. It's not

the pain, just the feeling you have that everything is so complicated that you want to let go. You want to sleep – or something
like sleeping – and then suddenly you are very frightened of that
feeling. You believe you are falling into a big, black hole, and the
fear makes you tell yourself this is not the right way to go.

'A nurse asked me if I wanted a priest. I nodded because I
thought, "A priest, yes, that can't be bad". I thought maybe he
would come in later or the next day. I didn't know what was
going on. Suddenly I felt a touch on my shoulder and I thought
the nurse just touched me or something. Then I thought, "Shit,
that must have been the priest". He quietly gave me the last rites
and left. But he said nothing directly to me.

'I think that's the worst thing you can do to anybody because
at least he should have come and said, "Here, my son, you are a
bit screwed up, but don't worry, with the hand of God you will
be all right again". It was after the last rites had been delivered
that my heart really started beating again.'

Niki's recovery started there, and he went on to tell how he
first saw his disfigured face, hugely swollen, in a mirror offered
by a nurse.

'I looked like a huge, ugly pig,' he recalled. 'The swelling
slowly went away, but not the scars. I looked at them and said
to myself, "What can I do? I will look like this for the rest of my
life so if I start worrying about that now I'll worry about it for
the rest of my life." So I finished at once the discussion with
myself about how I looked. It's not the way you look, it's the way
you think and the way you are.'

It was six weeks – six weeks! – after receiving those last rites,
and being given up for dead by some, that he was driving again
in a Grand Prix in Italy. He finished fourth – 'Which some people
thought was quite good,' he said in his matter-of-fact way. Quite
good!

Our day with him at the British Grand Prix was itself memorable. He gave us every cooperation. We had breakfast together
in a hotel behind Harrods – two eggs, bacon, toast, coffee and
mineral water then nothing until after the race – followed by a

helicopter flight from Battersea to the heart of Silverstone. We captured all the race-day preparations and with them a useful piece of Lauda philosophy that I afterwards modified and used on big match days and recommend heartily to others on their pressure days.

'You are tense and concentrating hard; not nervous, but tense. So I just switch a switch. Get there early and then do everything at half-speed. Whatever comes to me, I hear only half of it. I keep myself calm. I don't get carried away by emotions. I sign autographs at half-speed, everything at half-speed. None of my energy is wasted (mentally or physically). Then, when we are ready to race, I switch the switch again.' Then it's foot hard down.

On this occasion it was foot hard down for only six laps at which point he had to retire with brake trouble. While his competitors were still hurtling round Silverstone, Lauda, with me and the production team in tow, was on his way to Luton by helicopter to start his journey home. He flew the jet most of the way and did an interview for us, and we finished a day that had given us so much eye-catching material with a couple of beers in the café at Salzburg Airport.

We had gone to Austria hoping we might be able to film him in his home, from where all others previously had been barred. As a general rule he would give a quick decision and, after it, no arguments, but now he was unusually hesitant. He'd have to consult his wife Marlene. She, like Niki, was not sure about allowing the camera into their very private world. We all decided to sleep on it.

We met for breakfast with him that Sunday morning in a café next to the local garage where he had deposited all his trophies – 'most of them are too ugly to have in the house' – and we still had not been given an answer. It came eventually late in the morning.

'Be here at one o'clock,' was his terse order.

We now had the perfect setting for the backbone interview for the film. I was proud of it. I thought it captured not only the heat and intensity of the Formula One race, but also the inner character of a man who was – and is – a shining representative of a collection of sportsmen who, truly, are a race apart.

Television, for all the flair and imagination shown now by ITV's comprehensive race coverage, to say nothing of the super-charged commentaries from that marvellous duo Murray Walker and Martin Brundle, never quite matches the sights, sounds and smells of actually being at the racetrack.

In a sporting lifetime, I hear people say, everyone should at some time experience the Cup final (don't ask me for a ticket!), a Derby, a Grand National, a Test match and Wimbledon. That list is not complete without a Formula One race.

Lauda – like Brian Clough – had that knack of making a point with a piece of homespun philosophy. I asked him if the accident had changed his personality.

'I think,' he replied, 'that as long as you live and nothing happens to you, you can't realise how quickly you can die. Now I watch carefully everything I do. Sure I still have to take some risks, but now I even watch how I go down the stairs. I don't like to die going down stairs. I think that would be stupid!'

The words of the master remain in my ears. Now, when I go down a flight of stairs without watching where I'm going and with my hands in my pockets – and we all do it – I hear Mrs Moore saying: 'Don't forget what Niki Lauda told you.'

Sadly, our paths have never crossed since those few days almost twenty years ago. Motor-racing and football are not really comfortable bedfellows. But for me the memories of that film remain warm and clear.

Patrick Collins, so often a fearless and pungent critic with the *Mail on Sunday* – and on this occasion a particularly perceptive one! – called it a sensitive and totally absorbing documentary, and the *London Evening News* critic wrote: 'With Brian Moore setting the pace, in-depth sports documentaries will become a regular part of the television diet. But rarely will anybody match the insight given to the fantastic life and times of Niki Lauda. Moore gave us a rare and moving glimpse of the man behind the mask.'

The film was well enough received to get a second showing. I firmly believe it remains a fresh and worthy item for the screens to this day, and will always serve to show what can be achieved in life by the right mental approach. Niki Lauda is an example to us all.

Timing was the essence of the film about Willie Carson. For a start, he was married for the second time during our short filming – to Elaine Williams – and we were able to finish the film with scenes from their wedding day and all the frenzied press activity that went with it.

We were also at Doncaster when Willie returned to race riding for the first time after fracturing his skull – and, like Niki Lauda, narrowly escaping death – in a fall at York. And then we had a huge and totally unexpected bonus one morning when we turned up at dawn to watch him ride out.

It was a desperately cold morning at the West Ilsley, Berkshire, stables of Major Dick Hern, then the Queen's trainer. None of us, I can assure you, were exactly overjoyed to be called from our beds at four thirty to get to the gallops in time to find the pictures and words to go with this essential part of race preparation for horse and jockey.

Along with the cold, there was also a damp, clinging mist, and out of that mist a little Vauxhall Viva nosed its way slowly into the yard just before six o'clock.

'Not another interruption, please,' I groaned to the chilled production crew. We were already running late. Now who was this holding us up at this unearthly hour?

A small, elderly gentleman climbed out of the car and made towards Major Hern.

'Good morning, Gordon,' called the Major. 'Would you care for a ride?'

Sir Gordon Richards! One of the legends of racing, and arguably the greatest jockey of them all. He was now in his seventy-ninth year but, more importantly, he was also comfortably in range of our cameras.

'We must get Sir Gordon to give us a quote on Willie,' I whispered to the director Ken O'Neill. He'd already thought of that one. But then it got even better.

'Perhaps, Gordon, you'd like to stay and have a bit of breakfast with Willie and our television friends,' said the Major.

'Thanks very much, Major,' said the little man. 'I'd be delighted.'

So after ghostly shots of galloping horses and hunched riders, frosty breath and all, we sat down to breakfast. Sir Gordon was in wonderful form. He told, in a quite high-pitched voice and with twinkling eyes, how back in 1933 he'd once won the last race at Nottingham, all six at Chepstow the next day and then the first five races at Chepstow the following day for an all-time record twelve successive winners.

'What happened to stop you going through the card on the second day at Chepstow?' I asked.

'That's the funny thing,' the master recalled. 'It was the best of the lot, a red-hot favourite. I'll never forget the horse. It was called Eagleray. I struggle to remember the winners, but that was a loser that sticks in my mind. Doug Smith just got up on the line to beat me.'

He went on to tell us how it was in the old days and how it had all changed so much for the jockeys; not least, of course, in their ability to get around the country to so many meetings.

'If there had been motorways in my time, and private planes and the chance to ride at two meetings a day, lummee, I'd have ridden five hundred winners in a season!' he said. Willie Carson's cackle could be heard for miles but he and the rest of us knew that the little man was probably right.

As it was, Sir Gordon rode 259 winners in that year of 1933, a record that he himself beat in 1947 with an astonishing 269 winners. He broke the 200 barrier no less than twelve times during his thirty-four-year career. In all, he was first past the post 4,870 times and champion jockey an amazing twenty-six times. When you think of it, he was worth a full-length film in his own right. What a chance we threw away. Indeed, we *literally* threw it away!

After breakfast one of our film crews went out again to get some extra shots and I sat alone with Sir Gordon while he carried on with his story. I quickly motioned our other cameraman to join us and start filming. Sir Gordon had no objection, and so beside a blazing fireside he let the anecdotes roll. He came up with a priceless procession of stories about his life and times in and out of the saddle. I knew that we had gold-dust in the can when he finally climbed back into his little Vauxhall and drove home.

That's the good news. The bad news is that this irreplaceable piece of film mysteriously went missing.

I rarely lose my rag, but on this occasion I went mad. It was an unforgiveable piece of negligence. I have searched the film libraries at LWT and ransacked drawers, but have never been able to find a trace of it.

This was Sir Gordon's last major television interview before he passed on in 1986. We had lost a fascinating glimpse of a true sporting legend that could never be repeated. Even now it makes me boil just thinking about the mystery of the missing Gordon Richards film.

He told how as a sixteen-year-old he'd begun as a stable lad on the Wiltshire Downs. He had come to the attention of a financier called Jimmy White, who had a string of racehorses with the trainer Martin Hartigan. Now Mr White was also a keen football man and loved nothing better than to see his lads win their needle matches against other stables. Sir Gordon recalled he sometimes fluttered five-pound notes in front of his lads as potential win bonuses (in the thirties that would be at least two weeks' wages). There were even times when he in-filtrated his team with one or two ringers from nearby Swindon Town.

Sir Gordon told me how he got his first ride.

'Mr White came to me and said that if we won the football match against rival stable Kingsclere that afternoon, he'd give me my first ride at Leicester the following day. We won and, lummee, I played well enough to earn a ride.'

Racing record books were about to be re-written.

He talked also of that glorious Derby victory – his only one – on Pinza in 1953, of being knighted by the Queen just before his Epsom victory, of riding for royalty (he was once given a Munnings painting by King George V as a present) and of those happy days of high rivalry with the likes of Steve Donoghue, Freddie Fox, Charlie Elliott, Harry Wragg, Doug Smith and Charlie Smirke.

Like Niki Lauda and Willie Carson, Sir Gordon had cheated death. In the mid-1920s, he contracted tuberculosis and it was considered a miracle that he managed to beat a disease that wiped out so many of his generation.

I thought about my dear old dad and how, when he was alive, he'd have his hard-earned shilling each way on Sir Gordon's ride and listen for the results on the wireless that night. I'd have given anything for him to have been with me and his hero by the fireside that morning.

Of course, it was Willie Carson who was the main focal point for my programme and he was a good man to interview.

He had done enough TV work to know what was expected of him, and he filled the screen with his bubbling personality. Today, of course, he is a pillar of the BBC racing service. When I met him for the first time, I was amazed by his lack of inches. It was like shaking hands with a young schoolboy.

'I'm just over five feet,' he told me, 'and my riding weight is seven stone ten pounds.'

'Don't you sometimes wish that you were a few inches taller?' I asked.

'No, it's best to be small,' he said. 'Small people are lucky. The only trouble we have is getting good clothes. I either have to have them specially made or, if not, I go to the children's department at Harrods!' A small man with a big heart. 'I've had to work hard to be a jockey,' he told me. 'It didn't come naturally. I've polished up my style a bit, but even now I'm not a pretty rider.'

Maybe not, but the record books show him to be a special one. He rode more than 3,000 winners and was three times first past the post in the Derby.

He is still not worried about his lack of inches. When he talks head-to-head with his fellow BBC racing presenter Clare Balding, he stands on a box so that he is not dwarfed.

It was a delight meeting wee Willie Carson, always a big man in the world of racing.

What was so pleasant about our film on Bjorn Borg was that he chose to play in such warm and welcoming places! No freezing dawn gallops for him or windy training grounds. He practised at the plush Puente Romano Club outside Marbella, played for us in the Monte Carlo tournament, where he also lived and where we interviewed him, and he competed at an indoor event in Munich; all very agreeable.

Sad to say, Bjorn's show-stopping achievements on court were never quite matched by his descriptions of them in front of the camera. This superlative player who was just about to win Wimbledon for a fifth successive year just failed to deliver.

When we filmed him he was, of course, still a youngster – only twenty-three – with so much more of life to be tasted. He was due to marry his Romanian girlfriend Mariana Simeonescu later that summer, and together they invited us to film them in their ultramodern apartment with its predominantly black furnishings and, as a backdrop, astounding views over the Mediterranean.

Bjorn's behaviour on court was, of course, impeccable. He remains an object lesson for so many international sportsmen over these last years. Only professional golfers, in my view, remain untarnished. Footballers, rugby players, yes cricketers too and many others could do with a Borg talk-in about good manners in sport. Nothing seemed to rattle him. Ice-Borg the papers called him. Yet he told me how he was always a wild boy at heart.

'As an eleven-year-old I had a bad temper. I was behaving so badly on court that it was a joke. I was suspended by my club in Sweden for five months because I had still to learn how to behave on court. It was a shock but it was probably the best thing that ever happened to me. This was the turning point in my sporting life.'

The cool Swede had proved that he could improve his behaviour without losing the edge off his game. So why couldn't this work for others? Today's appalling bad manners, on pitches and courts the world over, are the biggest scourge in modern international sport.

Bjorn tried so hard to give us what we wanted for our programme, but in the end it was no more than an average film. What has stuck most in my memory was a meeting with Jimmy Connors. I decided we needed a few quick quotes from Bjorn's tennis rivals to give the film a necessary injection of pace and interest. John McEnroe, Vitas Gerulaitis and Ilie Nastase provided just what we wanted and, during that tournament in Monte Carlo, I approached Connors for two minutes of his time.

'Come back later,' he said tersely. I left it for a couple of hours. Again nothing doing. I thought I'd give it one last try towards the close of the day when he'd finished playing and was casually watching the last few games in the evening sunshine.

'Could we do that two-minute piece on Borg now?' I inquired. He proceeded to let fly a stream of invective – that will certainly not deface these pages – about being bothered so much, how inconvenient it was and so on, and so on and so on. It was a twenty-four-carat tirade, I assure you. I've never been on the end of such abuse, so I decided to quit. Then, still in bad grace, he suddenly agreed to sit down in front of our microphone and camera. The camera was switched on, and at once, as if by magic, he became the smiling, slightly naughty boy-next-door Jimmy Connors, the darling of the Wimbledon crowds. It was an amazing transformation.

I accept that he was a great champion and a gutsy fighter, but I had seen the other, unacceptable face of Jimmy Connors. I don't begin to understand what had annoyed him so much that day, but I do know I shall never forget it. Champions don't behave that way.

Seve Ballesteros also gave us some bumpy times when we filmed him for the series. However, he had more reason to be at odds with us.

I never really hit it off with the director for this film. We both had ideas about how the project should develop and they were some way apart. In fact, after his first cut I put my foot down and insisted on the whole production being reshaped and put together again. So the temperature and the spirit within our camp was not as it might have been.

When making films like these, it is essential that the whole crew pull in the same direction over several weeks of long sessions with the camera and even longer ones with the script and editing machines to get the structure right and the story faithfully told.

I think that Seve sensed all was not well among our production team, and this had a bearing on his attitude.

I watched the film of our interview again recently. For years I harboured the belief that Seve had been a difficult, uncooperative cuss. But, with the bridge of time, on this latest viewing he came across as quite a helpful young man who did just about everything we asked him to do.

Also, as a humble 19-handicapper (on a good day!) I shall always be grateful for the golfing memory to beat them all – the day I was caddy for the great Ballesteros.

We were filming one morning at his home in Pedrena in Northern Spain. As usual he had slotted some practice into the afternoon schedule.

'Would you like to caddy for me this afternoon?' he asked during a break in our interview. I could not say 'yes' quickly enough.

It led to the most illuminating afternoon in the golfing life of a high-handicapper. I had a close-up view of an astonishing performance. He went round Pedrena, his home course, in something like five or six under par – and he did it as easily and comfortably as you or I would go through the locker-room door.

He told me each time where he was aiming to put the ball, and proceeded to do it with stunning accuracy. There was none of the infamous Seve wildness about his play, and we made no visits to the car park! To be that close to a master at work is something I shall always remember.

I had hoped to lure another golfer into the series, a sportsman I admire above most others: Gary Player. Focusing on his beliefs, his approach to life and golf, the care of his body, his thought for others, his amazing decades of success would have made a dazzling addition to the series.

Seve could not match Player's oratory, but he performed well in front of the camera despite the disagreements going on behind it. His film was, in truth, the weakest of the series.

Michael Grade, as good as his word, proved to be a great supporter of the series. He set it all in motion, but when he left to join the BBC to be replaced as our Controller by John Birt, the future of 'Brian Moore Meets...' was firmly on the line.

Birt killed it off – and, if I'm honest, he may well have been right in his judgement, although I struggled to come to terms with it when the news was first passed down to me.

The programmes were simply costing too much for what they were producing in audience terms. I have now come to the conclusion that as much can be achieved in this documentary area by the famous old 'Face to Face' studio technique perfected all those years ago by John Freeman and now being used to good effect by my old pals Dickie Davies and Jimmy Hill on Sky. And even more recently by me.

But it was great fun while it lasted.

— 11 —

THE SACK THAT SAVED MY LIFE!

THROUGHOUT the 1980s I led a high-profile life with some-times four major television programmes to my name every week. The travelling, the preparation and the presentation work were hugely demanding, and it was an exhausting as well as an exhilarating time. 'Chase-arseing around' is how they would have described it where I come from. Rich rewards were on offer, but I also got the sack for the first and only time. It probably saved my life.

I presented 'Mid-week Sports Special' for about eight years. It was a live and lively Wednesday night magazine programme that ran usually for ninety minutes. It was designed to chal-lenge the BBC's 'Sportsnight'. Sam Leitch, who had already enjoyed a great career in newspapers as a columnist and Sports Editor on the *Daily Herald* and the *Sunday Mirror*, came across from BBC Television to shake up the midweek sports output of Thames Television. Sam, a formidable, square-rigged Scot, loved a laugh and nothing better than a good scrap to defend his beliefs. He had the journalist's instinctive feel for a good story, and he was a great pro to have on board.

But Sam more than met his match with those early midweek programmes. Thames TV were simply not geared up for them. Their ambition always outstripped their capabilities and it was a mystery how we kept some of those first transmissions from falling off the air. They were a shambles.

From breakfast-time on Tuesdays until we were off the air at midnight on Wednesdays, I gave a more than passing imitation of a man on his way to the gallows. I used to worry myself silly because there were so many loose ends as we approached transmission time.

'Relax and give us a smile,' the director would urge in my ear as the countdown got to ten seconds. He could as easily have asked me to jump over the moon.

I remember with a shudder how during one of the first programmes, the PA – the vital-cog lady with the stopwatches, scripts and running orders who is the director's right hand and who keeps the show on the rails – had her mind on other things. Two minutes before we were due on air – vital moments when only 200 per cent concentration everywhere will do – I could hear her ordering taxis to take the production team home after the programme! 'One to Hemel Hempstead, one to Leytonstone… one minute to opening titles…oh, and two can share one car to Beckenham.' All this on the threshold of a live network programme! Relax, indeed!

All hell was breaking loose a few weeks later before a live broadcast. The main camera had gone on the blink, the football team news had still not arrived, I had huge problems with my communications and everybody was shouting at once. 'Quiet!' yelled the PA. At last, I thought, somebody is going to bring some order to all this chaos. Having got us all hushed she turned to the director and said, 'Would you prefer a glass of red or white at half-time?' Relax, indeed!

Yes, dear Sam Leitch, now sadly no longer with us, had his problems, but from few materials eventually he built a sound working base.

The programmes did improve. Bob Burrows joined as Head of Sport from BBC radio after Sam's tragic early death, and he was later joined by Trevor East, now a power in the BSkyB sporting juggernaut. Better sporting contracts were signed – skating in the era of Torvill and Dean, gymnastics, then a television flavour of the month, and top-class snooker. Promoter Frank Warren brought us some good-quality boxing described for viewers by the excellent Reg Gutteridge and Jim Watt, and there was always a rich seam of football to be mined on those Wednesday nights. For a few seasons after that less than impressive start we more than matched the 'Sportsnight' output.

On Sundays – going straight from 'The Big Match' studio – I also hosted for several years a weekly football programme for the overseas market, that was transmitted from the Thames Studios down on the river at Teddington Lock. I completed my midweek experiences at Thames Television by presenting a late-afternoon programme on Thursdays called, with striking imagination, 'Thames Sport'.

That was an interesting addition to our sporting output, not least because the programme planners urgently required something to put a dent in the ratings of the perennial favourite 'Blue Peter' on BBC1. 'You must aim exclusively at a young audience,' we were instructed. So the producer John D. Taylor and I sat down each week to find topics, competitions, action and interviews, all aimed predominantly at the under-twelves. It was fast-moving, good-quality television and the ratings were excellent. A year after its opening, and following regular pleas from the programme planners to keep our thoughts on the under-twelves, Thames decided to do some organised research into this children-orientated programme. They discovered that the average age of the audience was fifty-five!

These were also the days of extreme union power. One of the competitions for 'Thames Sport', for a trip to a Wembley international, produced sackfuls of postcards and we got Jimmy Greaves to come and pull out the winner. Just before the programme was due on air, John Taylor emptied all the postcard entries into a large waste-bin.

'Oi, what's going on here?' called a stagehand. 'That's our job. We'll have to have a meeting about this.' Which they did. It was eventually resolved when another stagehand solemnly emptied the cards back into the black plastic sacks, and then returned them all to the waste-bin from which originally they had come. Then, and only then, the programme went ahead.

Once on 'Mid-week Sports Special' a strike by electricians robbed us of all but the everyday house lights. The show went on, and I was forbidden to mention the poor lighting because talks about the strike had reached such a sensitive stage. So it was that everyone at home was left bamboozled; either they thought their set suddenly and badly needed adjustment or that a permanent mist had settled over our studio. This was more like 'Carry On TV!' But what days they were.

In 1985, London Weekend decided that their leading luminaries should be featured in a glossy promotional brochure to put before potential advertisers and to use for on-screen projection. They hired Lord Snowdon to take the pictures and over a year or so twenty of us presented ourselves, one at a time, at his front door in west London. At his suggestion, each of us turned up at his studio with a prop pinpointing our particular beat. Cilla Black, for example, and for some reason that still escapes me, surrounded herself with woolly toys and teddybears; Bruce Forsyth balanced a top hat on the tip of a finger; Dickie Davies arrived with a copy of the *Sporting Life* and a pair of binoculars; Jimmy Tarbuck wore bow-tie, evening suit and carried a set of golf clubs; much-travelled Michael Parkinson sat on a cabin-trunk; Melvyn Bragg was in a director's chair and so on. I went along with a large sheepskin coat and a lip microphone.

I got trapped in an horrendous London traffic grid-lock and was almost an hour late for my lunchtime appointment, which was a torture for someone like me who, as I have described, gets to football grounds in time to put out the goalposts.

'Don't worry about it,' smiled his lordship. 'Come and join me. I'm having a pie and a glass of Guinness.'

It's called, I imagine, 'Putting Your Subject At Ease', and it worked. Soon there I was perched on a studio stool after a young assistant had smoothed out the plain blue background used for all these brochure pictures, adjusted the lights, loaded the camera and got everything just-so for the shoot.

Click, click, click – 'good, very good.' Click, click, click – 'little to the right.' Click – 'now look at me.' Click, click.

And so it went on, and for the want of something to say I mentioned that he had not once said, 'Smile, please.'

'Don't worry about that,' he replied, dismissing the very idea. Click, click, click. A couple of minutes passed. 'Why did you say that about "smile, please"?' he asked.

'It's only that when I don't smile I think I look a miserable old bugger,' I replied.

No response from his lordship. Click, click, click for another couple of minutes.

'You know,' he said eventually, 'I don't think you look a miserable old bugger at all when you don't smile.' I smiled. Click. 'That's the one,' he announced.

Perhaps that was a clever trick of the photographer's trade. At any rate, I was enormously impressed by his care and sheer professionalism. London Weekend presented me with a large framed copy of the smiling photograph. With my sheepskin collar turned up, looking slightly off camera and wistfully into the distance, I became a cross between somebody who had stepped straight out of a Spitfire and a 1940s cigarette ad – 'You're Never Alone With A Strand'. It hangs in my office. The 'Snowdon' signature in the corner is so small it's almost impossible to see, but, apparently, that's his hallmark. For the brochure, incidentally, they wiped the smile off my face!

It was a very happy experience, and so for someone with 'a head like the London Planetarium', 'a face like a tired old football', and once also dismissed as 'hardly with the looks of a matinee idol', I was especially pleased when, in the year before I hung up my microphone, I was asked to sit for the celebrated David Bailey. This was for the popular football magazine 4-4-2 who wanted a portrait of me with one of my friendly rivals at the BBC, Barry Davies.

Barry and I presented ourselves in good time at Bailey's studio just off London's Gray's Inn Road. It was cluttered and comfortable, there were three or four assistants and in the middle of them the man himself. That wolfish grin, stubbled chin, casual clothes apparently thrown on, and without an iota of interest in sport.

I noticed everybody called him Bailey, and that was how he introduced himself.

'I only know three sportsmen,' he told us, 'John Barnes, Gazza and Frank Bruno.'

'How come you know them?' I asked.

'I did a commercial for the Pru and they kept talking about John Barnes this and John Barnes that. In the end I had to say, who the f*** is this John Barnes?'

'What about Gazza?' I asked.

'*Hello!* asked me to do his wedding photgraphs.'

'And did you?'

'No,' Bailey said very firmly.

'And Frank Bruno?'

'I directed a commercial featuring him. I liked him.'

Bailey's studio is dotted with photographs of famous faces – The Beatles, Michael Caine and a whole box of slides labelled Jerry Hall. He'd just returned from South Africa and an assignment with Nelson Mandela and Naomi Campbell. I figured he was hardly likely to be fazed by the prospect of snapping Mr Davies and Mr Moore.

I asked him who in the whole world he would most like to photograph now.

'Castro is the only one,' he said, without hesitation. 'My choice is nothing to do with politics or whether he's a good man or not. It's just that he's an icon and the one man the world's photographers haven't got to. But I couldn't afford the time hanging around while he made up his mind.'

Barry and I perched ourselves on stools.

'Back to back…look right in the lens. Lovely, lovely, good, well done, fellas. Now face each other, closer, closer. No you don't have to kiss! Lovely, lovely, try a smile. Little more light…his eyes [mine!] are a bit heavy…good, good, nearly finished…'

It's always fascinating to see at such close range how the truly great pros work; and it was quite daunting to think of the famous faces that had looked into Bailey's lens. He was a masterful combination of technique, manipulation and choosing the moment – all at the range of one yard.

We talked briefly about football. He doesn't watch it, of course, but his feeling is that it's on TV all the time. I spotted my hobbyhorse galloping by, and I was quickly in the saddle once more.

'I totally agree,' I said. 'I believe there should be a scarcity value for everything.'

'Yes,' he agreed, adding with that famous smile, 'except sex.'

As I left I said that if ever he fancied going to a game of football I'd be delighted to fix it up.

'No, thanks,' he said. 'I also turned down Jack Nicholson recently when he invited me to a basketball game. And he was going to lay on a helicopter for me.'

I knew I was out of my depth.

On 'Mid-week Sports Special', I had four notable workmates for company. They came along each Wednesday to share some of the presenting and to read out various items of news. They have all since made impressive inroads into the world of television sport: Steve Rider, then a growing talent with Anglia Television, Helen Rollason, who was later to capture the nation's heart with her fight against cancer, Elton Welsby, who was to have a good run as frontman for the ITV network football, and Nick Owen, in the days before he teamed up so successfully with Anne Diamond. We were, I thought, a happy, successful band. Then, in 1986, I was sacked. The decision to remove me was taken by new bosses Bob Burrows and Trevor East, and it hit me like a sucker punch. I just never saw it coming.

Incidentally, I have never disputed their right to do it. It was their programme and they had the big decisions to take. They quite understandably set out to stamp their own imprint on the show, and they wanted Nick Owen in the main job. Me? They thought that I should concentrate on my commentaries.

My only beef was that they should have removed me with a

good deal more grace. The programme was a great success and I had played my part, particularly in those early years when it had been so difficult to keep the ship afloat.

The very least I deserved, I thought, was to be given the chance to say publicly that I had decided to give up presenting in order to concentrate on the commentary box and for them, a month or so later, to announce with trumpets that they were delighted that Nick had agreed to step into my shoes. It would have been an elementary piece of spin-doctoring. However, it was not to be. In fact it was a messy business, and left a bad taste.

As with so much in my career, it all came about with a telephone call. I had arrived home one Tuesday evening relaxed in the knowledge that the following night's 'Mid-week Sports Special' was in place and the 1986 World Cup in Mexico was just a couple of days away. Betty and I were about to go for a pleasant summer's evening walk over the Kentish fields with our two Jack Russell terriers, Tom and Daisy.

We were heading for the door when the telephone rang. On the other end of the line was my old friend and colleague Ron Allison, a Thames Sport executive; but it was not the usual, cheery Ron. He seemed embarrassed.

'Thames have signed up Nick Owen,' he said, 'to do some work on "Mid-week Sports Special" and "Thames Sport". And there are one or two other programme ideas for him as well.'

'Good idea,' I replied in all innocence. 'So he'll work alongside me?' Still I had not seen the punch coming.

'Uh, not exactly,' said Ron. 'Don't quite know how to say this, Brian, but he'll be the main presenter. It'll give you the chance to go back to full-time commentary, and we think that's the line we should take with the press.'

Mentioning the press alerted me to the fact that the story had obviously leaked out before the powers-that-be had wanted it to, hence this awkward telephone conversation.

'Do they know about this?' I asked, trying to grasp just exactly what was being said to me.

'Yes, I think the *Daily Mail* has got the story.'

Ron has been a good friend since our days together on BBC radio – he went on, of course, to become the Queen's Press Secretary – but now I sensed he was not happy making this call.

He was right about the *Daily Mail*. Within minutes they were on the telephone, followed by others. The dogs had to wait for their walk. To each reporter I stuck to the line about concentrating on commentaries, that I had been thinking of moving away from presenting for some time and that I wished Nick well. None of them fell for it. 'Moore Ousted By ITV' was the theme of the Wednesday morning headlines.

There were some interesting repercussions. By nine o'clock that morning the telephone calls started coming in. One was from Brian Clough.

'They must be barmy,' he said, and offered to come down to be a guest on the programme that night, which he did. Another call was from Ernie Clay, chairman of Fulham.

'There's always a job for you at Craven Cottage,' he said. I told Ernie that my life was still in television but the thought was a warm one and much appreciated.

Meanwhile in Mexico there were big rumbles in the ITV World Cup camp. I was due to host the programmes with the panel in London before flying out to commentate on the final. Already out there were Martin Tyler, who was to do the bulk of the ITV games and is now such a distinguished performer with Sky, and Jim Rosenthal, who has become one of television's outstanding all-rounders and was rightly recognised as such in the 1998 Royal Television Society awards. Where, Martin and Jim wondered, did they stand now? Nobody was prepared to give them an answer.

Martin, who had taken over main-line commentaries while I was in the studio, could only see his chances reduced by my return, and Jim saw his route to the top barred by Nick as a leading ITV presenter. It was certainly not the best preparation for any of us as we squared up to the BBC for a month of sharp-end World Cup competition. The camp was confused and most of the leading players dispirited.

So it was that several of our team, myself included, were emotionally bruised going into the World Cup, but it was nothing to the technical tangle the Mexican host broadcasters found themselves in for the first ITV match on the second day of the tournament.

The featured game was Spain against Brazil, and it developed into a nightmare for Mexico's sound technicians and just about every television station around the world. On reflection it was hilarious, but at the time it was anything but amusing.

To put it simply, almost all the plugs had been put in the wrong holes. The pictures were perfect, but the German viewers found they were getting the Japanese commentary, the French were hearing what the Spaniards were saying, the Italians were trying to make sense of the views of the Russian commentator, and it was all Greek to the Swedes. And so it was right around the world.

It was total mayhem. Peter Brackley had his microphone to his lips for ITV, but not a single word of his pre-match build-up was coming through to London. His vocal contribution had been re-routed to a confused audience somewhere on the Asian continent! Peter is a naturally funny man, and when the mood takes him there is no better mimic or after-dinner speaker on the circuit. But for once he saw nothing to laugh at as the news was fed back to him that he was coming to us in what sounded like double Dutch!

The teams were all ready to kick off in far-off Guadalajara, and in London we were facing a monumental crisis – peak-time television, our opening live game of the greatest football show on earth, and no commentary.

'Mooro, you'll have to do the commentary from here,' the producer Jeff Foulser decided.

'But I have no idea what the team line-ups are,' I half protested. As a soundman fitted me up with a microphone in front of a large monitor, I knew I would just have to get on with it.

'We'll get the teams to you as quickly as we can,' said Jeff. 'In the meantime busk it, and we'll sit Cloughie alongside you as your co-commentator.' Brian had been booked as one of our studio panellists, and rose to the emergency like a true pro.

We explained to the viewers that we had problems with the sound from Mexico, and somehow staggered through the match commentary. In the village world of television we often take ourselves far too seriously, but this was another of those occasions when, because we had come clean about our plight, the audience felt a part of an on-going drama and that somehow added to their enjoyment of it.

Brazil won the game with a fine goal by the immaculate Socrates, but even the Brazilians had been slightly wrong-footed before a ball had been kicked by more Mexican incompetence. The band managed to play the wrong Brazilian anthem, and goodness knows it had been played often enough in past World Cup settings for just about everybody to recognise it. Armed with the wrong sheet music, the band struck up with a patriotic song most often heard at Brazilian political meetings. However, Socrates and Co. soon got into that familiar winning rhythm.

After that stumbling start, the Mexicans got almost everything right. It was a delightful World Cup and I was glad to be able to get out there to enjoy some of their hospitality and sunshine and to commentate on the final.

It was not Brazil's but Argentina's year; and Maradona's. His 'Hand of God' goal against England in the quarter-finals has been replayed countless times. If you point the finger at Maradona, you have to point one at the referee and linesman, too.

Anyway, the controversial goal has sadly always been allowed to obscure the true brilliance of Maradona's other goal that day. It remains, without doubt, the finest goal of the many hundreds that I have seen in my broadcasting career.

With such great pace and such exemplary control Maradona ran from just about the halfway line, through almost the entire English defence (and you felt that if it was necessary he could have done it all again) before sliding the ball perfectly and at an angle past the oncoming Peter Shilton.

Perhaps for a moment we should overlook the down-turn later in Maradona's life, with all the drug allegations and off-field feuding, and instead recognise this goal as a supreme and sublime moment of the highest football skill.

Who else in the history of the game could have done it? Pele for one, Cruyff and George Best. That's where, for me, the counting stops.

Maradona at that moment finally put England and Bobby Robson out of the competition, and that's when the England manager moved over to join us for the rest of the tournament on ITV. This presented us with a minor problem. Bobby and Kevin Keegan were not hitting it off at all at this time. It was Bobby who had pulled the rug from under Kevin's international career when he had taken charge four years earlier. Kevin felt that, as a captain with great experience and know-how, he still had plenty to offer his country even if, as he told me, he didn't play in every game. Obviously, Bobby and his number two Don Howe thought otherwise.

We often tend in British sport, it seems to me, to discard talented players too soon. In industry, too, we pay only lip service to that old maxim, 'There's no substitute for experience.' Matt Busby used to say, 'If he's good enough, he's old enough.' But the reverse surely also applies.

Cloughie, of course, had the definitive view: 'Management is about judgements – not about reading birth certificates.'

I have often wondered about the judgement that, I believe, discarded Kevin Keegan much too soon from the international scene. Anyway, it took some thoughtful use of the rota system to ensure that he and Bobby were kept apart while working for ITV on the final stages of the 1986 World Cup.

Indeed, at the final itself, we had Bobby stationed at one end of the ground with a camera, and Kevin down on the pitch with another. Diplomacy won – and never did the twain meet that day!

It was not until I returned from Mexico that Bob Burrows and Trevor East talked to me about the pre-World Cup sacking storm that cast such a cloud over the final preparations. They were conciliatory and anxious to play up my role as a commentator, and I was grateful for that.

I know there were colleagues in ITV who felt I should have gone for the jugular because of the shabby way I had been treated, but I've never been one to stamp my feet and threaten resignation in high dudgeon. Stamp my feet, yes, but here there was no reason to go beyond that.

'Never resign,' has always been my watchword, 'and make sure there are cornflakes on the table for the family tomorrow.'

If a huge principle had been at stake it would have been different, but how stupid to resign from a job I enjoyed simply because my pride had been wounded by an unthinking lack of communication.

We sorted out our difficulties amicably – and to prove there were no lasting scars both Bob and Trevor were on my guestlist for my retirement dinner all those years later – and I settled back into the commentary box

However, there was something of deeper significance privately troubling me. I had not been feeling particularly well for the past few months. One episode, in particular, had caused me great concern. I had felt close to collapse while lunching one day in Mexico City with Kevin Keegan and Peter Brackley. I put it down to the high altitude but secretly worried that it was something more serious.

There was more evidence that all was not right when, following my return home, I would take the dogs over the fields for walks and, particularly on upward stretches, I often felt a discomfort that I conveniently put down to indigestion. 'I must have devoured my breakfast too quickly,' or 'That new brown bread must be the culprit.' But I knew that was unlikely to be the whole truth and that I was only kidding myself.

Fortunately my GP, Geoffrey Barker, is also a good friend. He realised my unease and insisted that I had a full medical check.

Frightening though the results were, thank goodness he did.

At a hospital in Blackheath they attached a web of wires to my chest and put me to work on a treadmill. After only three minutes at rapid walking pace the technician placed a chair for me and told me to get off.

'I'm afraid we've got to stop this test at once,' he said. 'Please sit down.'

It didn't take much imagination on my part to know that I was in trouble, particularly when I caught sight of the form he was completing where in the box marked 'Heart' he had written the one stark word: 'Abnormal'.

They arranged for me to have an angiogram – a process in which dye is squirted around the heart – and this revealed that a major artery near the heart was heavily and very dangerously clogged. It suddenly hit me that I was in real danger of hearing the final whistle.

But then came the good news. I was pronounced a suitable candidate for an angioplasty, these days almost a routine procedure, but back in 1987 a mighty and relatively new step forward in the battle against heart disease.

Albert Fenech, a cardiologist with a fine reputation and a great sense of humour, took over. 'Would you like Sinatra or Mozart?' was his greeting when they wheeled me into the operating theatre.

'You mean that I will be conscious enough to appreciate it?' I asked.

'Sure, why not?' he replied. 'There's no anaesthetic – in fact, you can watch the whole thing on that monitor. You might find it interesting.'

I chose the beautiful Mozart flute concerto for the background music, and watched the entire operation on the television monitor. I let Albert do the commentary!

He explained how they were making a nick in my groin area, threading a catheter up the artery, easing it past the blockage and then pulling it back down – a bit like sweeping a chimney or pulling through a rifle – to clear out all the gunge. Within thirty minutes it was all over. I was back home the next morning and working again within a week.

For a long time, Betty had been imploring me to ease up on my workload but, like many people before me, I found the contracts so tempting; easing up was something perhaps I would do the following year. Now, without 'Mid-week Sports Special' to worry about, my workload *had* eased somewhat. If I had continued working at such a rate 'you probably would not still be here,' the cardiologist said with a shake of the head.

It was all so quick but it was an experience that had a profound effect on my life, and the way I live it. For a start I prayed so hard in those worrying days leading up to the angioplasty, and was so grateful for the happy outcome that it brought me much closer to my church. It did not seem fair somehow to ask God for help in a crisis and then once that crisis had been resolved to say, 'OK, thanks, God. I know where to find you when I next need you.'

My faith is still not as strong as I want it to be but I hope and pray that I am gradually getting there. I now try to get to my lovely village church, St Giles in Farnborough, Kent, every Sunday, and that, for me, remains just about the most serene and rewarding hour of the whole week.

It also made me watch my diet more closely (I lost half a stone round the middle during the crisis), and I started to eat much more sensibly than in the past. It helped that I had already abandoned my pipe, to cheers from the family, some years earlier. I had been quite a dedicated pipe-smoker and one year even came second to Magnus Pyke in the Pipe-man of the Year award!

I have also recognised all the medical opinion about taking exercise. Apart from golf, I go on at least three lung-busting one-hour walks over the nearby fields every week, and I feel a whole lot better for it.

Even so, this new healthier regime did not stop another of my arteries giving a few problems back in 1995 when I travelled the angioplasty route once more.

This time the cardiologist was Graham Jackson, a true leader in his field, which is perhaps more than can be said, as I write, for his sporting love. He is devoted to Oldham Athletic!

Again it was a relatively painless thirty-minute experience and this time technical advances were such that Graham was able to send me away with a video of the operation. It won't be a bestseller, but it was a good enough example of a blockage being cleared for Graham to plan to use it as an illustration during his worldwide lectures on heart surgery.

Graham is, so I understand, one of those experts who also believes small amounts of red wine can be beneficial for a healthy heart. When I spoke to him about my exercise routine he said, 'Yes, all that and add to it a brisk walk to the off-licence and back.'

In any case, I figured I'd got plenty to celebrate, and I have raised many a glass of red wine to my continued good health, for which I thank God.

— 12 —

STITCHED UP
BY BIG RON

THE 1990 World Cup in Italy was one of the happiest and most successful assignments of my career. I should at once declare an interest. I love just about everything Italian. Indeed Betty and I always feel there is something missing in our year if we fail to take a holiday somewhere among their glorious lakes. The apparently easygoing lifestyle of the Italians, their devotion to the family and their undisguised passionate approach to life just bowl me over. I often think that if I were not British – and I'm certainly proud of that – being Italian might be quite an acceptable second option.

It was a month of good football, good organisation, good food and wine, naturally, and almost unblemished sunshine. In Rome, I would start the day with breakfast at a pavement café with my ITV team-mates, not least because our five-star hotel in the hills overlooking the city was charging an outrageous £29 for coffee and rolls. We would talk football from then until late into the warm and welcoming Italian night. I was in good company. Trevor Francis was on our team as a co-commentator, Graham Taylor, soon to take over as England manager, was also with us – and, of course, there was always Big Ron.

Ron Atkinson and I had first worked together ten years earlier – also in Rome – on the 1980 Euro Championships. He is now the master of co-commentary: good use of words, great feeling for the swaying motions and emotions of a game, and with an agile football brain that is as quick as anyone's to spot the small changes within a game that often turn out to be the crucial ones.

Over the eighteen years we worked together, we moved commentary from the often stilted two-man operation towards a more viewer-friendly conversation piece. Ron knew he could take up the mike whenever he felt the need and make his points. We hit a good balance between report and analysis, but Ron also knew that when the ball reached the penalty area it was the time when the match commentator had to do his important work, to build up the impending drama and put his foot hard down on the gas. It was always a joy working with him.

Ron would come to commentary positions around the world armed with a good supply of throat sweets – 'Come on, Mooro, keep those tonsils in tune' – and always with his latest quiz question. He has a thousand of them, and is a walking, talking Trivial Pursuit board. I often wonder how it is that TV has not twigged what a good host he would be for a quiz show, a genuine rival for 'Question of Sport', and I'm not joking. The man is a natural.

'Here's one for you,' he'd always say for openers. 'Name me seven major golf winners with the letter "z" in their surname,' or, 'Who are the five England football captains who played for the same club all in the same year?' or, 'After the last General Election there were only six Premiership or Football League clubs in Tory constituencies – name them,' and so on. Ron is never happier than when he's teasing answers from an eager audience, or when he's stepping back to pick out extravagant memories from his rich career in football – or when he's telling people about the day he stitched me up in front of a television audience of millions. That was in Rome, too. He loves reviving that one, like a fifties crooner continually singing an old hit! And, incidentally, he fancies himself as an old crooner, like Cloughie, out of the Sinatra school. 'New York! New York!'

It was the 1980 European Championship final between Germany and Belgium in the Olympic Stadium. It was also our first tournament together and at half-time, when we had handed back to the studio in London, I mentioned that the star of the show, Germany's Bernd Schuster, both in his running style and his passing technique, reminded me so much of Chelsea's Alan Hudson.

'What are you talking about, Mooro?' Ron countered. 'Hudson? You've got it wrong, pal. He's a dead ringer for Germany's great former international midfielder Gunter Netzer.'

'D'you really think so, Ron?'

'They're like peas in a pod, Mooro. Could be identical twins.'

The second half got under way. Schuster was again in fine form. A couple of minutes after the restart I turned to Ron and said into the microphone, 'This man Schuster continues to dominate the game. You know, Ron, he and that great former German midfielder Gunter Netzer are so alike in style they're like peas in a pod.'

'What are you talking about, Mooro?' Ron shot back into his microphone. 'You've really missed a trick here. You should be thinking much closer to home. Haven't you spotted that Schuster is, in fact, a dead ringer for Chelsea's Alan Hudson?'

Ron just loved it. He could not stop laughing about it for hours afterwards. For years afterwards, even to this day, he delights in telling his after-dinner audiences around the world all about it. One–nil to Big Ron.

I never did score an equaliser, but I certainly dug him out of a potentially dangerous and embarrassing hole, again in Italy, during those 1990 finals. It was when England played Cameroon in a quarter-final in Naples, a match I shall always regard as the best of the tournament. During the first half Cameroon showed great touches and were clearly going to be a considerable threat to England's progress. Yet from time to time they were let down either by their undisciplined lack of composure or their fragile temperament. One culprit was their giant defender Massing, who kept committing himself to unwise challenges. Ron was exasperated.

'That Massing,' he snapped over a big close-up of the player, 'he hasn't got a brain.'

Alarm bells clanged. In this politically correct world of ours, I could just imagine the phone calls of protest already humming towards the ITV switchboard.

'What I think you mean, Ron,' I said with a quick interruption, 'is that Massing at times hasn't got a *football* brain.'

Let me say at once that the colour of a man's skin or his background has never been a problem for Ron, but he raised the subject again at half-time. I said some people might have been offended by his remark. He still didn't see the warning lights and proceeded to make a flippant remark about those who'd be watching at home in Cameroon, a few ill-chosen words that could have been interpreted as racist by those who wished to twist meanings for their own ends.

What we didn't know – and should have been told – was that one television station, in Bermuda I believe, had stayed with our feed from Naples during the half-time interval, and their viewers heard every word. Reactions to Ron's cheeky comments were all over the newspapers the following day. Mind you, we had broken one of the first rules of broadcasting: 'Never say anything into a microphone that you wouldn't want your boss/spouse/public/newspapers to hear. It might just be live.' We've all done it, and mostly got away with it. Sadly for Ron, he didn't.

I greatly miss our regular jousting. The football public haven't got it quite right about Ron. They love to talk of his bangles and medallions, of the sunbed tan, the champagne and the fancy living, an image that he cultivated early in his career and was never able to escape. But with all the glitter, they sometimes overlook his vast knowledge of the game he loves, and what they wouldn't know is that he is, genuinely, a wonderfully entertaining and considerate companion. His retirement from football management at the end of the 1998–99 season has left a gap in the game – and certainly when it comes to post-match press conferences. He's a one-off.

The game in Naples against Cameroon was a corker. Bobby Robson's team improved as the tournament progressed, but in this quarter-final they required all their spirit to hold the capricious, green-shirted Africans, who had us gaping at their naivety one moment and gasping at their dazzling, effortless skill the next. England led 1–0, then it was 1–1, then 1–2, 2–2 and, finally, England triumphed at 3–2. This was, I believe, Gary Lineker's finest hour. Twice in this mighty stadium, watched by 55,000 spectators to say nothing of a nation at home stretched to the limit by the suspense, Gary faced up to taking a penalty – once to save the game and once, in extra time, to win it. What an over powering test of a man's temperament that was.

His forty-eight goals for England in eighty internationals are a monument in themselves. However, those two penalties in Naples told so much more about the real Gary Lineker and his strength of character and concentration. Amazingly, it was a missed penalty against Brazil at Wembley that cost him the chance of equalling Bobby Charlton's all-time record forty-nine goals for England, but he certainly came up trumps when it mattered in World Cup '90, the biggest stage of them all.

I worked a few times with Gary before he moved across to the BBC. As a co-commentator he had a good, light and slightly self-effacing touch which he has taken to his TV work on football and, of course, as an arch-stealer of crisps! What a pity he has been persuaded to be a part of the laddish, loutish 'They Think It's All Over' programme. It just does not sit comfortably with the image we all have of Gary or, for that matter, David Gower. Both they and Ken Wolstenholme's immortal words deserve better. Perhaps it's Gary's only own goal.

In Bologna, I bumped into violin virtuoso Nigel Kennedy. He denied himself so many of the blandishments of this wondrous Italian city to stay in his room for hours of practice. I was in the same hotel and the sounds reaching me were magical. It brought home to me, yet again, that for performers at the top of any profession, nothing comes easy.

I was once invited, with Betty, to join him in his dressing-room after a concert at the Royal Festival Hall. He had played Max Bruch's violin concerto like an angel, a piece of music that, like

STITCHED UP BY BIG RON

many others, simply reduces me to tears. But there was the young maestro, wearing only a pair of Aston Villa underpants, much more concerned about how his beloved Villa had played that afternoon at Millwall than any reaction to his own blissful work that night.

Nigel is a genuine football fan, not like that growing cloud of butterflies (or should that be moths?) from the arty, luvvy and yuppy world who have settled, temporarily no doubt, on the great game. He'll still be there, with all the joy and agony, when they have moved on to their next novelty. I have little patience with so many of them.

Italia '90 was memorable for so many things – a truly brave performance by the Scots before losing to a solitary goal against the Brazilians; Jack Charlton's Republic of Ireland boys winning friends worldwide with their laughter and fun to say nothing of results that took them to the quarter-finals and a narrow 1–0 defeat by hosts Italy; and I remember what was a really scary night in Milan with Trevor Francis.

The setting for our nightmare was the match between Germany and the United Arab Emirates which the Germans won 5–1. That provided fireworks enough, but it was nothing to the thunder, lightning and monsoon rains that accompanied almost the entire game. It proved to be the fiercest electrical storm to hit northern Italy in years.

All our commentary positions in the vast San Siro Stadium were open to those spectacular elements. It was like sitting under a shower, and the cascading rain hitting the millions of pounds worth of technical, highly sensitive equipment caused serious and potentially dangerous problems.

One station after another was knocked off the air by the elements, and soaked, sorry-looking and suddenly silenced commentators scurried for sanctuary in the stands. By half-time Trevor and I were about the only ones left broadcasting. Unknown to us our anxious producers were discussing whether or not, in these potentially lethal conditions, we should also bail out. The water was fizzing around high-powered electrical equipment, and around cables that led to our headsets and microphones. When Trevor and I were asked if we wished to take to the lifeboats, we looked at each other, shrugged and decided to carry on commentating.

There was nothing particularly bold about it. In truth, it would have taken more nerve to have called off a live commentary than to have gone on with it. Mind you, I'm not sure that Mrs Moore and Mrs Francis would have agreed.

Trevor and I finished the night like a couple of drowned rats, and with all the noise from the skies above and the tension from down below we were both nursing splitting headaches by the time it was all over. How appropriate, then, that the referee from Russia that night was A. Spirin! Another little gem for the Ron Atkinson trivia collection.

England went on from Naples to Turin for the semi-final against Germany. That's the game remembered for Gazza's tears and that losing penalty shoot-out, the forerunner of further agonies to come. Certainly there was little else to remember. I helped put together a World Cup video soon afterwards, and can vouch for the fact that for an hour this game was the most turgid encounter in the whole of Italia '90, except for the ill-tempered final between Germany and Argentina, which was even worse.

Paul Gascoigne's weeping hit the right emotional button with the nation that night. We all felt like shedding tears after first Stuart Pearce and then Chris Waddle made a hash of their penalties in an intense atmosphere. At the time Paul was among the top half-dozen players in the world, and still only twenty-three. He had been establishing himself as one of the best performers for the previous eighteen months and would stay at the pinnacle for just a few months more. His split-second of madness at Wembley the following summer – the irrational and suicidal challenge on Gary Charles in the 1991 FA Cup final – and the cruciate knee ligament injury that resulted from it, followed later by another serious knee injury, was the start of Gazza's slide. His injuries, plus a failure to live the right life off the pitch, were his undoing. Regardless of what he or anybody else might claim, he was never the same player after those knee problems.

Those injuries – from which he battled back so bravely – were enough to take maybe two per cent off the top of his game; and that was also enough to turn a great player into one who was merely very good. That in turn enabled opponents who previously could only tackle his shadow suddenly to find themselves within range. So his frustrations began to spill out in all directions.

Mostly, of course, he blamed the press for everything. He has continually played that favourite game of shooting the messenger while also having a hand in the Fleet Street pocket. One day Paul would be playing up to the media – and probably signing a big-money contract with one of the tabloids – and the next pointing accusing fingers. Relations with the press must be a two-way street, but it's too late now for him to learn that lesson.

By now, Paul might so easily have been regarded as one of the greatest players in the history of the game. Sadly there is no such reservation for him at that top table. He had the God-given talent for a place alongside the immortals, but regrettably not the character.

Anybody who loves the game and loves to see it played almost as an art form should regret those serious injuries to Gascoigne, and those demons that have been on his back and in his brain all these years. But, oh, those blissful memories of that shining talent displayed on the 1990 World Cup stage. Then we had no idea it really would, after all, end in tears.

Graham Taylor was a fellow-traveller during that Italian adventure. He was filling several roles for ITV as well as writing an excellent column for *The Times*. He was then a man in big demand. Success at Watford, on the way to more of it at Aston Villa, a clean-cut, purposeful reputation, perhaps too much long-ball in his strategy for some, pretty good with the press – no wonder there were only a few dissenting voices when he was measured for Bobby Robson's shoes as England manager even before the World Cup shooting and shouting was over.

He was very keen to learn. I recall a meal in Bologna with

Graham (before England's dramatic last-minute win over Belgium following an exquisite free kick by Gascoigne and a glorious volleyed shot from David Platt). Also in our company was a Belgian TV commentator friend of many years, Rik de Saedeleer. Graham was anxious to know how the Belgian manager Guy Thys, with limited resources, so often got a team together that played above itself and got results to match.

'He likes to start each season with seven or eight certainties in the national team,' explained Rik to an attentive Taylor. 'They are fixtures in his side. If they are fit, they play. He experiments only with those other three or four places. It is a system that produces stability, a great team spirit and results.'

Graham was getting his information from one of the very best sources in Belgium. Rik is unrivalled among commentators in his knowledge of the game, and I am proud to call him a staunch family friend of more than thirty years' standing. Along with his understanding of football and the broadcasting business, he has an excellent sense of humour, a never-ending fund of stories and a nose for the very best restaurant wherever we might meet on our travels in this whole, wide world. He's a great companion.

His information about the Belgian team selection plan impressed Graham, who made a note. Unfortunately, when he became England manager this advice slipped his mind, or perhaps non-availability of players made it unworkable. He rang the changes more than any other manager.

The Belgians still make the consistency selection system work, but it all went horribly wrong for Graham. His reign as England's manager – played 38, won 18, lost 7 – virtually came to an end after that infamous defeat against the Dutch in Rotterdam that just about killed off England's interest in the 1994 World Cup. His judgement, I suspect, had been shattered by the sheer size of the job and the relentless pressure.

How else can one explain his agreement to be centre-stage for that damning, and at the same time riveting, Channel 4 fly-on-the-wall documentary, riddled with the 'f' word, but without taking the right of veto if the results were, as turned out, a disaster? Do I not understand that.

And how else can one explain that embarrassing press conference on the eve of the Rotterdam game that was allowed to develop into a slanging match when he was being, quite legitimately, grilled by Rob Shepherd, then of the *Daily Star* and now with the *Express*?

I was there, and I felt embarrassed for the beleaguered England manager as he lost the plot completely. His performance in front of the media that day was the nearest thing I've ever seen in real life to the breakdown of Humphrey Bogart as Captain Queeg in 'The Caine Mutiny'. It was a sad business, like watching a friend about to fall into a pit and not being able to lift a finger to help.

Graham is a good, decent man but at this time he was also a broken man. I dropped him a note after his sacking with commiserations and telling him of my genuine thanks for the help he had always given me. His handwritten reply was typically upbeat and in his pain he still found a plus to set against the minus. He said that he had not expected support from the FA, and – as with Alf Ramsey twenty years earlier – he was not disappointed. 'But on my return from Rotterdam,' he wrote, 'I was given the news by our youngest daughter that we were to become grandparents for the first time. Talk about lows and highs in such a short period of time.' There is, thankfully, always something around the corner that can put the problems of life into perspective.

It was a racing certainty that Graham would soon get his values back in order and his football reputation, too. The next decade will be a thriller for all who follow Graham Taylor and his illustrious chairman up that Yellow Brick Road to Watford. And nobody cheered louder than me when he took the club back to the Premiership.

That fateful Rotterdam match provided another illustration of how doing your homework can pay off. It was always a discipline of mine that I should watch any international opposition in training during the build-up to a match against England, not only to familiarise myself with the players but also to note any tactical information that might help me give a wider picture to the viewers.

I took a taxi for a thirty-mile journey to watch Holland train, and one of the things I noticed was that free-kick specialist Ronald Koeman practised with alternate shots, first his feared swerving drive and next a delicate chip – drive, chip, drive, chip. I made a note. The next day, moments after being allowed to stay on when he should have been sent off for a professional foul on England's David Platt, who was clean through on goal, Koeman took a free kick from twenty yards. His powerfully driven shot was charged down, but a re-take was ordered. As he replaced the ball I was almost off my seat as I shouted into the microphone, 'He's going to clip it, he's going to clip it.' I think that subconsciously I was trying to get the message not only to the viewers but also to the England defensive wall and goalkeeper David Seaman. Sure enough Koeman chipped the ball rather than hammering it as England were anticipating. I was spot-on, and so was Koeman; the ball floated into the net to signal the beginning of the end of England's World Cup chances for 1994 and Graham Taylor's uncomfortable stay in the manager's hot seat.

There must be something about working with Trevor Francis because during the World Cup in the United States the jinx struck again. We had commentated on Brazil's afternoon victory over Sweden in Detroit, and a gap of a few days before the next stage of the tournament gave me the chance for a quick family break back home and for Trevor to put in some pre-season work at Sheffield Wednesday, where he was then the manager. It looked simple enough: a short internal hop to La Guardia Airport in New York, a good night's sleep and then an early morning flight out of Kennedy Airport to Heathrow. What it turned out to be was a genuine journey from hell.

We checked in for the 6.15 p.m. flight, but within minutes we were told of a technical problem and the prospect of a lengthy delay. A nuisance, but at that point we were quite philosophical. Then there was an unexpectedly quick announcement: 'Would all passengers for the flight to La Guardia report at once to Gate 11 for an imminent departure.' Off we bustled, accompanied now by some 200 New York-based Brazilian supporters, decked out in their national colours and in great spirits. It was samba time. Trevor and I laughed along with these partying people as we made our way to Gate 11.

We boarded the plane, and almost at once the pilot was telling us of another problem.

'We have a slight technical hitch, folks,' he revealed. 'A small part has been found to be faulty, and the fact is that we have no replacement inside this airport, so I'm afraid you'll just have to sit it out with us.' Not the Brazilians – they were still dancing in the aisles. Trevor and I did not join them! Forty-five minutes later there was a fresh development.

'We think we can get that part from one of our planes inside this airport,' the pilot informed us breezily. 'That should cut down the delay. Again, we offer our sincere apologies. Have a nice day.' The Brazilians took him at his word, and continued to dance. Trevor and I were certainly not in a dancing mood. Another half-hour passed.

'Thank you for your patience, ladies and gentlemen,' announced our friendly pilot. 'Glad to say we are about to push back and get you on your way to La Guardia.' The Brazilians were now strapped in – but singing still – as we taxied towards the end of the runway. Then we stopped.

'Uh, I don't know how to tell you this, folks,' the pilot said, sounding for all the world as if he was doing a Bob Newhart impersonation, 'but the control tower have just told us about a massive storm developing to the east over Milwaukee and, as that's the way we first have to head, we've got to stay here and sit it out.'

We sat there – everybody in silence now – for the best part of an hour. Even the Brazilians had had their spirits quashed. Then the pilot came on again.

'I've been doing this job for twenty-five years,' he confided, 'and I've never known anything like this. Now, you poor souls, I have to tell you that La Guardia is closed for the night and we are diverting to Newark in New Jersey. And, in order to miss those storms, we are being rerouted by way of Canada. I'm afraid that will add some time to the journey. But at least we are on our way now.'

Trevor and I along with the silenced Brazilians eventually reached Newark shortly after 1.30 a.m. The airline had put on buses for what could be anything up to a two-hour journey into New York. Trevor and I opted for a taxi.

'That'll be eighty dollars,' said the driver, spotting a kill. We handed him our bags and followed him to his taxi. America, land of the streamlined car, and here we were clambering into the back of a scruffy old banger that could have come straight out of the 'Beverly Hillbillies'. Still, at least all our experience told us that it would be quicker than an airport coach. Wrong!

What we couldn't have known was that we had chosen a cowboy driver whose recognisable English vocabulary did not stretch much further than, 'That'll be eighty dollars.' We had not even left the terminal before he was stopping to get directions to New York and Kennedy Airport. Trevor and I looked at each other. We were too tired and depressed even to raise a smile.

It was shortly after 3 a.m. when we pulled up at the Kennedy Hilton. This was by way of an unconducted tour of the entire airport and two trips down a dual carriageway where we could see the hotel sign, but the driver couldn't find a way to get in.

Eighty dollars lighter and at least an hour behind the coach party, we presented ourselves at reception, but that wasn't the end of the torment. I produced a World Cup hotel voucher for my room. Trevor had mislaid his.

'We have a room for you, Mr Francis,' the receptionist said as if continuing with the Bob Newhart sketch, 'but without the voucher it will cost you one hundred and forty-nine dollars.' By now the famous Francis control was broken, and the sparks began to fly.

'A hundred and forty-nine dollars?' he raved. 'It's because of your country's inefficiency in the air and on the ground that I'm only going to be in the room for a couple of hours. It's not the price, it's the principle...' and so on, all in that mix of native Devon and adopted Brummie accent.

Trevor had met his match. The receptionist was out of the New York Jobsworth school. Thou shalt not pass.

'Sorry – one hundred and forty-nine dollars is the price. Now do you want the room or not?'

At that moment I found a spare voucher. Trevor saved himself apoplexy and a fistful of dollars as well. It was close to 4 a.m. when we finally went to our rooms. But wait, there's more.

I was just about to climb into bed when I realised my feet were wet. I looked down to find water coming up over my bare feet from the carpet. There was a major leak somewhere from the room above.

I got dressed again and went wearily down to reception once more. The receptionist showed little sympathy as he booked me into another room. I dragged myself to the elevator and five minutes later collapsed into a dry bed. After less than two hours of fitful sleep I got my early morning wake-up call. It won't surprise you to learn that I slept most of the way home across the Atlantic.

I have not worked with Trevor since the 1994 World Cup and I am glad to hear him in good form with Sky now. I must ask his co-commentator, Alan Parry, if Trevor has been anything of a jinx on him!

That was a curious World Cup in America, not helped by what in all honesty was a below-par performance from the ITV team. The distances that we all travelled between each game were enormous. I covered a match in Boston one afternoon and then flew six hours across several time zones to San Francisco to work on one at Stanford the next day.

The organisation for World Cup '94 was, as you would expect in the States, of the highest order, but most Americans passed the tournament by on the other side. I even overheard one local say, 'Gee, I didn't realise they could hit the ball with the head as well as with the feet.' That's how much ground has to be covered there.

FIFA's view was that it was a worthwhile missionary exercise, but the facts hardly stack up. Football is still a hit-and-miss affair throughout the States, despite the imaginative pioneering work by British gospel spreaders like Gordon Jago, Phil Woosnam and Clive Toye. I think that will always be the case.

I remember that World Cup for one match in particular – the stirring victory in the first week by Jack Charlton's Republic of Ireland against Italy in the spectacular Giants Stadium in New Jersey. It was shown live on ITV and produced an astonishing audience of 18 million. They saw a thrilling match, sparked off by Ray Houghton's goal for the Irish early in the game.

There followed a sustained onslaught from Roberto Baggio, Franco Baresi and Co. in the stifling heat. At one point Jack got involved in an angry confrontation with officials on the touchline when they tried to restrict his players' use of water bottles in conditions where there was serious risk of dehydration. The Irish held on for a famous victory in one of the most dramatic matches of a strange tournament. It was an extraordinary performance against an Italian team talented enough to carry on to the final and the disappointment of a penalty shoot-out defeat by Brazil.

On ITV we got great value from Jack Charlton over many years as an opinionated panel member. His views were never less than forthright and positive, even if sometimes his tongue and brain found it impossible to get in tune when it came to dealing with players' names

Jack is another, like Jimmy Greaves, who was dropped by television with little warning. A worldwide football figure from 1966 onwards, a remarkable hero for the Irish in 1990, again in 1994, he was ignored and forgotten four years later when the team was being selected for France '98. I am not blameless in this. When Jack's name came up and was discarded in all those pre-World Cup meetings, I should have argued louder than I did for his inclusion. He deserved another shout.

There was a ground-shift towards a fresher feel, using people who have an affinity with the younger audience. That seems to be the case in most areas of television. However, I refuse to join that headlong rush towards the modern doctrine that the young must be served ahead of everyone else. I believe in 'believability'. Jack Charlton had it in bundles. This is, I hope, not simply a veteran looking after his own. But I'm listening when people such as Big Jack or Jimmy Hill tell me things about football, or Reg Gutteridge gives me a view on boxing, Bill McLaren on rugby, Peter Alliss on golf, or when Peter O'Sullevan used to talk about racing, and, outstandingly, when Richie Benaud talks about cricket. I overwhelmingly respect the written views of Ian Wooldridge of the *Daily Mail* and Michael Parkinson, when he's writing in the *Telegraph* or appearing on TV. They served their time, and are the voices of experience. You can't beat it.

Youth must be served, but all in good time. In America the legendary newscaster Walter Cronkite was able to defy hugely advancing years because he was supported by his broadcasting bosses. They knew the American view: 'If Walter says so, it must be true.'

Jack Charlton is a champion of many parts, but he is not an advertisement for self-organisation. He once almost missed a live ITV Coca-Cola semi-final at Birmingham when he fell asleep behind the wheel of his car in the St Andrews car park. We found him, with five minutes to spare.

He was wide awake and working well for us at the 1992 European Championships in Sweden, but even here we often heard his cries for help! The first came in a phone call to my hotel room in Malmö where I was preparing for England's game against France.

'I'm in trouble, Brian,' wailed Jack in that unmistakable Geordie voice of his. 'I made a phone call from the airport, and I left my pocket book with all my phone numbers and tournament accreditation in the booth. What shall I do?'

'It might be a good idea to start with the lost property office at the airport,' I suggested. Ten minutes later he was back again.

'Yes, they've got it. Can't tell you how relieved I am. Now, Brian, shouldn't we be getting off to the match?'

'The match is tomorrow, Jack,' I said. Click. He had gone.

The tournament was won thrillingly by the Danes, who defied all the odds to beat the Germans in the final in Gothenburg after getting a back-door entrance to the finals when war-torn Yugoslavia pulled out. England made a disappointing exit following a defeat by Sweden, a miserable match in which Graham Taylor inexplicably substituted Gary Lineker.

I was packing for home the morning after the final when I had a call from the hotel manager.

'Your friend, Mr Charlton, has checked out,' he told me, 'but has left a number of things in his room. Could you collect them?'

Jack had somehow managed to leave his room without a couple of shirts, some socks, a pullover, a collection of toiletries, a packet of small cigars and some papers. But he *had* remembered to take his pocket book!

He had caught an early flight to Stockholm to appear in our programme rounding up the tournament, so I rang our Chief Mother there, Pauline Hamilton, who is normally never ruffled and has an answer for everything and a solution to all problems posed by less-than-disciplined television personnel.

'Don't talk to me about Jack Charlton,' she hissed. 'At the moment, we are scouring the whole of Stockholm looking for the taxi that brought him in from the airport. He's left his fishing rod in it!'

13

URCHINS NO LONGER

GETTING the FA Cup final back was a huge boost to ITV, and the 1998 match at Wembley between Arsenal and Newcastle was a big one for me, my last as a commentator. It was an even bigger one for ITV. It was our first for ten years after being cast into the contractual wilderness when the Football Association preferred the looks – and the money – of Sky and the BBC.

Now we were back, knowing that the vultures with press badges would be waiting, supported by the hordes of traditionalists who can see no wrong with BBC output and nothing right with anyone else. But *we* had the contract now, and we were aware of our responsibilities to the audience and to the game – and we set about trying to get things right.

I knew I had to be on my toes on this major Wembley occasion, and in the days leading up to it. David Welch, the sports editor of the *Daily Telegraph*, invited me to write for him my diary of a commentator in Cup Final week. This was how it appeared in the *Telegraph* on the Monday morning after the final played at Wembley on 16 May 1998:

Saturday, 9 May: Considering the Cup final is still a week away, I'm getting disturbingly nervous about it. Perhaps it's because it's such a huge day for ITV – our first final for ten years – or, more likely, because, after thirty years, it's my last before retirement. In any case, I'm anxious that the butterflies don't become demons before the week is out.

I'm keeping busy enough. Lunch at the Variety Club awards alongside Kenneth Wolstenholme, who has a cheerful beef about today's commentators. 'Too many statistics,' he grunts. From there to a late-night televised sports debate, where I'm given a dressing-room equipped with chaise longue for an early evening nap; except that in the next room someone at once starts practising the xylophone and goes on for two hours. Turns out to be Patrick Moore, no less. He's about to make a guest appearance on 'Have I Got News For You' in another studio and this, apparently, is his second string. I'd prefer him to stick to telescopes.

Alec Stewart is a guest on our show. In all my dealings with sportsmen over the past forty years or so, I've rarely met a more pleasantly up-front young man or one who is sharper-witted.

Sunday: To Blackburn to watch Newcastle's last game before the final. A long trip, but homework is never wasted. At lunch I bump into Newcastle's chief executive, Freddie Fletcher. 'It's the first and only time this season I feel relaxed about a game,' he says.

It seems that, with Premiership survival secure and a Cup final to enjoy, Newcastle are at last beginning to stir from their nightmare. For Blackburn, it's clear that their dreams have mostly been sweet ones all season. Their chairman, Jack Walker, gets a huge ovation when he presents Blackburn's Player of the Year award to Chris Sutton. The volume goes even higher when he says: 'We all know Chris should be playing for England.'

Newcastle are beaten and David Batty is sent off for the third time this season. Kevin Keegan once told me that Batty was one of his best signings, but I wonder how he can possibly survive a World Cup campaign.

Monday: A call from Granada Television today, inviting me to choose my favourite hymns for a future Sunday morning half-hour. One of them will be the Cup final hymn 'Abide With

Me'. It moves me to tears every year and will do so again this Saturday. I require a couple of deep breaths and a few reviving seconds before I can go on.

Incidentally, 'Abide With Me' was sung at every peace-time final until 1959, when it was dropped, presumably on the whim of some trendy committee, but restored a year later after a huge public outcry. Quite right, too. Enough football traditions have gone to the wall.

Tuesday: I fly to Newcastle for their media day. On the plane, a Sunderland supporter tells me he'll be rooting for Arsenal. So much for north-eastern solidarity!

I worry that I might be overcooking my preparation. But then I'm always haunted by a slogan I once saw in a Howard Wilkinson dressing-room at Leeds –'Fail To Prepare Prepare To Fail'.

The art of good commentary, I believe, is to find the right, delicate balance between describing the action and imparting information. I've always tried to go with the flow of a game, its drama and emotion, and leave everything else – statistics in particular – simply as an essential insurance policy to be brought out only when it's needed.

Then my clanger of the day. I'm talking to Stuart Pearce about his new lease of life at Newcastle. 'And still France '98 to come,' I venture brightly. 'No,' he says. 'While you were flying up here, Glenn announced his preliminary thirty, and I'm not in it. In fact, he told me two days ago.'

Wednesday: Call from John Motson, with good wishes for the final. I'd expect nothing else from such a thoroughly nice broadcasting colleague – funny how people think we must be at daggers drawn.

I telephone Paul Durkin, the Cup final referee. Says he'll just be happy when three o'clock on Saturday arrives. He's not alone in that. He's also our World Cup representative, of course, and next week he'll spend the week – at Glenn Hoddle's invitation – with the England squad at Bisham. He tells me he'll talk to the players about FIFA's latest directives (with emphasis on the red card-rated tackle from behind) and will referee their practice games, with reds and yellows, in true World Cup mode.

I also ask the time-honoured question that goes with the close-up picture of the toss-up. He'll use an Australian 50 cent piece, a gift from an aunt. Wonder if Motty knows? At any rate, slowly the jigsaw of a thousand pieces is coming together.

Thursday: At the Royal Television Society awards dinner I sit with Murray Walker, whose passion and commitment I've long admired; Jim Rosenthal, who is honoured for his all-round TV work; and Bob Wilson, still buzzing from a good meeting with the Prime Minister at Downing Street at breakfast time.

Bob was given ten precious minutes for an interview for our Cup final programme and Mr Blair, a Newcastle fan, named his all-time Newcastle team. But the PM misses the final because of the G8 meeting.

Friday: Today is a long day. Head down and I get on with filtering a thousand facts. My system is to divide a sheet of paper into twenty-two boxes and fill them with relevant facts about every player – that's the master copy. Then I have enough sticky white labels to cope with all late changes. Tonight, for example, the unfortunate Bergkamp is eliminated by such a label.

I have sheets of general facts about the clubs and their cup history and also one of obvious statistics – the last Cup final hat-trick (Stan Mortensen, 1953), biggest final victory (Bury 6, Derby County 0, 1903), quickest goal (Roberto di Matteo, forty-two seconds, last year) and so on – in red ink and marked 'use only when relevant'.

A brisk one-hour walk this evening through Kentish fields to lift some of the tension and then an early night.

Saturday: I'm up at seven, a car arrives at eight, we pick up a television crew, who are to follow me all day for a documentary on commentators – and I arrive at Wembley at 9.15. Still almost six hours to kick-off, and that's early even for someone as cautious as me.

Papers to read – several have been most generous about my last Wembley final. Then a swift editorial meeting in our trailer park before I take myself off to the commentary gantry to sit quietly for an hour or two.

Ron Atkinson arrives. He's a good friend of many years and I don't know anybody who is quicker at spotting the nuances within a game.

The match flies by. I use about five per cent of all my preparation and, like all commentators, I'm grateful that the goals are clear-cut – Overmars gives a good sighting on his No. 11 shirt before getting the first and Anelka his No. 9 before striking the second.

I take one abiding memory from my last Cup final in the commentary box and it is the sight and sound of Newcastle's wonderful supporters applauding Tony Adams and his men up the steps. The game for a few moments is wrested from its tightening corporate grip and is handed back to the people.

Home exhausted. To the local Italian, a couple of glasses of red and then to bed.

Friendship is what I have enjoyed with so many workmates over all my years in broadcasting, and it delights me now to see ITV enjoying such a sporting renaissance. The spirit in the camp has never been higher, or more united.

The ITV portfolio is as strong as it has ever been. For so many years we were cast as the urchins with our noses pressed to the windows of BBC's sumptuous sporting banquets, but not any more. ITV now have every right to regard themselves as the leading terrestrial channel. They have men and women both in front and behind the camera to make their future large audiences feel comfortable and secure.

BSkyB, with its many contracts, now dominates so much sport on television, but without being able to reach the vast audiences available to BBC and ITV. With the Champions League, FA Cup, England's internationals, and the Worthington Cup among their contracts, ITV are powerfully placed. Add to that the magnificent coverage of Formula One racing and the rugby World Cup and you can see why ITV Sport is so buoyant these days.

The ITV football commentaries are as good as you will hear when the likes of Clive Tyldesley, Peter Drury, and Peter Brackley are at the microphone, and I have to admit that deep down I envy them, just a little, the years of excitement and professional fulfilment that lie ahead in the new digital age of television.

Presenters don't come better than Bob Wilson and Jim Rosenthal, who is comfortable and authoritative whether he is anchoring programmes about football, boxing, rugby or Formula One (what, I wonder, does Jim do with all his air miles!).

Then, of course, there is always Gary Newbon. There is nobody in the business better liked than Gary, particularly by himself. He will enjoy that because he has got a lovely larger-than-life outlook and nobody laughs louder than Gary when things go wrong for him. Viewers know him as the man who asks the tough questions at the end of football matches and boxing contests. Nobody can touch him as a foot-in-the-door on-screen reporter who will get the interview that everybody else wants. But he is also a highly respected backroom tactician who has kept Central Sport at a high profile since taking over as the top man in the Midlands from the splendid Billy Wright.

Yes, the ITV team is a first-class crew, and there are firm hands on the tiller. Jeff Farmer is energetic and innovative as the Head of Sport Production. Jeff was a top-notch football reporter with the *Daily Mail* before switching to the world of television, and his strong journalistic background shows in the editorial direction of ITV football programmes in which he plays a big part behind the scenes. Rick Waumsley is a producer with a sharp eye for detail and a sharp wit to go with it. Like me, Rick is a great admirer of all things Henry Purcell, which sometimes helped enormously when the television going got tough!

In my last year, ITV poached Brian Barwick from BBC where he was the driving force behind the top sports programmes. He is now Controller of Sport for ITV and also the man in charge of the launch of ITV2. A Scouser with Liverpool red blood, Brian has just the right sort of enthusiasm and talent to lead ITV Sport into the new millennium. I will be with them in spirit.

ITV are the urchins no longer.

— 14 —

MY FEARS FOR FOOTBALL'S FUTURE

WHEN I reluctantly peep into football's future, I do not like the view at all. My father was born in the days of the horse-drawn carriage but lived long enough to see a man walk on the moon. That was, truly, a giant step for a single generation. However, a ten-year-old child today has lived through a convulsion no less striking or startling in the world of football. During the 1990s the sporting rocket has gone into orbit but, sadly, I predict with little chance of a happy landing.

In the months since I left the commentary box I've been able to take stock of a broader picture. What I see is the nation's number one sport in serious crisis. Financially, the boat is rocking dangerously; morally, it has already gone down. I find it a bit like looking at football through a cracked and distorted mirror. Some of it remains the thrilling and emotional spectacle I've loved all my life; much of it, however, has made my leaving of it far less painful than I could ever have thought.

When I started in broadcasting, and before Jimmy Hill's triumphant campaign to abolish it, players were on a maximum wage of twenty pounds a week. In the new era of wage freedom, I remember so well the shaking of heads and the doom-laden mutterings when Fulham's chairman Tommy Trinder decided to pay his star player Johnny Haynes a hundred pounds a week. 'Now we know the game has gone completely mad,' we said.

But when they were on that twenty pounds a week could

anyone truthfully say that Stanley Matthews, Tom Finney, Billy Wright, the Busby Babes, Nat Lofthouse, Haynes himself and so many more gave anything less than everything on those distant Saturday afternoons? There was a special code among them. The money, or lack of it, was secondary. They were aware that they had a moral commitment to their contract – one-sided though it was – to their club and to the supporters, but most of all to the game they loved.

What do we have today? On the right side, there are many good pros who would have felt quite at home and comfortable with the philosophy of the stars of less affluent days. But on the worrying downside, we also have a breed of players, blinded by their celebrity and the vast money that goes with it, who are betraying the sport that has brought them riches beyond the dreams of most working men.

When Dave Bassett, as good a trouper as you will find in the game, fell victim to the raised voices of the Nottingham Forest fans – yes, they've changed too – and perhaps the power of the players, he commented: 'You detect a nonchalance, a diffidence in them [the players]. When you are talking to them you can see them thinking, "I've got my house, my cars, I've got this, I've got that. I don't need you." It's the disease of greed, the disease of "me".'

One Premiership manager told me, 'The problem I have is that my players don't want to improve. They are sitting on huge contracts – their ambition has gone. It's almost impossible to motivate some of them. They have simply got too much.'

So we saw at Nottingham Forest how the Dutchman Pierre Van Hooijdonk went on strike when he made it known that, in his view, his team-mates were not going to be up to the job in the Premiership. His contract, to say nothing of the season ticket money already forked out by Forest fans, obviously meant little to him. Yet he survived and Dave Bassett, the man who defied him, didn't. Another dubious battle-honour for player power.

I was a guest on a sports phone-in with Alan Parry on Talk

Radio the night Bassett was sacked. 'I agree with Van Hooijdonk,' said one caller after another. 'It proves he was right about his Forest team-mates.' In despair, I tried to defend Bassett's record and the true values of the game. In despair, I also came to realise that the epidemic of unprincipled self-interest had spread wider than I thought, to fans as well as players.

Money is the root of all evil, they say. It is if it is not properly used. Football's biggest problem is that it has all come so quickly. If the growth to the game's present prosperity had been a gradual performance over the last, say, forty years the experience would have enabled clubs to handle their wealth more sensibly. But gold was struck only in the last decade when Sky Television came riding into town. Ever since then it's been drinks all round in the Crazy Horse Saloon. How soon before it becomes the Last Chance Saloon?

It's there for all to see how the game in every direction – players' wages, transfers, directors' holdings – has started to go off the financial rails. There's no point in my raising examples here because it's a racing certainty that by the time you read this everything will already have gone up a notch or three in any case. In fact, as I write Rodney Marsh is making the headlines by predicting that within a year of the new millennium we will have British football's first £100,000 a week player.

The money, largely, has been badly handled by club directors – not least in their headlong chase, with their managers, for talent on the field. Whatever the players, or their agents, have wanted, they've got. There's no point in blaming the players for that, and no point in wishfully thinking that they will prune and modify their demands. They won't because of the 'me' culture. Sky, for whom I have great professional admiration and who have transformed so much of football coverage over the last ten years, began with the slogan 'There's No Turning Back'. For them it was the perfect pitch. It has, however, a sinister echo for British football as a whole. No turning back to sanity!

So the clubs got the money, it passed to the players, and they found a new power in their hands. The clubs asked the fans for more money, the fans paid up, and now their voice is more strident and less tolerant than it's ever been; and that, in turn, has put greater demands on clubs and managers and players. A frightening circle has been drawn. We have entered a volatile era that great managers such as Matt Busby and Bill Shankly would not begin to recognise and, for all their legendary skills, would probably find beyond them.

In the 'good old days', small clubs were kept alive by transfer fees; the money paid for a player circulated around the football world. Now – post-Bosman – much of it goes into the pockets of the players and their agents never to be seen again. It is a recipe for disaster.

Unsolicited support for my theory comes from no less a person than 'Deadly' Doug Ellis, the power behind and often in front of the throne at Aston Villa. Doug, as shrewd on football business matters as anyone in the game, was addressing the Villa shareholders when he called for an upper limit on what clubs can spend on their squads to prevent pay demands from spiralling out of control. So, in much glossier circumstances, is this a return to the days of the maximum wage? Doug has been around long enough to know that his cautionary view will not be shared by all – least of all the players and their agents. The spiral will continue until there is a sad and spectacular crash.

Will digital television or pay-for-view provide another rich dividend for the game? I don't know – and neither does anybody else. In the meantime, I fear for our football in the next few years. The golden honeymoon is almost over.

The spending simply cannot go on. There are no answers and no remedies. Football has gone spinning out of control, and very soon there will be blood on many a boardroom carpet.

In 1988, I made a film about the Olympics held in London forty years earlier. Sporting life and sports stars were different then, my how they were different!

This was a one-hour documentary about an age of sporting innocence, lost forever, the last of the true Corinthian events and it was all so close to my heart that I look back on it with nothing but pride.

The idea was cooked up by Bob Burrows, Trevor East and the team at Thames Television from an original concept by my old Fleet Street friend Norman Giller. Norman and I shared the scriptwriting duties, and John D. Taylor, a respected colleague from our days on 'Thames Sport', was the editor and producer. We had a budget generous enough to attract a collection of golden winners from those 1948 Games. For the three of us it was a true labour of love, meeting our heroes and heroines and not being disappointed by any of them.

Fanny Blankers-Koen, winner of four gold medals and still arguably the greatest woman athlete of all time, flew in from Amsterdam with a smile and a fund of stories. I sat for one morning at Wembley with the incomparable Emil Zatopek, and found it so hard to believe that this was the same man I watched on my grandmother's little black and white TV all those years ago as he took the world by storm in this very stadium. We went to Henley to meet oarsmen Jack Wilson and Ran Laurie, rare British gold medallists at those Games. Laurie, incidentally, is the father of that fine comedy actor Hugh Laurie, himself a first-rate oarsman. Both Ran and the unassuming Jack Wilson could themselves have stepped straight from any British stiff-upper-lip silver-screen production.

'We weren't national heroes,' they each insisted as they reflected on their victory in the coxless pairs.

'Well, maybe for ten minutes,' said Laurie. 'But I think in a rather low-key British way, one felt one was rowing for the old country. There were certainly no financial benefits. But young people asked us to go and coach them at their colleges, one is asked to talk to rowing clubs and, we suppose, a little bit of gold-dust hangs on to one for the rest of one's life.'

Jack Wilson revealed that he also had free haircuts for life from his local barber. Ah yes, the way it used to be!

The programme budget for 'The Games of '48' was stretched enough for me to take a film crew for a couple of days to Orange

County in southern California – John Wayne territory, indeed the local airport is named after him – to meet Bob Mathias, who as a seventeen-year-old schoolboy became the Daley Thompson of his day when he took gold in the decathlon.

Now in his fifties, Bob could indeed have doubled for Wayne himself. He's a big, handsome man with an easy, relaxed manner and his Olympic glitter – including a second gold medal in 1952 – put him on the path to an eventful career, first as a film actor under Wayne's guidance. 'Don't act, Bob, just be yourself,' was the great man's advice. He made four films and then went into politics to serve eight years in Congress as a Republican until he was swept out of office by the tide of disillusionment that followed the Watergate downfall of Richard Nixon.

Bob seems to have suffered little. He still has ties with American athletics, has a spectacular home and pool just a short stroll from the endless sands of Laguna Beach and fits comfortably into his life in the Californian sunshine. It would be hard to find a pleasanter man to interview, but what made his contribution so valuable to our film was the contrast he threw up to the preparation of Daley Thompson and all modern athletes. Today the mental and physical conditioning is exhaustive. Bob Mathias, however, was only entered for the 1948 decathlon a few weeks before leaving for London. When he started training for it, he didn't even know what a decathlon was. His coach knew, but even he could not be sure what the ten events were!

'I had nothing else to do so I thought I might as well go for it,' Bob recalled. Ah yes, the way it used to be!

The entire Thames TV team fell in love with Fanny Blankers-Koen. She was a delightful subject, always smiling and somehow giving the impression that she couldn't really understand what all the fuss was about. Today she would be cosseted by coaches, surrounded and protected by agents, and worth a fortune. No wonder she giggled as she told me how back in 1948, a mother, housewife and an expectant mum, she nearly missed her final in the women's sprint relay. She went by tube to Oxford Street on the morning of the race to buy a raincoat, only to get caught up by the crowds on the train back to Wembley. Her coach was livid with her, but could say little when she romped to her fourth gold medal half an hour or so after getting off the packed tube train!

She thought that was a hoot, and couldn't stop laughing when we also talked of the perks that came her way as a four-time gold medal winner. There were none; except that her neighbours clubbed together on her return from Wembley and bought her a bicycle. I wonder what her countryman Pierre Van Hooijdonk would make of that? Ah yes, the way it used to be!

Emil Zatopek's story was not only about his triumph on the track but also the love story of the Wembley Olympics that would make a wonderfully romantic film. He had come to London with his eyes on the young Czech javelin thrower Dana Ingrova. Men and women competitors, however, were housed miles apart in North London. Emil saw a chance to grab a few moments with Dana during the opening ceremony. Czech officials had banned him from attending because he was competing in the 10,000 metres the following day, but he defied them, joined up with the Danes, who were marching just behind the Czechs, and slowly infiltrated his way forward among his team-mates to Dana.

He told the tale in front of our cameras with all the rosy-cheeked animation he showed on the track. He avoided any punishment by racing away with the 10,000 metres the following day, the first gold in track and field for Czechoslovakia in the history of the Olympics. That evening he set off alone, map of London in hand, to Paddington, Harrow-on-the-Hill and eventually to Northwood to the women's camp to show the gold medal to Dana. But there was another hurdle – he found that men were not allowed in the women's headquarters, not even gold medallists.

Suddenly to my surprise and to the delight of the director Ian Little-Smith, he started to sing an old Moravian love song. He'd sung it at the gates of the women's camp that evening until Dana heard him and recognised the man who was to become her husband.

'I'll meet you by the swimming pool,' she called.

So he climbed over the twelve-foot high wall and made his way to the swimming pool. He showed Dana his gold medal which he swung around with such force that it slipped out of his hand and dropped straight into the deep end of the pool.

'What to do?' he asked, looking directly into our camera with a twinkle in his eyes. He knew, of course, what had to be done. Emil quickly stripped off in front of Dana and dived in to retrieve his precious medal.

At this point, the director of the Olympic Village arrived and, as Emil quickly dressed himself, ordered the new Olympic champion out of the camp in the best Hattie Jacques tones.

'Get out – at once,' she demanded. In his confusion, Emil ran to the main gate, looked back over his shoulder to blow a final kiss to Dana, tripped over backwards and fell headlong into the street laughing wildly. What a way to celebrate a golden triumph! He enjoyed every moment of it, he said, as he recalled it all for us at Wembley forty years on.

In Helsinki four years later he won the 5,000 metres, 10,000 metres and the marathon, and Dana won the javelin. By then they were married and they are still together. Their lives today are far removed from the athletics arena. Now, he told me, their competitive instincts are confined to their gardening. Dana's love is her flowers. Emil specialises in growing vegetables.

There has been no braver man than Emil Zatopek, who stood with proud defiance against suffocating communist doctrine in his country's darkest days. At his lowest point he was forced to sweep the streets as an exhibition that free speech would not be tolerated. They took away some of his dignity, but none of his pride. There have been few Olympians over all the years to match his worldwide popularity, or to be more greatly revered.

As we were starting to pack the cameras away at the end of my unforgettable morning with him, he recalled the great fun he'd had at Wembley in the 5,000 metres. He lost that race to the outstanding Belgian Gaston Reiff. His tactics that afternoon were, as he all too readily admits, faulty and midway through his tiredness got the better of him. He was settling for silver half a lap behind Reiff when he suddenly got a second wind. He saw that Reiff was tiring badly and set off in wild pursuit, bringing the spectators to their feet with his lung-bursting run. But he had left it too late, and Reiff just held on to win by a yard. Emil knows to this day that the gold could have been his.

He shook his head as he turned to me that morning at Wembley and said, 'From that moment, though, Gaston and I were great friends. And maybe friendship is more valuable than any medals.'

Ah yes, the way it used to be!

'The Games of '48' struck a very favourable chord with the critics. There seems to be a growing movement in television to turn back to the archives and it is a trend that I applaud to the full. Certainly there are rich seams to be dug in all sports. It makes fascinating viewing, it's inexpensive and, more than anything, it is a worthwhile exercise to remind ourselves and to show future generations of the standards and the talents of earlier years, of the way it used to be before greed threatened the structure of our sport in general and football in particular.

I hope I have conveyed both sides of a still shining coin. In its way it encapsulates my years in broadcasting, from an age of 'here's to a jolly good game and may the best team win' to one that is becoming ensnared by greysuits for whom profit is the one and only motivating force. Football just happens to be the current gravy train, but it has spread even to that one-time beacon of amateurism and high ideals, the Olympic Games.

What, I wonder, do those spotless Olympians I interviewed for 'The Games of '48' think, for example, of the drugs issue that so regularly commands such disturbing headlines? Fanny Blankers-Koen told me the only substance she ever took was a daily teaspoon of cod liver oil, and she knew, unfailingly, that she competed against women who kept to a level running track. Could you imagine Emil Zatopek ever being tempted to take the cheat's route to glory?

What would Emil think of an Olympic movement that has the stench of bribery about it as nations dip into slush funds in a bid to buy the right to host the potentially devalued Games. What was that he said to me? 'Friendship is more valuable than medals.'

I compiled a series of half-hour programmes for Sky Television, with great footballers from past generations. Like the greaty Olympians, they revived memories of a sport before so much madness overcame it.

Les Allen, who played every game for Spurs in their memorable Double season in the Blanchflower era of 1960–61, was given a bonus of twenty-five pounds and a watch. That was for the entire season!

And Nat Lofthouse told me that as a magnificent centre-forward for Bolton and England he never earned more than twenty pounds a week. 'But as my father was earning only two pounds a week down the pits, it made me feel like a millionaire,' he said.

There were contented and fufilled men, and like so many of that era they now look with apprehension at the game they love.

Like me, they also look in vain for a solution.

— 15 —

MAGICAL MOMENTS

I'VE no idea how many matches I have covered for radio and television, but some undoubtedly loom larger and are more vivid in my memory than others. It may seem inconceivable that, having commentated on England's triumph in the 1966 World Cup final, another game should take the prime spot. However, first place goes to England against Argentina in St Etienne in the 1998 World Cup. I've written about it earlier, not least my shopping of my co-commentator Kevin Keegan at the end of the penalty shoot-out, and I nominate it simply because of the enormity of the occasion and the bizarre, cruel rollercoaster ride it gave us all on that balmy summer evening; to say nothing of the sights and sounds of a nation magnificently united by a stirring sporting defeat.

So England against Germany in the 1966 World Cup is nudged into second place – a day when a nation was united in victory. Somehow the passing years have dimmed my memory and emotions of that glorious day, though for a series on Sky Sports I recently interviewed George Cohen, the galloping right-back on that afternoon. Pragmatic as ever, he auctioned his winner's medal to help buy a pension for his family. It delights him, incidentally, that it was bought by his old club Fulham and rests in their museum. George says his memories of that campaign are so sharp that he could just have finished wiping the sweat off his brow. An England captain holding the golden trophy aloft is an image I despair of seeing again in my lifetime.

A game I will never forget is Liverpool against Arsenal, the epic battle in 1989 when Michael Thomas scored the second for Arsenal at Anfield with almost the last kick of the game – and the season – to snatch the title away from Liverpool and whisk it south to Highbury.

'It's up for grabs now,' I croaked into the microphone as Thomas, unbelievably, found himself behind all of Liverpool's renowned defence before beating the advancing and astonished Bruce Grobbelaar. In my commentating life I've churned out few repeatable lines, I suppose, but this one, even a decade later, Arsenal fans are happy to use as a form of greeting. I was in a taxi driving round Piccadilly while I was writing this book when the driver suddenly and joyfully started repeating the last full minute of my commentary on that night. He knew it word for word. His video of that game must be worn out – and probably his family with it!

In fact, the video was a remarkable success. 'Gunning For Glory' we called it. It was attractively packaged and we had it in the shops in a matter of days. Within a week it had sold 25,000 copies. One theory has it that even the most optimistic of Arsenal fans could see no sign of a two-goal victory and didn't set their video machines. When victory came in the dying seconds it was too late anyway to flick the video switch. To this day I still receive the occasional royalty cheque as a new generation of Arsenal fans catch up with the famous victory.

England against Holland in the 1996 European Championship is my fourth choice. The 1966 World Cup final apart, this was the most skilful, uplifting and exciting exhibition I had seen from an England team at Wembley. Terry Venables had coached and talked his players to the peak of their powers and the Dutch were swamped 4–1. Everything was right, including the quality of the goals by Alan Shearer (2) and Teddy Sheringham (2). The atmosphere in the stadium was helped in no small measure by the Dutch with their bands and their singing. It was a joyous occasion. Even the weather was in winning form.

In broadcasting there are nights when the words come out as you would wish and the commentator feels on top of his game; and there are nights when, inexplicably, they don't. This was one of the better nights. A pooling of resources for this tournament gave me the enjoyable experience of working for the first and only time with the BBC's highly regarded director John Shrewsbury and our words and pictures went out that night to seventeen million viewers on ITV.

Match number five is the European Championship final of 1976 between Czechoslovakia and Germany in Belgrade. It came at the end of the most riveting week of football – the championship was over in a week in those days. There were only four teams playing out the final stages – Yugoslavia, the hosts, Holland, Czechoslovakia and Germany – and there were just two venues, Belgrade and Zagreb.

The final had everything, including extra time and a penalty shoot-out. It was 2–2 at the end of extra time and there was nothing to choose between the penalty-takers until Uli Hoeness missed for Germany and Antonin Panenka won the championship with the cheekiest penalty I'd ever seen. The title and unexpected glory for the Czechs rested on that one kick. Sepp Maier, brilliant World Cup keeper, was in goal for Germany. Up stepped Panenka. With no more than a two-yard run, he sent Maier the wrong way and gently chipped the ball over him virtually in the centre of the goal. It scarcely reached the back of the net. Dwight Yorke is the only man I've seen do it since, but not in a European final!

My sixth choice is another European final. I considered Aston Villa's unexpected triumph over Bayern Munich in Rotterdam in 1982 when Peter Withe scored and Nigel Spink arrived as a heroic young stand-in goalkeeper; the Mark Hughes night in 1991 for Manchester United in the Cup Winners' Cup, also in Rotterdam, when they edged out Barcelona in a thriller; and perhaps the gutsiest performance of all when George Graham sent out an understrength Arsenal side with such conviction against Parma in the Cup Winners' Cup final of 1993 in Copenhagen that the goal by Alan Smith was just enough. But my choice is Liverpool's victory over Roma in the European Cup final of 1984. It was played in the Olympic Stadium in Rome and the Roma supporters came swaggering up to the match already planning their celebrations. Liverpool stuck their jaws out as never before. I can't recall a more stubborn, inspiring display by a British side in Europe with so much hostility all around. Graeme Souness, a magnificent captain, set the mood by parading his team in front of the noisiest Roma supporters before the start. 'This may be your place,' he seemed to be saying, 'but you don't worry us.' It was a master-stroke.

Phil Neal scored for Liverpool, Roberto Pruzzo equalised for Roma and we eventually came to another of those penalty shoot-outs. Joe Fagan, canny old campaigner and one of the most genuine men in the game, was Liverpool manager and he played his part. Just before the shoot-out he took Bruce Grobbelaar aside and quietly said, 'Just do what you can to put them off.' So it was that Bruce unveiled his famous quaking legs act as each Roma player prepared to take his penalty. It worked, as Joe Fagan probably knew it would. Both Bruno Conte and Francesco Graziani missed from the spot and Liverpool added another notch to their long honours list.

One of the huge luxuries for anyone working in television is the opportunity it provides to rub shoulders with the mighty. For me they came no mightier than Denis Compton, the last of the great all-rounders who was able to combine careers in both cricket and football. My microphone on this occasion was not live to the nation, but just to a couple of hundred privileged and bow-tied diners at the Café Royal in Piccadilly for a tribute night to Compo. It was my honour to be the host for this salute to a hero of heroes.

The big perk was that I sat with Denis during dinner, and in all things he was everything you would want a superstar to be; this at a time, in his late seventies, when his health was beginning to fail. Yet still there was enough of the old cavalier on show. His former team-mates were out in force for him, and it was like looking at a life-sized pack of cigarette cards from my youth: Alec Bedser, Peter May, Trevor Bailey, Brian Statham, Godfrey Evans, all there to pay their respects to the Brylcreem Boy of old. Incidentally, for that unmissable, nationwide advertising campaign in the forties and fifties – in newspapers, on hoardings and even on the sides of buses – he received a princely £1,000. 'And that wasn't at all bad for those days, old boy,' he said.

Previously, Steve Hamer of the National Sporting Club and I had gone along to a pub near Maidenhead for a spot of lunch with Denis and a friend to research the forthcoming night of celebration at the Café Royal. It was a fairly modest lunch, so we were somewhat taken aback when the bill for four came to £185. Before we arrived, Denis had spotted a table of young ladies out on a spree, and he promptly sent over a couple of bottles of the best pink champagne. All his life he had a certain style!

So, too, did Juste Fontaine. I was thrilled to meet him, a footballing legend, at the World Cup in France last summer. He lives in Toulouse in a house that he calls 'Thirteen' – for the very good reason that he scored thirteen times in the World Cup finals of 1958 in Sweden, and that is a record unlikely ever to be beaten. In France '98, Davor Suker of Croatia was top-scorer with six, and we thought he did well!

It took FIFA twenty-eight years to recognise Fontaine's achievement and at the 1986 tournament they presented him with a commemorative medal. When I spoke to him last year, his own French federation had so far kept their hands in their pockets, but at least the Swedes had recognised him. They gave him a rifle. For a hot-shot marksman, what better!

I listened with respect and fascination as Juste gave me his list of greatest players. There was Pele, of course, who he saw as a gifted seventeen-year-old in that Sweden World Cup. He put Alfredo di Stefano and Pele together on the top rung; Puskas, Cruyff and Maradona one rung below; and one below that

Bobby Charlton. How would Juste have coped in today's football world? I wondered.

'Certainly,' he said with a smile, 'I would be making a lot of money.' Of that there is no doubt.

From a legend of the football field to a legend of broadcasting – anyone who ever picked up a microphone professionally, whatever the sport, was in awe of Sir Peter O'Sullevan, the Voice of Racing across five decades. For more than fifty years, this superb commentator, effortlessly and with immense authority, got just about everything right. He was the perfect ambassador both for his sport and his profession. Nearing his eightieth birthday, Sir Peter was honoured at a Royal Television Society dinner with – and not before time – a lifetime achievement award. His acceptance speech, as you might expect, was both gracious and elegant. He finished off by saying in that rich, distinctive voice of his: 'When you get to my age you find that three things happen. The first is you start to lose your memory…' and after a long dramatic pause, '…and I can't quite remember what the other two are.'

A year later, at the Royal Television Society dinner, I, too, received – to my great surprise – the judges' special award for my lifetime of work in television. It was the crowning moment of my working career. On a glittering night for Betty and myself at the London Hilton, Murray Walker, another commentator who has stood the test of time and whom I admire greatly, was at our table. So too was Jim Rosenthal, also up for a much-deserved award as a gifted all-rounder. The dinner and the award seemed to set the seal on a full-time career that was approaching the final whistle.

On the subject of 'medals', on the morning of my last FA Cup final I was the subject of a warm editorial in the *Sun*. It meant a lot to me, not least because I remember so well how my dear father was such a strong supporter of the old *Daily Herald*, which made way for the *Sun* back in 1964. I could imagine what satisfaction that editorial recognition would have given him. The *Sun* said:

For thirty-one years he has been the voice of Football on ITV. Today Brian Moore commentates on his last Cup final. The man with the golden tonsils is retiring – after he's covered his eighth World Cup that is.

Soccer fans everywhere will wish Brian a long and happy retirement. He has given us all a huge amount of pleasure and excitement.

Have a great game today, Brian. And see if you can win the World Cup for us before you go!

I was heartened by that support but while I felt I had a good FA Cup final, winning the World Cup was way beyond me. I'm no Zidane!

Public recognition – and sometimes acclaim – are the lifeblood of all of us in television.

'Store away the good notices and remember them,' Betty said to me years ago, 'because the nasty ones are sure to follow.'

It was good, sensible advice from somebody who has given me the best support a man could ask for throughout his career. Betty has been proved right. There have indeed been some articles that have hit their target and wounded. But I believe that, on the whole, I bowed out of full-time television with my account just about in credit.

Like my dad before me, my memories have made me a millionaire. You will not have heard of Vera Houghton or Bob Rounthwaite, but Vera, until passing on last year, and Bob have not missed sending me birthday and Christmas cards for the last twenty-five years. Vera, from North London, lived in a residential home in Sussex and was an avid QPR fan; Bob, a Geordie living in Kent, is Newcastle United to the core. These are just two of the many people to whom I have been privileged to be a messenger and, more importantly, a friend.

You can't put a price on that.

EPILOGUE

I'T's a cliché I have heard often enough from greybeards who survived their retirement parties long before me. 'I'm so busy,' they'd say, 'I often wonder how I found time to go to work.' I, in turn, wondered if they were simply kidding themselves. They were not – I know that now from personal experience.

Since my own 'retirement' I have returned with pleasure to my first love, radio. Among other programmes, I enjoyed a couple of high-profile Friday nights on BBC Radio 5 Live, standing in for Alan Green, and had first Ron Atkinson and then Kevin Keegan as my guests. The timing of the Keegan broadcast could not have been better. It came in the week when he was named as the stop-gap England manager and it was his only one-to-one interview that week. I was grateful for his generosity to an old friend. There was not a sports desk anywhere that did not turn an ear in our direction. The following day's banner headlines were the proof. Perhaps there will be more, perhaps not.

The voice-over work was still forthcoming and then Sky Television came knocking. Trevor East, now a Sky mogul, made the first approach. Andy Melvin followed it up and invited me to do a series of full-length interviews with some of the football greats of the last thirty years. These were men with whom I grew up and grew old – it was the perfect assignment. My producer

Mark Pearman and I consider it a labour of love – and to think that we get paid for it too!

My golf clubs, sadly, come clanking out of my study even less frequently now than when I was in full-time television. Do you know, I can't think how I found the time to climb into the commentary box for all those years!

INDEX

Statham, Brian 222
Stein, Jock 58–60, 119
Stengel, Casey 12
Stepney, Alec 137
Stewart, Alec 202
Stiles, Nobby 48, 54, 67
Stock, Alec 75
Stokoe, Bob 77–8, 94–5
Sugar, Alan 141–2
Suker, Davor 222
Summerbee, Mike 75
Sunderland 119
    v Leeds United 77–8, 94–5
Sutton, Bill 100
Sutton, Chris 202
Swanton, Jim 34–6
Sweden
    v Brazil 194
    v England 200

Tarbuck, Jimmy 171
Taylor, Graham 184, 191–4, 200
Taylor, Jack 114
Taylor, John D 45, 170, 212
Taylor, Peter 87, 127, 142
Taylor, Shaw 111
Thames Television 168
    'Mid-week Sports Special'
        174–5
    'Thames Sport' 170, 175, 212
    'The Games of '48' 211–16
The Times 39–40
Thomas, Michael 219
Thompson, Daley 213
Thys, Guy 192
Todd, Leslie 31
Tottenham 56–8, 86
    v Anderlecht 128, 149

    v Atletico Madrid 52–4
    v Coventry City 102
    v Gornik 57–8
Toye, Clive 67
Trinder, Tommy 208
Tunisia v England 14
Turner, Graham 96
Tyldesley, Clive 51, 206
Tyldesley, J.T. 37
Tyler, Martin 176

United Arab Emirates v
    Germany 189

Van Hooijdonk, Pierre 209, 214
Vaughan Thomas, Wynford 62
Venables, Terry 3, 6, 16, 54–5, 116
Venison, Barry 6, 81, 141
Vine, David 58

Waddle, Chris 190
Wales v Scotland 60
Walker, Jack 30, 202
Walker, Murray 159, 204, 223
Warren, Frank 169
Warsap, Jimmy 29
Washbrook, Cyril 31
Waterman, Dennis 45
Watford 89, 193
Watt, Jim 170
Watts, John 17, 78, 85
Waumsley, Rick 206
Webb, David 84, 87
Webster, John 41
Welch, David 201
Welsby, Elton 115, 174
West Germany v England 111;
    (1966) 67, 218; (1985) 98